T0255436

# Mastering ARKit

Apple's Augmented Reality
App Development Platform

Jayven Nhan

Apress®

*Mastering ARKit: Apple's Augmented Reality App Development Platform*

Jayven Nhan
Waterloo, ON, Canada

ISBN-13 (pbk): 978-1-4842-7835-2          ISBN-13 (electronic): 978-1-4842-7836-9
https://doi.org/10.1007/978-1-4842-7836-9

Managing Director, Apress Media LLC: Welmoed Spahr
Acquisitions Editor: Aaron Black
Development Editor: James Markham
Coordinating Editor: Jessica Vakili

Distributed to the book trade worldwide by Springer Science+Business Media New York, 233 Spring Street, 6th Floor, New York, NY 10013. Phone 1-800-SPRINGER, fax (201) 348-4505, e-mail orders-ny@springer-sbm.com, or visit www.springeronline.com. Apress Media, LLC is a California LLC and the sole member (owner) is Springer Science + Business Media Finance Inc (SSBM Finance Inc). SSBM Finance Inc is a **Delaware** corporation.

For information on translations, please e-mail booktranslations@springernature.com; for reprint, paperback, or audio rights, please e-mail bookpermissions@springernature.com.

Apress titles may be purchased in bulk for academic, corporate, or promotional use. eBook versions and licenses are also available for most titles. For more information, reference our Print and eBook Bulk Sales web page at http://www.apress.com/bulk-sales.

Any source code or other supplementary material referenced by the author in this book is available to readers on GitHub via the book's product page, located at https://github.com/Apress/Mastering-ARKitFor more detailed information, please visit http://www.apress.com/source-code.

Printed on acid-free paper

# Table of Contents

# About the Author

**Jayven Nhan** has worked with the biggest international and national enterprises in the health care, financial banking, and entertainment streaming industries. He has published books and over 30 App Store apps. Jayven is an Apple scholar who contributes his best work to passion, fitness training, and nutrition. Passion makes problem-solving an enjoyment. Outside of coding, you may find him listening to audiobooks and podcasts, reading, or learning from YouTube videos.

# About the Technical Reviewer

**Felipe Laso** is a Senior Systems Engineer working at Lextech Global Services. He's also an aspiring game designer/programmer. You can follow him on Twitter at @iFeliLM or on his blog.

# CHAPTER 1

# Why Augmented Reality?

Every now and then, there comes a special time in history where things really change humanity for the better. One day, when you look back, I believe augmented reality will be a special time in history.

What's so special about augmented reality, and why should you care? Here's the deal. Really, you don't have to care. In hindsight of the last centuries, a handful of people could care less about today's latest gizmos. And they may be just as happy as anyone you can imagine.

The iPhone has existed for a long time. The device itself is a force of nature. It enables people to do things that they otherwise could not without it. And I have a feeling that many of us reading this book can share a story adhere to the statement. As special as all these smart devices may seem, you can actually live without them.

Where does the technology stand with humanity? Technology has a neutral moral system on its own. Neither good nor bad. However, technology can do good and bad depending on the hands the technology lands into.

Technology has enabled humans to live longer and healthier, communicate further and simultaneously with more people, and enjoy the most lucrative career and life paths where people may not have even dared to dream of in the past.

© Jayven Nhan 2022
J. Nhan, *Mastering ARKit*, https://doi.org/10.1007/978-1-4842-7836-9_1

Intelligent medical devices can detect and prevent diseases, enhance various parts of the human body, and empower us to make better and more informed decisions. Smartphone gives us the ability to speak to people from various parts of the world in real time. YouTube combined with Internet access lets video gamers become millionaires within months, beauty experts showcase their art from their bedroom, democratize education of all subjects to be available to the world, and more.

Heck, technology has allowed this book to be distributed digitally onto a MacBook, iPhone, iPad, and more.

The existence of augmented reality will be no different. It will exist to serve the enhancement of humanity. However, it's a device that may be in front of our eyes as close to 24/7 as any device will, from when we wake up and put on our augmented reality glasses to when we place them down at night for charging. Hence, it is worthwhile to pay attention to the most up-close, personal, and interactive technology the world has yet to know.

Let's rephrase that succinctly. Augmented reality may be in front of our eyes as close to 24/7 as any device will, from the time we wake up to the time we sleep. Hence, it is worthwhile to pay attention to this technology.

Imagine yourself 10, 20, or 30 years from now. Apart from the amazing accomplishments you envision yourself to have achieved by then, some parts of your body may deteriorate. As much as you want this to be false, your vision is likely and may deteriorate as nature allows. You have glasses, contact lenses, and laser treatments to enhance our vision needs.

Augmented reality can enhance your current vision needs and adapt to your future vision needs. The latter is possible with augmented reality. When a person's vision quality deteriorates, augmented reality, combined with computer vision algorithms, can render the world in a way that optimizes a person's vision needs.

The accessibility feature dramatically reduces a person's cognitive loads from looking into the world, trying to fixate jigsaw pieces into place, and comprehending vision ambiguities.

Moreover, for people who love to multitask, such as walk and message, augmented reality's world-facing camera can act as an extra pair of eyes to assist you in your overall world awareness. Fewer people should run into health-damaging objects. And steel poles.

How about when you travel to a galaxy far far away? You seek adventure, and you have found yourself on a mystery planet. Landing on a mystery planet, you plant your feet into this mystery planet. You have stepped out of your rocketship. Black clouds surround you. The sky slowly fades darkly. Then, pitch-black.

You see a dark and habitable cave. One foot after another, you get closer to the cave. You are standing at a cave entrance. You walk-in, you see nothing. Your world-facing camera maps your world with infrared light. Safely, a step at a time, you have mapped the cave.

Now, you have yourself a man/woman cave. In addition, augmented reality can project the cave into your eyes. Even if you walk with your eyes closed, augmented reality can guide you through a world that is pitch-black to the eyes.

# The Three A's: Accessibility, Assistance, Automation

Now, let's talk one of today's most prominent setbacks in academia, ADHD.

When augmented reality kicks in, the technology is an integration into the human body. Imagine this. Your future self came home and got some work to knock out the park and into the moon. You have found your desk and chair. You let gravity kicks in, and you are well situated on your chair.

You do the subtle shoulder shimmy, stretch shoulder slightly back, and then stretch your arms in front of you. You feel ready for flow. You say: "Hey Siri, start a 30 minutes timer." Siri says, "Your 30 minutes timer has started."

You see a single piece of paper document sitting on your desk. It looks you right into your eyes. You look right back at it. Siri suggests, "Hey Jayven Nhan, would you like to start focus mode?" You say, "Yes, Siri." That is all it takes to keep notifications, phone calls, text messages, room access, and any other Apple devices from distracting you.

All your Apple devices understand that you are in focus mode. Hence, they empower you by giving you the focusing power. The devices lock themselves up for 30 minutes—under the exception that you need access to your devices before the time is up.

Okay, your Apple technologies empower you to stay focus and go into flow. You start to read the document beginning with the header. It spells "P." The rest is a tad blurry and small for your eye to figure out the letters easily.

Siri suggests, "Hey Jayven Nhan, would you like me to amplify the text size?" You nod. Siri says, "Okay, I've applied the document's text size."

The document is accessible to the eyes. You read 70 papers front and back. Timer rings. Siri suggests, "would you like to start a 5 minutes breather?" You nod. Siri begins the 5 minutes voice-guided breathing exercise.

As of now, you may be wondering how Siri suggests these events? Starting with iOS 12, Siri Suggestion is a feature that works behind the scene. Siri suggests tasks by learning from donated events. Donated events are events that developers give to Siri for Siri to make helpful suggestions based on repetitive activities.

For instance, if you have watched *Game of Thrones* every Monday at 7 PM at home for 4 weeks straight, Siri may suggest that you head home from work when the time is 6 PM so that you can catch the latest episode of *Game of Thrones*.

Because you have repeatedly entered work mode, set up a 30 minutes work timer, set up a 5 minutes breather, and set up a 30 minutes work timer, Siri suggests the following since the 5 minutes breather is up: "Would you like to start a 30 minutes timer?" You nod. Siri says, "30 minutes timer begins."

After an intensive reading session, your cognitive computing power is slightly taxed. The 5 minutes breather gives your brain some breathing space. You look left. You see the 70 documents you've read. You look right—another pile of documents.

Wait.

The letters are jumping around on this one. Perhaps, this is not a dyslexic-friendly font. Your cognitive computing power is taxed. Do you need to power through this?

Fortunately, Apple has always cared for accessibility users. Thanks to the built-in natural language processing and OCR in your augmented reality glasses, you can say: "Hey Siri, read me the document in front of me." Siri begins naturally reading the document: "Empower everyone by first and foremost treating everyone with dignity and respect...."

Ah, another productive work block. You look to your right. There's only the empty table surface to be found this time. In front of you, you see a flat table surface. To your left is a productively read stack of documents—given productivity is more work done toward achieving one's objective in the least amount of time possible.

These are three examples of vision accessibility. Now, let's talk space.

# Real Estate

Space, space, and space. Real estate. As more buildings are built, more people occupy space, and more city areas become dense. Particularly, earth space becomes exponentially valuable over time.

Take San Francisco, for example, the heart of Silicon Valley. San Francisco's real estate has spiked exponentially valuable over the last decade due to and not limited to innovation, culture, human talents, and prosperities.

The exponential growth in the last decade isn't limited to San Francisco. Some of the most in-demand cities in the world include New York, Hong Kong, Singapore, Zurich, Seoul, and many more.

In the particularly land-scarce places, including, but not limited to, cities, could be your backyard, front porch, or whichever room could use some extra space. These spaces remain very much a constant and less of a variable. Augmented reality can become an extremely viable option for solving space limiting problems. Augmented reality can provide state-of-the-art space reusability features.

Imagine yourself heading into a state-of-the-art fashion design museum in New York City. You walk out of your hotel in New York City with your augmented reality glasses. You see art posters on cab doors, building with art posters, and street signs that point you toward the art museum.

The art museum aggregates fashion designs designed by artists from all over the globe. There are incredible European artists from Italy, Germany, France, and many more European cities.

You line up for an hour now. Finally, it's your turn. You strut through the automatic glass doors. A lady greets you with a hello. Then, she hands you a pair of augmented reality glasses.

You take a couple more steps forward into the museum. Another automatic glass door meets you. This time, there is a biometric camera to verify that you are a guest.

The glass door fades green. Then, it turns white. The door opens. You walk through the doors.

You put on your augmented reality glasses. Virgil Abloh, Louis Vuitton's menswear artistic director, greets you. The museum tells the story behind each masterpiece—the manifestation of an idea.

Fast-forward, it's the next day. You walk into yesterday's museum. This time, you sign up for music creation.

The day after, you learn about wine brewery at the same museum.

Fast-forward to next week. It is an electronic sports week. You walk out of your hotel in New York City with your augmented reality glasses. You see sport team flags, banners with players' quotes, and street signs that point you toward the sports stadium.

Then next week, you want to catch your plane. Taxi available for hire has an Uber sign on the roof. You flag down an Uber.

You scan the QR code on the door with your glasses and hop in the car. On you go with your ride.

At destination arrival, you verify the payment with voice biometrics. You step out of the car.

Arrows greet you toward your check-in counter. You do your usual check-in. Then, arrows on the floor point you toward your Gate 1.

However, before heading to the gate, you would like to spend an hour at the First-Class lounge. You say, "Hey Siri, show me the way to the First-Class lounge."

Siri says, "I've updated your path to walk towards the closest lounge. Please follow the arrows in front of you."

Without much cognitive load, you are inside the majestic Emirates First-Class round.

An hour passes. Siri suggests, "Hi Jayven Nhan, your flight is boarding in 30 minutes. It's a good time to head over to the Gate 1 if you'd like to reach Gate 1 by boarding time. Would you like me to show you the way to Gate 1?" You respond, "Yes."

Siri, using arrows as visual aids, guides you toward Gate 1. You board the plane.

Augmented reality can personalize spaces for you. Whether you want to attend a museum presented in a language foreign, experience special events, or direction, augmented reality can seamlessly augment and personalize the world for you.

So that's space. Now, let's talk about education.

# Education

Edgar Dale states that the human brain remembers 10% of what we read, 20% of what we hear, and 90% of what we do. It is time we make learning intuitive to the human brain.

Ever wonder what it's like to live as a marine or ever felt anxious prior to an event. Do you know what could help you reduce anxiety and increase your confidence? Practice. Again. And again. And again. Over and over and over again. Augmented reality can simulate reality to prepare you for an event. Say, you are about to join the marines; your role, in particular, is to strategize and deliver the strategy to your team.

You happen to be anxious to deliver your first speech to your team. Hence, you open an app that simulates your team in augmented reality. You practice giving the speech over and over again. Although a computer can give a speech precisely word by word, there has yet to be a close replacement for having a physical human-to-human interaction. In addition, to an audience simulation, your augmented reality device can show you your speech text as you speak. This reduces the need to memorize. Computers happen to keep text preciseness in memory better than humans. Hence, using computers to remember text can mitigate the time spent on text memorization.

Imagine a personal tutor for your homework. A simple "Hey Siri, tutor me" can make a homework or test preparation tutor accessible to you and anyone with an augmented reality device and access to the tutoring app.

The universe is the limit with such an app. In addition, the app can learn about you and personalize functionalities to optimize for your desired learning experience.

Accessible and personalized education for people around the world. Wow. Every kid deserves a good education. If every kid has access to augmented reality, this technology can help the human race take an excellent step forward.

People will also have education options and personalizations. You identify with particular courses, professors, tutors, mentors, etc.

Say you have a load of homework and an upcoming test. You can choose your tutor, human or artificial intelligence, to help you with your homework and test preparation.

Want to take an interactive and engaging computer course from your bedroom, perhaps due to dangerous weather conditions today? You can. The class can continue.

A professor can create an augmented reality class. A class experience where students can learn from anywhere and learn by doing. Augmented reality unlocks students' ability to interact seamlessly with the virtual world—at the comfort and safety of their homes.

More students than ever face mental issues. The world is catching up in raising mental issue awareness. No kids should go to school to put their mental health at risk, whether it's terrible weather, bullying, or haircut.

Education affects everyone. This space is ready for a revolution.

## Closing

The number of augmented reality devices is at an all-time high, with over augmented reality capable devices on the iOS platform alone, and the number continues to grow. We are at a phase where we prepare for the augmented reality and human integration.

I believe that augmented reality glasses will be a very personal device. And it will be a more significant extension of the human body than smartphones.

Augmented reality is a technology that looks into the world with us 24/7. It will learn about you, me, and the world.

Augmented reality will empower people to do things that we could not do otherwise. Augmented reality will give some people independence with accessibility features.

Augmented reality will give us a personalized world.

Augmented reality will also give us an accessible and personalized education.

And this is the very beginning of augmented reality.

Let's build the world for today, tomorrow, and centuries after.

## Why ARKit?

Choosing a technology is deciding to make an investment. Analogous to investing in stocks, investing in a company's technology can become a sizable investment of your effort, time, and potential outcome. This chapter covers the following considerations when choosing ARKit:

- Apple's core values

- Versus cross-platform software

- Riding the technology momentum

- Apple's documentation

- Apple's developer community documentation

By the end of this chapter, you'll have a better idea about why you'd want to choose ARKit to develop your augmented reality apps.

## Apple's Core Values

Why does anything you choose matter? When we buy a branded product, we resonate with a brand to an extent. A brand stands for values, and people buy branded products that say something about them. Apple has long stood for the following core values: accessibility, education, environment, inclusion and diversity, privacy, and supplier responsibility. From Apple's core values and my observations of Apple, Apple always seems to strive to do the right things that fundamentally push humanity forward.

Big companies such as Apple bring excellent values to the world—as a byproduct, their business seems to take care of itself healthily. Companies the size of Apple have the spending power to hire top talents from all around the world. These talents can develop and push forward Apple's augmented reality platform in a particular direction.

The direction in which a platform is heading toward is dependent on the company's talents. Certain companies attract certain talents—usually, talents whose ambitions align with the company's core values.

Based on a company's core values, you can expect certain features in the company product/platform. Apple's hardware and software are accessible. Apple works toward providing education, such as teaching students to code on the Playground app.

Apple strives toward creating processes, buildings, and products using 100% renewable materials. Apple creates products and environments for its customers to experience for people of all backgrounds. Apple creates products responsibly by taking into Apple's high standard of human rights, environmental protection, and business practices. These are products/ events that are to be expected from Apple.

Apple's augmented reality product and platform are expected to have included these constants. History doesn't always repeat itself, but it does tend to rhyme at the very least. If Apple's core values resonate with you, they are a fantastic reason to develop on Apple's platform and aid in fostering those core values in the products you build for the world.

# Versus Cross-Platform Software

Beyond having a secure cultural connection with a brand like Apple, some people may ask: How about a cross-platform development for augmented reality? Would that be more efficient for developing a single code base for platforms inclusive of Apple's platform and others' platforms?

Everything is case by case and has its exception. Nevertheless, every cross-platform development environment requires a layer of abstraction to handle Apple's platform and others' platforms.

Adding a layer of abstraction may result in a non-native feel of the resulting app built from the cross-platform development environment. This reduces the user experience because a user may need to relearn a non-native app's navigation pattern. An abstraction layer can frustrate your users when your users can yet to operate specific functions within an app. What you want is to build an exceptional app experience for our users.

Moreover, by having an abstraction layer, you practically have to build for Apple's platform and others' platforms. This means you need to build for Apple's platform, non-Apple supported platform, and the cross-development platform.

You may not be the one to create the abstraction layer every single time. However, this requires your attention to ensure all features carry over as expected to your app.

For instance, a subsection of native app features, can your view controller (pushed onto the navigation controller) navigate back to the previous view controller with a native swipe gesture?

Another instance here. Does your app support accessibility features, such as a label or text field, to work as intuitively as the native app? Or is every single line of code in the abstraction layer necessary app's code base? Having ambiguous layers of abstractions is the beginning of days to security flaws.

Some codes may not trigger a security flaw or app crash today or tomorrow. Yet that doesn't stop it from ever happening.

The app may trigger a security flaw years from the release of your app. Or there may even be unexpected crashes due to the code architecture flaw in the abstraction layer.

In this case, it may take extensive time to debug the app's surface code. Then, under the awareness that the crash may be due to the abstraction layer, someone will need to read and understand the abstraction layer.

Afterward, debug and fix the abstraction layer flaw yourself, which you may not know if fixing this part of the code may lead to other leakages unless the abstraction layer is fully tested. Or, hopefully, given time, the team which publishes and maintains the abstraction layer releases a fix.

Also, due to having an abstraction layer, a cross-platform development environment has historically released its version of newer frameworks at a later time than the native framework publisher.

The reasons are that the native solution is first released, the cross-platform team has to coordinate and create the abstraction layer for all supported platforms, and then hopefully thoroughly test the abstract solution before public release.

Having the cross-platform development tool at your disposal at a later date could lead to a reduced time spent with the latest technology, a reduction in technological competitive edge, and deadlines, which add a framework's cross-platform support variable on itself.

How about when a framework such as ARKit releases a version update? Are you going to be able to tell that the cross-platform solution works like a native? When your app crashes, are you going to have the resources to go through the abstraction layer when the client code works? Will the cross-platform solution support all features from the latest framework or merely a subset of features at a particular date? Timelines can become an issue when working with cross-platform development tools.

# Riding the Technology Momentum

Another reason to choose Apple's development platform is that Apple seems to push its proprietary augmented reality technology with more force than any other company in the respective industry. This means you'll be riding the more influential or most influential wave if Apple continues its momentum and push for augmented reality.

Apple first announced ARKit at WWDC17. Since then, Apple's augmented reality technology has only continued to progress, becoming ever more precise in world tracking and growing new features that push ARKit forward. These features include vertical plane tracking, image recognition, object detection, USDZ file format, motion tracking, geographic locations, and much more.

Based on Apple's push for augmented reality, Apple seems to believe that augmented reality is a technology sector that is well worth investing in.

One more reason to choose Apple's development platform is that Apple's technology has historically been relatively well documented. Apple provides the Apple Developer Documentation archive. The archive is a collection of API references, articles, and sample codes.

# Apple's Documentation

The APIs are generally organized, structured, and user-friendly. Apple also has WWDC videos that cover mostly high-level technical and design-focused presentations. The WWDC videos are usually great for understanding the high-level overview of technical and design-focused topics.

# Apple's Developer Community Documentation

For when Apple's documentation fall short, Apple's developer community is there to catch the apple and make sure it doesn't fall flat on the ground and break—sometimes.

Apple is fortunate to have an open-minded, supportive, and very active iOS developer community. A considerable percentage of the developer community will translate over to the augmented reality platform when the augmented reality glasses have essentially become the iPhones. This means when you are stuck or are spending more time than you want on a specific problem, it's unlikely that you'll feel alone and helpless. There will be enough people who have experienced what you have and are willing to share their experience toward finding a desirable solution. This is evident with some of the well-defined questions and succinctly in-depth answers on StackOverflow. Moreover, there's also a growing library of video tutorials.

## The Apple Audience

Finally, a decision-making point for choosing Apple's augmented reality platform is the audience it attracts. Apple is known to sell highly priced premium products and attract users willing to spend more than any of Apple's competitors. Consequently, your augmented reality users are more likely to make an in-app purchase benefitting your company's revenue growth.

## Conclusion

In conclusion, reasons to choose Apple's augmented reality platform include Apple's core values, benefiting from native app development, Apple's heavy investment into augmented reality, Apple's technical documentation, the unique iOS community, and the users that Apple attracts. These are the six core reasons for choosing ARKit.

# CHAPTER 2

# Introduction to ARKit: Under the Hood and Matrixes

Ever wonder what makes up the engine of a plane? What's inside a machine capable of transporting hundreds of people from across the world? What makes Boeing 747-300 able to take off from gravity, soar into the air, and go distance beyond the human imagination just a century ago?

Ever wonder what magic makes specific technology so powerful is? What is the magic behind ARKit? Time to roll up the sleeves and uncover the engines behind ARKit.

Augmented reality is the blending of the physical and virtual world. And ARKit works like magic from the consumer point of view. From the engineering standpoint, the gears that power the augmented reality engineer become more apparent. You'll uncover the gears behind the engine.

ARKit utilizes the visual-inertial odometry technique to create a correspondence between the physical world and the virtual world. The visual-inertial odometry technique composes of the motion sensor and computer vision.

© Jayven Nhan 2022
J. Nhan, *Mastering ARKit*, https://doi.org/10.1007/978-1-4842-7836-9_2

You feed ARKit the video frames. ARKit will try to make sense of the world for you by creating a world map resulting from notable image features and motion-sensing data. ARKit runs intense ongoing algorithms to shape the world with the presented world modeling knowledge.

Given the fact that ARKit needs notable image features to paint the shape of the world, lighting can play a significant factor in designing the augmented reality app. In particular, this applies to iOS devices with the world-facing camera like the iPhone 11 Pro. The TrueDepth or front-facing "selfie" camera, on the other hand, is equipped with an infrared emitter and infrared camera.

The infrared emitter emits over 30,000 points onto the user's face. Yes, 30,000. Afterward, the infrared camera captures an image with the emitted infrared points for face model analysis.

The TrueDepth camera has additional sensors to map our faces. It takes an essential role in powering features and apps FaceID (face detection and tracking), Animoji (real-time expression tracking), Clips (creating depth for iPhone photography and videography), and more. Moreover, the TrueDepth camera is relatively more prodigal with battery expenditure.

The world-facing camera uses video frames and motion-sensing data to map out the world. The TrueDepth camera uses video frames, motion-sensing data, infrared emitter, and infrared imagery to create a 3D model of our faces. ARKit utilizes the visual-inertial odometry technique with the help of cameras, sensors, and world mapping software to create a correspondence between the virtual and physical worlds.

Now understand that ARKit is the framework to create a correspondence between the virtual and physical worlds. To create the 3D experiences in augmented reality, you will need to utilize graphics APIs such as SpriteKit, SceneKit, and Metal.

SpriteKit enables you to create a 3D experience with 2D assets. SceneKit enables you to create 3D experiences with 3D assets. Metal enables you to create 3D experiences that can utilize Apple's low-level graphics frame to improve heavy graphics experiences potentially.

Before progressing from ARKit's visual-inertial odometry technique to code, I'll talk matrixes. Particularly, 4 × 4 matrixes. 4 × 4 matrixes play a critical role in positioning virtual objects onto the physical world. Having a solid understanding of 4 × 4 matrixes can help you make world positioning decisions.

# What Is an Array?

You'll start at a sub-complexity of a matrix—array. An array is a collection of elements.

Here's an array:

```
[1, 2, 3]
```

Here's another array:

```
[1]
```

And here's another array:

```
[]
```

# What Is a Matrix?

Now, put a collection of the array together, and you have an array of arrays. A matrix is a two-dimensional array (an array of arrays).

Here's a matrix:

```
[[1, 2, 3],
 [4, 5, 6],
 [7, 8, 9]]
```

Here's another matrix:

```
[[1],
 [2],
 [3]]
```

And here's another matrix:

```
[[]]
```

At this point, you know:

- What's the definition of an array?

- What's the definition of a matrix?

When you alter a 3D object's property, such as changing a 3D object's position in the virtual world, you modify a value within a matrix.

# Matrixes: Addition and Subtraction Operations

Beginning with matrix addition and subtraction, you may encounter a scenario where you want to move, translate, rotate, and scale an object by increasing or decreasing a property's value by a certain amount—understanding how matrix addition and subtraction will help you achieve those intentions.

University math matrix addition.

```
[[1, 2, 3],
 [4, 5, 6]]

 +

[[6, 5, 4],
 [3, 2, 1]]
```

```
=

[[1 + 6, 2 + 5, 3 + 4],
 [4 + 3, 5 + 2, 6 + 1]]
```

or

```
[[7, 7, 7],
 [7, 7, 7]]
```

This applies to university math, not Swift. When applied to two matrixes, Swift's addition operation combines the two matrixes into a single matrix.

Swift matrix addition.

```
[[1, 2, 3],
 [4, 5, 6]]

+

[[6, 5, 4],
 [3, 2, 1]]

=

[[1, 2, 3],
 [4, 5, 6],
 [6, 5, 4],
 [3, 2, 1]]
```

This applies to Swift. It is essential to take note to mitigate this logic pitfall when handling matrixes, communicating matrixes, or even in a coding interview. To apply the university math matrix addition, you can create a simple algorithm to do so.

The subtraction operator in Swift, on the other hand, simply returns a compiler error. This is due to the fact that binary operator "-" cannot be applied to two [[Int]] operands.

When dealing with a 3D object in the real world, addition and subtraction are commonly used for dealing with translations—for example, moving a 3D object one meter positive on the x-axis, one meter positive on the y-axis, and one meter negative on the z-axis.

```
X: +1
Y: +1
Z: -1
```

In the scenario where you are facing a 3D object, the 3D object's positive z-axis points toward you, the positive y-axis points toward the earth's sky, and the positive x-axis points toward your right. Also, the scenario is taken place in the real world with the utilization of ARKit and SceneKit.

The translation application would move the 3D object one meter to your right, one meter up to the earth's sky, and one meter away from you. It is important to note that position relativity is important when dealing with any 3D object transformation(s).

# Matrix Identity

If you make changes to your 3D objects, whether it'd be a translation, rotation, or scaling, you can call the identity method onto the matrix to reverse the changes. You can also change the identity of a matrix to set its origin translation, rotation, and scaling values. You can use the identity property of a matrix as a "reset matrix to origin" button. The identity property is what the object starts out as.

# Setting Up Playground

Great. Enough matrix theories for now. It's time to pull up Swift Playground and warm up your fingers' biceps.

Open up **Xcode**.

Create a new Playground by clicking **File/New/Playground...** or press the ⌥⇧⌘N keyboard shortcut.

---

**Note**    For machines running on an M1 chip or ARM-based system, ensure that Rosetta is turned off when running Xcode. Also, Swift Playground (Version 3.4.1) from the App Store has limited framework support and would disrupt following the upcoming instructions.

---

You should see the following screen.

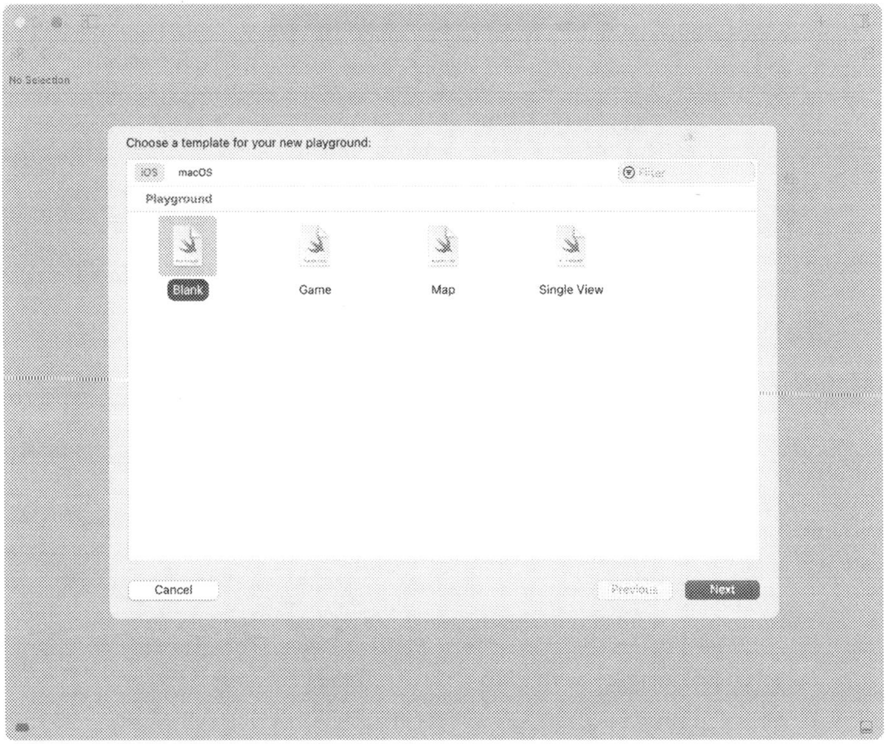

Click **Next**.

Enter **matrix .playground** for the file name.

Click **Create**.

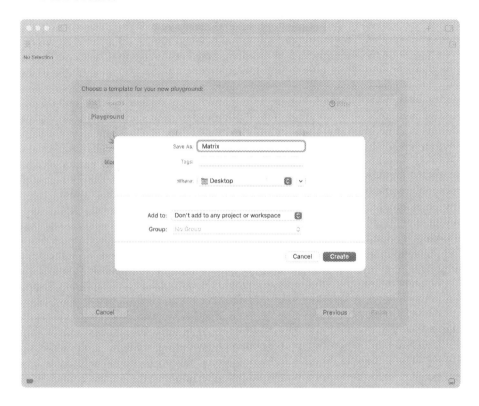

You should see the following screen.

Replace the page with the following code:

```
import UIKit
import ARKit
import PlaygroundSupport
```

Here, you imported Apple frameworks for utilization later on for this tutorial.

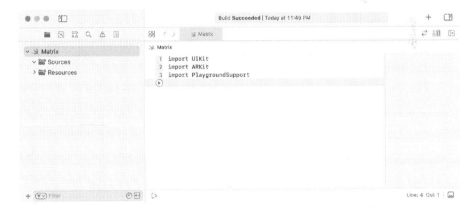

There are many ways of creating a matrix in Swift. You'll work with SceneKit and simd matrixes because of their convenience and descriptive built-in class methods. The additional benefits of simd matrixes are computational optimization. As you can imagine, having many objects update different properties while optimizing for full-frame rates is no walk in the park. Hence, Apple has introduced simd which is part of the Accelerate framework and optimizes computational speed for matrixes.

# Setting Up Scene View

It's time to bring visualization into the components that make up the different matrixes of augmented reality experiences.

Okay. For visualizations, you can create a scene view environment with lights, camera, and cube node action!

First, add the following code to your Playground to set up the scene view:

```
// Scene View Setup
let frame = CGRect(
    x: 0,
    y: 0,
    width: 512,
    height: 512
)
let sceneView = SCNView(frame: frame)
let scene = SCNScene()
sceneView.autoenablesDefaultLighting = true
sceneView.scene = scene
PlaygroundPage.current.liveView = sceneView
```

You have created a frame of a fixed size—512 floating points in width and 512 floating points in height. With the frame constant you created, you initialize a SCNView object with the frame property. Then, set the sceneView's auto enables default lighting property to be true. This gives the objects in sceneView color contrasts over its surfaces.

Afterward, you set the scene view's scene to the scene property you initialized. Lastly, you set the PlaygroundPage's current live view to the sceneView property. This allows you to see an interactive playground with the scene view as your live view's canvas.

To see the interactive live view, you'll need:

First, click **Adjust Editors Options**.

Second, ensure **Live View** is enabled from the jump bar. If not, select it to enable the Live View.

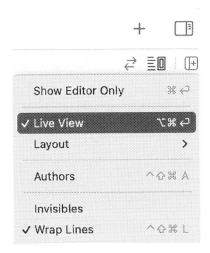

Press the **Execute Playground** button on the bottom left window. Now, you should see a blank view on the right.

# Matrix Translation

It looks like the stage is ready. Now comes the light!

Add the following code to the page's end:

```
// Light
let lightNode = SCNNode()
let light = SCNLight()
light.type = .omni
lightNode.light = light
lightNode.simdPosition = simd_float3(-2, 10, 5)
scene.rootNode.addChildNode(lightNode)
```

Here, you've initialized a light node of type omni. The position of the light will be situated relative to the root node. It will be two units to the left, ten units to the top, and five units away from the root node. Then, add the light node onto the root node.

The stage is ready. The light is available. It's time to bring on the camera. A camera directs what the user sees, much like a movie.

To add a camera to the scene, add the following code to the page's end:

```
// Camera
let camera = SCNCamera()
let cameraNode = SCNNode()
cameraNode.camera = camera
cameraNode.rotation.y = GLKMathDegreesToRadians(45)
cameraNode.position = SCNVector3(x: 0, y: 2, z: 5)
scene.rootNode.addChildNode(cameraNode)
```

With the code above you:

Initialize a camera node object.

Rotate the camera node in the y-direction by 45 degrees. This gives the camera a tilt downward so you can look at the cube node later at an angle. Get that beautiful 45 degrees photoshoot shot!

Move the camera two units upward and five units backward.

Add the camera node onto the root node.

Okay. This is starting to look like a movie casting scene. Now, you need the star. Alright, cube node. Come on in.

To bring a cube node to the scene, add the following code to the end of your Playground's page:

```
// Cube
let cubeLength: CGFloat = 1
let cube = SCNBox(
    width: cubeLength,
    height: cubeLength,
    length: cubeLength,
    chamferRadius: 0
)
```

```
cube.firstMaterial?.diffuse.contents = UIColor.red
let cubeNode = SCNNode(geometry: cube)
cubeNode.simdPosition = simd_float3(x: 0, y: 1, z: -0.5)
scene.rootNode.addChildNode(cubeNode)
```

The preceding code initializes a cube node with its width, height, and length equal to 1 unit. The cube's color is red. In addition, you've also set the cube's position. Then, you've added the cube node onto the root node.

The x, y, and z make up the 3D position in the world anchored to a relative position. The x, y, and z dictate the horizontal, vertical, and distance position, respectively.

Imagine a scenario where an object's positive z-axis points directly at you, the positive y-axis points toward the sky, and the positive x-axis points to your right.

The last row and first three values are the translation values.

```
[[1, 0, 0, 0],
 [0, 1, 0, 0],
 [0, 0, 1, 0],
 [x, y, z, 1]]
```

Go ahead and add the following code:

```
print(cubeNode.simdTransform)
```

This prints the cube node's transform matrix. You can see that the last row and the first three values reflect the cubeNode.position values set earlier.

Storing the translation coordinates in the last row and first three values of the array is called the row-major form.

**Execute Playground** and you should see a red cube in the scene view.

# Matrix Rotation

You will work with x, y, and z. Oh, and there's a w. A w represents the fourth component of a rotation vector.

W is useful for when you want to describe a quaternion rotation in a three-dimensional space. Imagine a 3D earth object in the physical world. Then, imagine a person walking around the 3D earth object with their feet intact to the earth.

The quaternion components play a beneficial role in computing the person's mathematical world position relative to the earth. Now, you'll back to the x-, y-, and z-axes.

Add the following code to the end of your Playground page:

```
// Rotation
let rotationDuration: TimeInterval = 6
let xRotation = CGFloat(GLKMathDegreesToRadians(-390))
let yRotation = CGFloat(GLKMathDegreesToRadians(45))
let zRotation = CGFloat(GLKMathDegreesToRadians(60))
```

31

```
let rotationAction = SCNAction.rotateBy(x: xRotation,
                                        y: yRotation,
                                        z: zRotation,
                                        duration:
rotationDuration)
rotationAction.timingMode = .easeInEaseOut

cubeNode.runAction(rotationAction)  {
print("Cube Node Rotation:", cubeNode.simdRotation)
print("X:", GLKMathRadiansToDegrees(cubeNode.simdRotation.x))
print("Y:", GLKMathRadiansToDegrees(cubeNode.simdRotation.y))
print("Z:", GLKMathRadiansToDegrees(cubeNode.simdRotation.z))
print("Cube Node Transform:", cubeNode.simdTransform)
}
```

The preceding code rotates the cube around its x-axis by -390 degrees, y-axis by 45 degrees, and z-axis by 60 degrees. Positive and negative degree rotation plays into the clockwise and counterclockwise rotation, respectively, around the axis rotated on. With the rotation action in place, the cube node is assigned with the action to rotate around the x-, y-, and z-axes.

In the scenarios where you want to rotate around any of the axes individually or simultaneously other axes, you can input the rotation radian CGFloat value type into the appropriate axis parameters as you see fit. Do note that the x, y, and z rotation parameters are in radians. You can convert degrees to radians with GLKMathDegreesToRadians(degrees).

The rotationAction is given an .easeInEaseOut timing mode. This gives the rotation variability in the speed at which the rotation takes place. The added acceleration effect makes the action look more natural to the physical world. The simple and elegant timingMode property can bring your augmented reality experience to greater heights.

After computing the rotation action, the console prints the cube node's rotation property. Since the values from the rotation property come in radians, the next three lines print the x-, y-, and z-axes in degrees with GLKMathRadiansToDegrees.

Finally, the cube node's action completion handler prints the cube node's transform matrix. The transform matrix is calculated as such:

```
[cosθ, -sinθ, 0, 0]
[sinθ, cosθ, 0, 0]
[0, 0, 1, 0]
[0, 0, 0, 1]
```

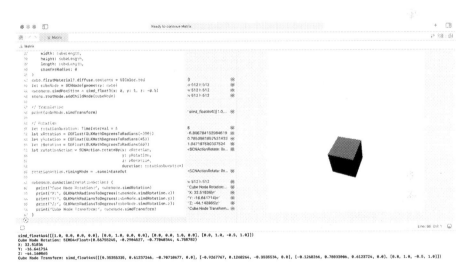

## Matrix Scaling

Scaling allows you to make an object greater or smaller in size in a particular axis. Like the rotation, you will work with the x-, y-, and z-axes when scaling.

Add the following code to the end of your Playground page:

```
// Scaling
let scaleActionDuration: TimeInterval = 4
let scaleDownAction = SCNAction.scale(to: 0.5, duration:
scaleActionDuration)
let scaleUpAction = SCNAction.scale(to: 1.5, duration:
scaleActionDuration)
let scaleSequenceAction = SCNAction.sequence([scaleDownAction,
scaleUpAction]) scaleSequenceAction.timingMode = .easeInEaseOut
cubeNode.runAction(scaleSequenceAction) {
  print("Cube Node Scaling:", cubeNode.simdScale)
  print("Cube Node Transform:", cubeNode.simdTransform)
}
```

The preceding code declares a TimeInterval duration for the cube node actions to come. The three actions are a scale-down, scale-up, and sequence action.

The first action scales a node by a factor of 0.5 from its identity in the x, y, and x scale.

The second action scales a node by a factor of 1.5 from its identity in the x, y, and x scale.

The third action combines the first and second actions into a sequence of actions. The scale-down action comes first, and the scale-up action comes after. The timing mode for the action sequence is to ease in and ease out. This gives it a more natural movement effect.

Finally, cubeNode runs scaleSequenceAction.

On scaleSequenceAction completion from the cube node, you print the cube's scale and transform. The scale of the cube node is direct. The cube node's transform takes the scale and node into the calculation.

# Up Next

Great work on the matrixes. As you continue to build knowledge on creating augmented reality experience, next is a chapter on the graphics frameworks for augmented reality.

# Graphics Frameworks for ARKit

Once upon a time, there probably was a 3D experience that stuns, amazes, and delights you.

Do you remember the first time you experienced a 3D movie? Yes. Those 3D glasses that you put on your head and used to be one of the coolest technologies in the world.

I remember my first 3D movie experience with Mickey in 3D at Disneyland. In the 3D experience, you get tackled into the jungle in the Lion King. You get drowned under the sea with sea creatures. You get lifted into the air on a magic carpet. The trumpet trumps, the violin strings, and the drum goes boom—all in all, a fantastically orchestrated experience.

There's something absolutely intuitive and fascinating during the 3D experience—the fact that almost everyone has once tried to put their hands out and grab what's in front of them. You believe what you see.

When you get tangled inside the jungle and a lion opens his jaw and takes a crunch at you, you may make a quick flinch or dodge. When you rocket sky-high into the clouds and spear toward the ground like a meteorite on a magic carpet, you may close your eyes or even take your 3D glasses off. When an orchestra harmonizes with perfect tones across the room, you may just feel the need to lay back and smile.

Here are the native graphics frameworks you can use to create your delightful 3D experience in augmented reality:

- SpriteKit

- SceneKit

- Metal

# SpriteKit

Let's talk SpriteKit. Sprite is Apple's graphics framework to create 2D experiences. In regard to augmented reality, SpriteKit is anything 2D in the 3D space. Imagine a video player hanging on a wall, a watch face wrapped around your wrist, or a screen of an arcade machine. These are three examples of where SceneKit can improve the 3D experience of your app.

# SceneKit

SceneKit is going to be your de facto or second-choice graphics framework. Even when you work with SpriteKit, there will be a time where you'd want to position and orientate a 2D shape a certain way. SpriteKit on its own without SceneKit will be a 2D asset that continuously faces you no matter how you move.

The SceneKit framework is not lower-level graphics frameworks like Metal. SceneKit is a high-level graphics API. Unless you are creating a graphical performance intense game, you may want to get the hang of SceneKit at least before working with Metal.

The strength of learning a higher-level graphics framework is that you can get the gist of how everything works (the big picture), before working on the optimizations.

Having said that, make no mistake that SceneKit is a high-performance rendering engine. It can handle animation, physics simulations, particle effects, realistic physically based rendering, and more while bringing you descriptive APIs to work with your 3D assets.

SceneKit is the way to go for more apps that don't require supporting graphically intense performances.

# Metal, RealityKit, Reality Composer

Once you've mastered SceneKit and would like to take graphics performances steps further, then look into Metal. Working with Metal means you'd have to worry about a lot more than SceneKit. This is not saying SceneKit is a walk in the park at all.

Metal has a higher learning curve. You'd need to worry about more detailed configurations—even for something simple. Hence, for people who need the maximization of graphical and computational power for their apps, this may fit you. Metal is a graphics framework that provides near-direct access to the graphics processing unit, according to Apple.

It's also good to note that SpriteKit, SceneKit, and RealityKit are general-purpose graphics frameworks that leverage Metal to achieve high-performance rendering. These higher-level frameworks are simply for not having to worry about writing a rendering/graphics engine from scratch and instead focus on delivering the experience at hand.

With the introduction of RealityKit and Reality Composer, the high-learning curve of creating augmented reality experience with Metal has been drastically lowered. This is because RealityKit is built for augmented reality with ease of use in mind. You'll also learn to make use of Metal with RealityKit and Reality Composer later in the book.

# Up Next

Warm up the engines. Before launch off into building augmented reality apps, you're going to learn about ARKit's session life cycles and tracking quality.

# Session Life Cycles and Tracking Quality

When developing an ARKit app, there are many factors to take note of for optimal app performance and user-friendly experience. Sometimes, especially with augmented reality apps, you'll find yourself needing to find the balance between the two because of mainly hardware or environment limitations. Nevertheless, you will need to handle your app's augmented reality session life cycles, keep track of the tracking quality of the app, and create the appropriate user interfaces to bind the two together.

# Session Life Cycles

There are session life cycles to an augmented reality app. The normal flow of your app goes as follows for the augmented reality camera's tracking states:

1.  Not available

2.  Limited with reason

3.  Normal

All of these values are a part of an enum value type, `ARCamera.TrackingState`.

# Not Available Tracking State

Beginning with the not available tracking state, it indicates feature point deficiency to recognize the device's position within the world. Hence, in `ARCamera.TrackingState.notAvailable`, ARKit needs an additional feeding of feature points.

# Limited Tracking State

After your app has gathered some feature points, ARKit can use the feature points to make sense of the device position.

Depending on the feature points and the world map ARKit can generate, the current feature points may not be enough to map out, say, a flat horizontal or vertical plane surface, for various reasons. As a result, this is when ARKit returns the position-tracking status of `ARCamera.TrackingState.limited(_:)`.

There are many reasons for which an app's tracking could be limited. The first reason can be insufficient feature points. ARKit may throw this error when the camera faces a blank wall, receives poor lighting, etc.

The second limited position-tracking quality reason can be the AR session's initialization state. The AR session initializes and needs to accumulate enough camera or motion data.

The third reason for poor position-tracking quality can be due to excessive motion. This happens when the user moves the device way too quickly for the images to make sense. You can imagine how blurry images are fundamentally incompatible for accurate image-based positioning.

The fourth limited position-tracking quality is when an AR session is interrupted and needs to relocalize. For example, you accept an incoming FaceTime video call.

In the limited tracking state, an ARKit app can function with imperfect conditions. However, the performance and accuracy of object positioning and device position have plenty of room for improvement.

At this state, plane detection is limited from adding or updating a plane anchor and hit-testing results. Hence, this condition is best met with more quality feature points for ARKit to make better sense of the world.

## Normal Tracking State

Finally, after going from no feature points to workable feature points, you have the ARCamera.TrackingState.normal tracking state. This is when ARKit can provide all available ARKit features. At this stage, your app works with a reliable world map. In adjunction, you'll be able to work with optimal feature points and surfaces to create a consistent and realistic augmented reality experience for the time being.

Do note that what is defined as the optimal state is based on ARKit understanding. If ARKit sees a flat surface, it will report a flat surface. However, ARKit may provide a false positive in contrast to what a user sees. ARKit may not always be right. Hence, providing users with the option to reset tracking can be vital to set the stage right before the performance starts.

Okay, so you've gathered the feature points, and the tracking state has gone from not available to limited to normal. Your app's AR camera tracking state is normal. Does this mean happily ever after? Or could a polar bear fall from the sky and crash into you? Let's look at the latter.

## Tracking Quality Transitions

If you've used augmented reality apps, you'll notice that sometimes objects slide away, or some odd interactions which you've yet accounted for. At this point, what do you do? Many times, this is simply ARKit's understanding of the environment changes. Previously, we've mentioned that ARKit can do its best work once it has gotten to the normal tracking state. With time passing after situating at the normal tracking state, your app is vulnerable to experience interruptions.

Anytime that your app fails to collect camera or motion-sensing data, your app session has been interrupted. Your app can be interrupted by a phone call, switching to another app, locking the device, or anything that removes your augmented reality app from the foreground. An interruption is the same as your app's AR session pausing.

After the hair force polar bear crashes into you to give you a friendly hug, the next event that occurs is making a friendly call to his friend for a drink. The bear passes you back the phone, and on he goes. You are flat on the ground from the bear hug. You switch from the Phone app to your AR app. At this stage, your app experience is interrupted due to the momentarily pause in camera and motion-sensing data input.

Interruption reconciliation should be available to bring your user back to the normal tracking state. Without the interruption reconciliation, your users may find themselves needing to quit the app and relaunch the app to give the app another chance. It is possible to mitigate the need for your users to relaunch your app to continue to experience an augmented reality app. Instead, ARKit can recover from session interruption.

# Relocalization Without a World Map

Once a session is interrupted, it is more likely than not that the virtual content is no longer positioned relative to the session's running real-world environment. Instead, the virtual content will look out of place. At this time, your app runs the session configurations once again.

Unlike the first time running the session configurations, one option available is relocalization. This can be set with the sessionShouldAttemptRelocalization(_:) *delegate method. If relocalization is enabled, ARKit tries to mesh together with the real-world environment from the last session.*

This process's success depends on the device's relative position and orientation to the last camera and motion-sensing data input. The closer the device is to those inputs, the higher the chance of relocalization.

Do note that the user can be stuck in this relocalization state indefinitely for when a user has moved to an entirely different environment. What happens is that ARKit tries and tries to relocalize only to be left with the action of trying. At this point, the user's option to reset the session is vital to your app's navigation.

Now, what about resuming a session after an app is quit or relaunched? Here comes the help of a world map.

# Relocalization with a World Map

From iOS 12 onward, ARKit uses world maps to relocalize from a session interruption. In addition, world maps persist as a means of aggregating space-mapping states and anchors of a world tracking AR session.

The beauty of world maps is that it can be saved as a file. This opens a particular session to a new realm of possibilities like world map persistence and multiuser experiences in augmented reality. A world map saves anchors from an AR session. As a result of these features, you can save virtual content from sessions.

Handling world map persistence is a feature up for timing considerations. Do you want your app to save world maps like a Mario game level where a session is saved once a checkpoint is reached? Do you want your user to save the virtual content for privacy discernment manually? Or do you want the app to automatically save a world map any time the app enters the background?

The first two cases vary depending on your app content. In the case of automatically saving a world map for when an app enters the background, a structured location to save this information is the AppDelegate's
`applicationDidEnterBackground(_:)` method. Upon the app's revival to

the foreground, set the session configuration's `initialWorldMap` property
to the world you have saved. On the topic of automatically saving world
maps, every session has a different world map. Hence, every world map
may be worth saving.

For a world map to succeed in relocalization, it would also need to visit
the environment its data amasses from. Upon successfully returning the
normal tracking state, a possible flow up to the normal track state is

1.  Run configuration with an initial world map

2.  Limited tracking state from initialization

3.  Limited tracking state from relocalization

4.  Normal tracking state

Similar to relocalization without a world map, in the scenario where a
user is in an entirely different environment coming from an interruption.
The user will stay in the relocalization state indefinitely unless given
the option to reset the configuration with the session configuration's
`initialWorldMap` property set to nil.

As you can see, many events can lead to an augmented reality session
off course. It is in the magic of the users not needing to understand all the
technology behind ARKit that makes an app feel like "it just works."

Behind the scene, it is you who can make this happen. By
understanding the session life cycles and tracking quality in ARKit, you
can handle the augmented real-world environment tracking edge cases
optimally.

# Up Next

Direction determines the destination. You will learn about designing an
exceptional augmented reality experience.

# CHAPTER 3

# Designing an Augmented Reality Experience

There are times when inspiration strikes. There are times when the iron is hot. When inspiration strikes and the iron is hot, that is usually when you have the greatest of momentum, and that is when you go all in. Right?

This exciting topic gives me the jellies just thinking about it. I believe what wakes up developers with jellies in their bellies is the thought of creating something world empowering, personal, or for the heck of fun. Okay, okay, drinking this grande caramel macchiato seems only to boost the jellies in my bellies. Before the jellies get out of control, who knows what will happen, let's begin on the design processes this chapter covers:

1. Ideas

2. User environment

3. The startup

4. Prototype

There are two efficient and effective ways to go about designing an augmented reality experience. Both ways begin with the idea of prototyping.

© Jayven Nhan 2022
J. Nhan, *Mastering ARKit*, https://doi.org/10.1007/978-1-4842-7836-9_3

# Ideas

There are good and bad ideas. Yet good or bad ideas are opinions. What defines a good or bad idea varies dramatically from person to person. It's not uncommon to contrast like night and day. This is great because it brings diversity that draws from different individuals' experiences. Now, let's move on to talking about augmented reality ideas.

The common question goes along the line: What do you think about building an augmented reality app? What if we put this into an augmented reality experience? How do we make this app great on augmented reality? Those questions sometimes drive me a bit crazy and are many times fundamentally flawed.

You're indeed at a stage of augmented reality where there's not much to look back on, and what works or doesn't work is still experimentation. The enthusiasm toward what's possible is a positive drive toward using technology to push humanity forward. However, many questions stem from technology and not the user experience.

## Why Start with the User Experience?

Every technology has its strengths and weaknesses. Augmented reality is no different. Many ideas can work with different technology with adaptations. Some works are better than others. For example, a game like *Clash of Clans* works rather well on iOS, iPadOS, and Android platforms. Hey, why don't we put the game into an augmented reality experience?

At first, this idea may sound fun. Let me be the fire extinguisher and say this idea is horrendous. It will probably get a lot of initial traction because the game has a solid brand and a loyal user base. The problem is that merely converting *Clash of Clans* from a flat-screen into 3D world won't cut it. You have to start with the user experience first and see if bringing such an experience into augmented reality makes sense.

Simply thinking about using a specific technology will result in lackluster user experiences. Because as obvious as it may sound, the user experience isn't the focus here.

Today, apps like *Notes* or *Clash of Clans* offer magnitudes of convenience compared to starting an augmented reality experience. In addition, those experiences work consistently and effectively. So what may compel users to choose an augmented reality experience?

# Augmented Reality Benefits

Augmented reality offers unique benefits that other technologies do not provide. These benefits are enablers of an app that would not be possible otherwise. Here are the top three benefits you get for building on top of augmented reality:

1. Physical world environment

2. Physical world objects

3. Overlaying virtual objects

Those are the three differentiating benefits of choosing augmented reality.

## Physical World Environment

The technology feels real because you are using the real-world environment. An environment such as time of the day will play an essential role in how your app feels as well.

Is it night or daytime? Is it a sunny or rainy day? How big is the room that you are currently experiencing your augmented reality app on?

## Physical World Objects

If there's a puppy in the real world in front of you, there's a puppy in front of you in augmented reality as well. You can have physical objects to work with. Physical objects combined with the world environment, you also get the best physics engine in the world—real-world physics.

## Overlaying Virtual Objects

Now, by having a layer on top of the world, augmented reality allows you to add objects or create events in the physical world with technology virtualization. You get to amplify the physical world with augmented reality. You can enable physical environment or objects to do things which they otherwise could not without the technology.

Whatever virtual objects are in augmented reality will feel natural. Users will expect second-nature user interfaces and interactions.

The technology will eventually head to a state where the virtual and physical world is blended so well that it'd take quite the brainpower to distinguish the material from the virtual.

# Idea Case Studies

Those are the unique benefits of augmented reality. Now, let's look at idea case studies for why some ideas may be better than the others. Let's take a couple of case studies that consider the unique powers of augmented reality into account.

## Case Study 1: Virtual Shoe Store

Imagine an app that enables people to try on shoes virtually. Theoretically, this sounds like a promising concept. However, digging deeper, the app doesn't give the user greater business value than trying on the shoes physically.

Shoes, for many people, represent fashion and culture. People have a very personal connection with shoes. Putting on the virtual shoe isn't remotely close to putting on a physical shoe. If connecting the shoe with the customer is the goal, the virtual solution stales in comparison to the physical solution.

Imagine putting on a pair of Adidas Ultraboost. Currently, augmented reality doesn't equate how a shoe fits your feet in real life.

Even by giving the technology the benefit of the doubt, say it becomes perfect. The virtual shoe looks in every respect as it would at the store. The shoe's material wraps naturally around the shape of your feet. The shoe absorbs and bounces the lights flawlessly off the shoe material.

Even with these conditions met, trying on a pair of virtual shoes doesn't give the user the actual experience of putting on a shoe.

From taking a pair of shoes out of a box to feeling the materials, you can't even feel how the shoe feels on your feet. You also can't test the traction of the shoe or how the outsole rubberizes the floor. And you can't experience the lacing of your shoe and feel inside materials.

If you're going for seeing a pair of the shoe look on your feet, privacy, or convenience, those are more convincing reasons for using the app.

An alternative to the app is to go to a shoe store. And try on the actual pair of Adidas Ultraboost. Here are some benefits of the physical solution.

The first benefit, what you see is what you get. And it's as real as the shoes get. The shoes are real.

The second benefit, you can try on the pair of shoes and feel the shoes. The shoe adopts the world physics engine.

You can feel how materials wrap around your feet. You can wiggle your toes around to experience how the material stretches. You can feel and test if the shoe is too tight or too loose.

You can stand up, jump up and down, walk around, jog around, or even do burpees with the shoes. You can lace your shoe to your personal preference. You can feel how the heat distribution is like with the shoe on.

The third benefit, the "workflow" for trying on the pair of shoes, is native experience. You wear your shoe in a physical world, and your shoe works for you in the physical world.

In other words, the app could simulate the physical shoe all its want. However, the virtual solution will always fall short of the physical solution.

What if you put on a pair of jeans and a Nike tee to see how it looks? Will you have to position your camera somewhere optimal to see how you look with those clothing on? Are these features solid enough? Does it mean that I may have to place my iPhone on the ground and use the front-facing camera to see how I look at a distance? This sounds like a horrible experience and humans adapting to technology and not technology adapting for humans.

The big question here is, will the experience be better experienced in the augmented reality or physical world?

# Case Study 2: Computer Science Education

Do humans study better from textbooks or personal experiences? Are humans more likely to believe and remember what they see and feel or what they read? Do computer science students prefer to study concepts by reading abstraction or working familiar physical objects? Let's see the potential benefits of a computer science education augmented reality app.

The first benefit—the "workflow" is natural. You can touch and move objects to see how they respond. Professors choose virtual objects to present, amplify an object's scale, change the material's color for emphasis, etc.

The professor can also have students come up to the front of the class and demonstrate their understanding of a computer science data structure or algorithm by moving elements around. Or a student can be location agnostic. He/she can have a real-time model copy in front of him/her and answer the question from his/her desk. The students will also be in "the front of the class" and see clearly.

The second benefit—professors can livestream and interact with students. Once again, a location-agnostic virtual class available worldwide. And students can interact with the class virtual objects.

An often-overlooked factor in education is learning resources for every student. In the virtual world, a lack of monetary resources doesn't limit a school's ability to buy, maintain, and update learning resources. In fact, every student "can" have the most up-to-date learning materials always.

Plus, professors can build around augmented reality experiences or lessons. Prepared lessons empower students with the ability to launch interactive lessons anytime and anywhere. Even students who are working day and night shifts, with little time, can have an impressive education. It only takes the best teacher to create a world-class course once to share with the world.

The third benefit—students can have an optimized learning experience. Some students require accessibility features. Imagine yourself as a student and catching a cold one day. You decide to stay home to prevent the risk of flu transmission to others at school.

You feel depleted in energy. Can't move, but you can speak. Guess what? You can still engage in the computer science lesson with Voice Control.

Also, in a traditional class and particularly in colleges with 800 students in a room, what a professor is doing in front of the class can be difficult to see without big monitors. Even then, it can be hard to follow what the professor is doing without the camera to follow the action appropriately. With augmented reality, you can have a copy of what your professor has and scale/color your assets to fit your needs. Plus, you can also work with your team/friends on solving a computer science project together.

This computer science education app example fits naturally in the physical world's existing workflows. Furthermore, there are student interactivity, accessibility, and personalization benefits.

# The Startup

Every augmented reality experience has to be given data about the real world. This usually means having enough lighting and moving a device around to feed data about space. This part of the experience is going to be experienced by all your users. Hence, it is especially important to make this process a great experience as well.

Based on your app's context, you can make this experience feel magical by invisibly detecting the physical world. Here's an example.

Instead of asking a user to scan a surface in a treasure hunting game, the app can ask the user to look around his/her space to see what he/she can find. *Pokémon Go* makes good use of this. Instead of asking the user to move his/her device back and forth, it makes the user explore the tall grasses.

As the user explores the tall grasses, the surface detection is done invisibly. Once the user has helped the app detect a surface area, the user can take on the grass to uncover the Pokémon.

Not every app needs to detect surfaces invisibly. Some apps could make more sense to be direct. It can feel foreign and mysterious to have different instructions with every app.

Part of easing the onboarding experience is to use standard user interfaces—user interfaces that users have either experienced before or will experience again in other apps. Apple has provided an API to standardize ARKit's world tracking onboarding. You would want to work with `ARCoachingOverlayView` in this case.

# User Environment

## Scale

An augmented reality experience can take precedence on multiple scales. They can range from table scale, room scale, and even world scale.

# Table Scale

Table scale is a small and defined area experience. Think about a slingshot game. Apple has a sample project introduced in WWDC18 called *SwiftShot*. That's one example of an augmented reality experience taking place on a table scale.

# Room Scale

The room scale takes on an initially defined surface area. Then, the experience can expand to take account of larger surface areas—for example, an augmented reality experience that asks you to continue to move around a room to discover more treasures after discovering the first treasure.

Room-scale augmented experiences handle potential surface area more significant than the initial exposure. This experience, however, still bounds to a specific space. For example, the experience could limit to a specific room at a particular place. Or the experience can only support an experience up to a certain amount of space like 10 meters square at most.

# World Scale

World scale is an augmented reality experience that has no area bounds. This experience continues to create the physical and virtual blend as you move throughout the physical world. You could have an augmented reality app that has an AI tour guide. You can walk anywhere around the world with this app turned on. The tour guide will show you the path to the landmark of a city, provide information on mysterious dishes, and even tell you about the city's culture and policy as the app explores the world with you.

# Defined and Undefined Space

The three scales explain environments that augmented reality applications can take place. However, it is more advantageous to think about the app experience in a defined or undefined space. This way of thinking supports a broader range of edge cases.

A defined space is a specified space where all content will take place. On the other hand, an undefined space is a growing space where content can continuously adapt to new space.

The table scale falls in the defined space category. The room and world scales fall into the undefined space category.

Part of defining the staple to place your virtual objects is to define the user environment. It comes down to choosing between building for defined and undefined user environment.

# Augmented Reality Experience Prototyping

Getting an augmented reality experience prototype up and ready today can be time-consuming and effort-expensive without using the fitting tools for the fitting occasions.

At times, a naive method toward going about prototyping an augmented reality app is building the full fletch app. Then, continuously go back and forth between code implementations and running the app on a device.

This approach looks fine for app maintenance. But for app prototyping, it can be incredibly time-consuming and effort-expensive. Perhaps, there's a couple of approaches that help you prototype faster and without wasted efforts.

This chapter introduces the following prototyping methods:

- Physical prototyping

- Reality Composer

Now, let's get started!

# Physical Prototyping

The idea behind physical prototyping is simple. You need the Camera app and creativity with the objects you have around you.

Say, you want to build a Starbucks merchandise app. Where can you start?

You could be prototyping for a price tag label for your app. If this is the case, you can simply use paper and pen to prototype.

You can cut/fold a piece of paper. Write on the piece of paper. Then, position the piece of paper based on how you see fit.

For example, here's a Starbucks merchandise app in the prototyping phase.

I open the Camera app. Switch to video mode. See the physical objects through the camera lens. This took about 1 minute to get up and running.

Depending on your app's complexity, your surrounding materials are likely more than enough for the prototype. However, for certain scenarios, there are more exceptional solutions.

For example, you find your surrounding materials insufficient for a prototype. Or your app has come to a complexity where the effort doesn't justify the physical prototype solution. I'm here to tell you that there's a powerful Apple developer tool that you can use that makes prototyping a piece of cake, under the condition that you're familiar with the tool.

# Reality Composer

Apple announces Reality Composer in WWDC19. The announcement is unanticipated, but I surely won't be the last person to tell you how great of a prototyping tool Reality Composer is.

Reality Composer is like an augmented reality focused version of Xcode. It's powerful. It helps developers build amazing augmented reality experiences. But also like Xcode, there's a steep learning curve to become efficient and effective with Reality Composer.

Once you get over the learning curve hump, you can prototype augmented reality experiences like a madman or madwoman. The beauty with Reality Composer is what you see is what you get. Unlike physical prototyping, where the physical assets typically don't resemble the preciseness of virtual assets, Reality Composer takes you to a real augmented reality experience with the physical and virtual world blend.

What can you do with Reality Composer? Reality Composer comes with a library of assets. This includes assets that are mutable geometry like a rectangle prism or actual 3D assets provided by Apple like a toy. You can create animation chain, on-hit sound effects, gravitational and object collision physics simulation, and occlusion effect and see how virtual objects look when you place them on a wall or even your face.

Using Reality Composer gives you a convenient way to bridge from prototyping to actual production code. I believe people who invest time in developing augmented reality experience should understand Reality Composer well. Not only can you design, but you can also help others see how an augmented reality experience can play out in record time.

For now, the takeaway is that Reality Composer is typically the overall best prototyping tool for realism, efficacy, and workflow integration. You'll learn more about Reality Composer in the later chapters.

# Conclusion

Two augmented reality experience prototyping methods are physical prototyping and utilizing Reality Composer. The former utilized the camera and physical objects. The latter allows you to leverage augmented reality experience building tools provided by Apple that you can import into your project without a sweat. Both are fantastic prototyping tools.

As a matter of fact, you can start prototyping your next great augmented reality experience now. After this chapter, you will essentially do one thing and "build" all kinds of augmented reality experiences to the end of the book. Woo-hoo, can't wait for all these exciting chapters!

# CHAPTER 4

# Building Your First ARKit App with SceneKit

Augmented reality is here. It is coming in a *big* way. Remember *Pokémon Go*? Well, that's just a taste of augmented reality. Apple is bringing augmented reality to the masses, starting with iOS 11. With iOS 11, hundreds of millions of iPhones and iPads are going to be AR capable. This will make ARKit the largest AR platform in the world—overnight. Yes—overnight. If you are interested in building augmented reality apps for iOS 11 and above, then you are in the right place.

## Purpose

This chapter helps you familiarize the fundamentals of ARKit using SceneKit by building out an ARKit Demo App.

It's time to get your feet wet, have you see the process of building out an ARKit app, and let you interact with the AR world through your device.

The whole idea of this tutorial is to learn the technology and its APIs by building an app. By going through the process, you understand how ARKit works in a real device to interact with the awesome 3D objects you create.

© Jayven Nhan 2022
J. Nhan, *Mastering ARKit*, https://doi.org/10.1007/978-1-4842-7836-9_4

Before getting too fancy, let's understand the very fundamentals first, and that's what this tutorial aims to do.

# Content

Here are the content topics I will walk you through:

- Creating a new project for ARKit apps

- Setting up ARKit SceneKit View

- Connecting ARSCNView with View Controller

- Connecting IBOutlet

- Configuring ARSCNView session

- Allowing camera usage

- Adding 3D object to ARSCNView

- Adding gesture recognizer to ARSCNView

- Removing objects from ARSCNView

- Adding multiple objects to ARSCNView

- Updating objects from ARSCNView

# Creating a New Project

Go ahead and open up Xcode. In the Xcode menu, select **File ➤ New ➤ Project....** Select **iOS**. Choose **App**. Click **Next**. Xcode has the Augmented Reality App template. But you can just use the iOS App template to build an AR app.

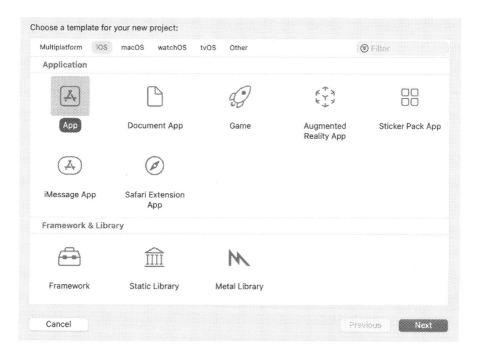

You can **name your project** whatever you want. I've named my project ARKitDemo. And then press **Next** to create your new project.

# Setting Up ARKit SceneKit View

Now open up **Main.storyboard**. Look inside the **Object Library** for the ARKit SceneKit View. Drag an **ARKit SceneKit View** onto your View Controller.

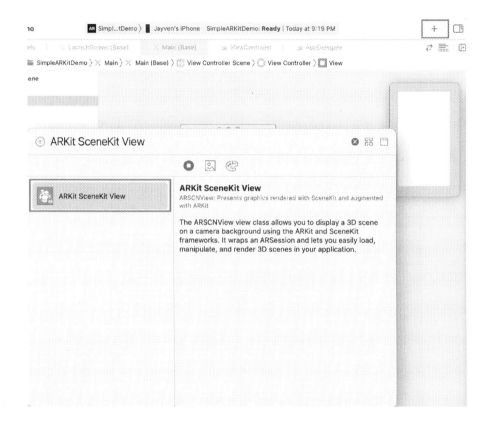

Then give your ARKit SceneKit View **constraints to fill out** the entire View Controller's view.

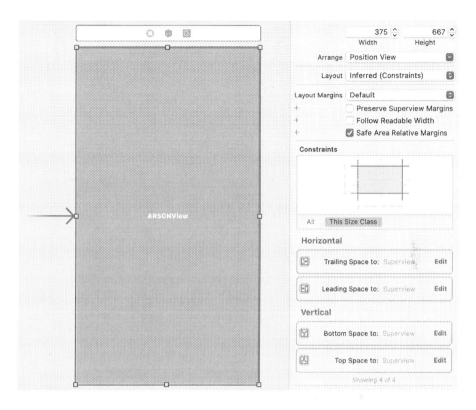

It should look something like this:

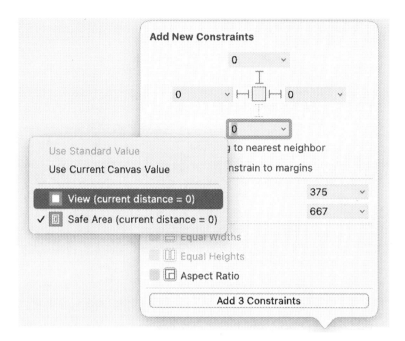

Cool. This ARKit SceneKit View is where we will display SceneKit content with augmented reality.

# Connecting IBOutlet

We are still on the Main.storyboard file. Go up to the toolbar and open up the Assistant Editor.

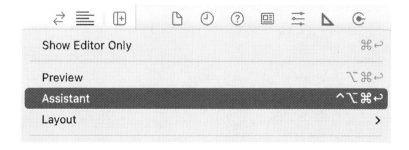

Add an import statement at the top of the ViewController file to import `ARKit`:

```
import ARKit
```

Then hold control and drag from the ARKit SceneKit View to the **ViewController** file. When prompted, name the IBOutlet `sceneView`.

# Configuring ARSCNView Session

We want our app to start looking into the world through the camera lens and start detecting the environment around us. This is quite an insane technology if you think about it. Apple has made augmented reality possible for developers without developing the entire technology from the ground up. Thank you, Apple, for blessing us with ARKit.

Okay. Now it's time to configure the ARKit SceneKit View. Insert the following codes to `ViewController`:

```
override func viewWillAppear(_ animated: Bool) {
  super.viewWillAppear(animated)
  let configuration = ARWorldTrackingConfiguration()
  sceneView.session.run(configuration)
}
```

In `viewWillAppear(_:)`, you initialize an AR configuration called `ARWorldTrackingConfiguration`. This is a configuration for running world tracking.

But wait, what is world tracking? According to Apple's documentation:

> *World tracking provides 6 degrees of freedom tracking of the device. By finding feature points in the scene, world tracking enables performing hit-tests against the frame. Tracking can no longer be resumed once the session is paused.*

— Apple's Documentation

The world tracking configuration tracks the device's orientation and position. It also detects real-world surfaces seen through the device's camera.

Now we set the `sceneView` AR session to run the configuration we just initialized. The AR session manages motion tracking and camera image processing for the view's contents.

Now add another method in `ViewController`:

```
override func viewWillDisappear(_ animated: Bool) {
  super.viewWillDisappear(animated)
  sceneView.session.pause()
}
```

In `viewWillDisappear(_:)`, you simply tell the AR session to stop tracking motion and stop processing images for the view's content.

# Allowing Camera Usage

Before you can run your app, you need to inform our users that we will utilize their device's camera for augmented reality. This is a requirement since the release of iOS 10. Hence, open up Info.plist. Right-click the editor and choose **Add row**. Set the Key to **Privacy—Camera Usage Description**. Set the Value to **For Augmented Reality**.

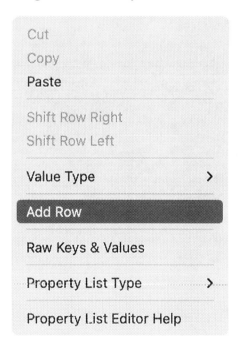

Before moving on, let's make sure that you have everything set up correctly up to this point.

Take out your device. Hook it up to your Mac. Build and run the project on Xcode. The app should prompt you to allow camera access. Tap okay.

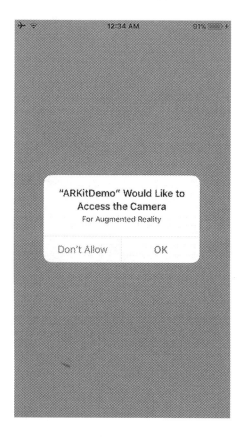

Now you should be able to see your camera's view.

We have configured our sceneView's session to run the world tracking configuration. It's time for the exciting part. Augmented reality!

# Adding 3D Object to ARSCNView

The time has come. The moment we have all been waiting for.

Without further ado, let's augment reality. We are going to begin by adding a box. Insert the following code to your ViewController class:

```
func addBox() {
```

```
let box = SCNBox(width: 0.1, height: 0.1, length: 0.1,
chamferRadius: 0)

let boxNode = SCNNode()
boxNode.geometry = box
boxNode.position = SCNVector3(0, 0, -0.2)

let scene = SCNScene()
scene.rootNode.addChildNode(boxNode)
sceneView.scene = scene
}
```

Here's what we did.

We begin by creating a box shape. 1 Float = 1 meter.

After that, we create a node. A node represents the position and the coordinates of an object in a 3D space. By itself, the node has no visible content.

We can give the node visible content by giving it a shape. We do this by setting the node's geometry to the box.

Afterward, we give our node a position. This position is relative to the camera. Positive x is to the right. Negative x is to the left. Positive y is up. Negative y is down. Positive z is backward. Negative z is forward.

Then we create a scene. This is the SceneKit scene to be displayed in the view. We then add our box node to the root node of the scene. A root node in a scene defines the coordinate system of the real world rendered by SceneKit.

Basically, our scene now has a box. The box is centered on the device's camera. It is 0.20 meters forward relative to the camera.

Finally, we set our sceneView's scene to display the scene we just created.

Now call addBox() in viewDidLoad():

```
override func viewDidLoad() {
  super.viewDidLoad()
  addBox()
}
```

Build and run the app. You should be able to see a floating box!

You can also refactor addBox() to simply:

```
func addBox() {
  let box = SCNBox(width: 0.05, height: 0.05, length: 0.05,
  chamferRadius: 0)
```

```
let boxNode = SCNNode()
boxNode.geometry = box
boxNode.position = SCNVector3(0, 0, -0.2)

sceneView.scene.rootNode.addChildNode(boxNode)
}
```

It is easier to explain some components individually.

Alright. It's time to add gesture recognition.

# Adding Tap Gesture Recognizer to ARSCNView

Right below the addBox() method, add the following codes:

```
func addTapGestureToSceneView() {
  let tapGestureRecognizer = UITapGestureRecognizer(
    target: self,
    action:  #selector(ViewController.didTap(withGesture
    Recognizer:)))
  sceneView.addGestureRecognizer(tapGestureRecognizer)
}
```

Here, we initialize a tap gesture recognizer with the target set to the ViewController with the action selector set to the didTap(withGestureRec ognizer:) callback function. Then we add the tap gesture recognizer onto the sceneView.

Now it's time to do something with the tap gesture recognizer's callback function.

# Removing Object from ARSCNView

Insert the following method in the **ViewController** file:

```
@objc func didTap(withGestureRecognizer recognizer:
UIGestureRecognizer) {
  let tapLocation = recognizer.location(in: sceneView)
  let hitTestResults = sceneView.hitTest(tapLocation)
  guard let node = hitTestResults.first?.node else { return }
  node.removeFromParentNode()
}
```

Here, we created a didTap(withGestureRecognizer:) method. We
retrieve the user's tap location relative to the sceneView and hit test to see
if we tap onto any node(s).

Afterward, we safely unwrap the first node from our hitTestResults.
If the result does contain at least a node, we will remove the first node we
tapped on from its parent node.

Before we test the object removal, update the viewDidLoad() method
to add a call to the addTapGestureToSceneView() method:

```
override func viewDidLoad() {
  super.viewDidLoad()

  addBox()
  addTapGestureToSceneView()
}
```

Now, if you build and run your project, you should be able to tap the
box node and remove it from the scene view.

Looks like we are back to ground one.

Okay. Now it's time to add multiple objects.

# Adding Multiple Objects to ARSCNView

Now our box is a bit lonely. Let's give the box some boxes. We are going to add objects from the detection of feature points.

So what are feature points?

According to Apple, here is the definition of a feature point:

> A point automatically identified by ARKit as part of a continuous surface, but without a corresponding anchor.

It is basically the detected points on the surface of real-world objects. So back to the implementation of adding boxes. Before we do that, let's create an extension at the end of the `ViewController` class:

```
extension float4x4 {
  var translation: SIMD3<Float> {
    let translation = self.columns.3
    return SIMD3<Float>(translation.x, translation.y,
    translation.z)
  }
}
```

This extension basically transforms a matrix into `float3`. It gives us the x, y, and z from the matrix.

Also, we need to modify `addBox()` to the following:

```
func addBox(x: Float = 0, y: Float = 0, z: Float = -0.2) {
  let box = SCNBox(width: 0.1, height: 0.1, length: 0.1,
  chamferRadius: 0)

  let boxNode = SCNNode()
  boxNode.geometry = box
  boxNode.position = SCNVector3(x, y, z)

  sceneView.scene.rootNode.addChildNode(boxNode)
}
```

We basically added parameters to the initial addBox() function. We also gave it default parameter values. This means that we can call addBox() without having to specify the x, y, and z coordinates like in viewDidLoad().

Cool.

Now we need to modify the didTap(withGestureRecognizer:) method. We want to add an object to the feature point if there is one that can be detected.

So inside of our guard let statement, add before our return statement. Add the following code:

```
let hitTestResultsWithFeaturePoints = sceneView.
hitTest(tapLocation, types:
  .featurePoint)

if let hitTestResultWithFeaturePoints = hitTestResultsWith
FeaturePoints.first {
  let translation = hitTestResultWithFeaturePoints.
  worldTransform.translation
  addBox(x: translation.x, y: translation.y, z: translation.z)
}
```

This is what we are doing.

First, we perform a hit test, similar to how we hit test the first time around. Except that, we specify a .featurePoint result type for the types parameter. The types parameter asks the hit test to search for real-world objects or surfaces detected through the AR session's processing of the camera image. There are many types of result type. However, we will focus on just the feature point in this tutorial.

After the hit test of feature points, we safely unwrap the first hit test result. This is important because there may not always be a feature point. ARKit may not always detect a real-world object or a surface in the real world.

If the first hit test result can be safely unwrapped, then we transform the matrix of type `matrix_float4x4` to `float3`. This is possible because of the extension we created earlier. This handily gives us the x, y, and z real-world coordinates that we are interested in.

We then take the x, y, and z to add a new box upon tapping on a detected feature point.

Your `didTap(withGestureRecognizer:)` method should look like this:

```
@objc func didTap(withGestureRecognizer recognizer:
UIGestureRecognizer) {
  let tapLocation = recognizer.location(in: sceneView)
  let hitTestResults = sceneView.hitTest(tapLocation)
  guard let node = hitTestResults.first?.node else {
    let hitTestResultsWithFeaturePoints = sceneView.
    hitTest(tapLocation, types: .featurePoint)
    if let hitTestResultWithFeaturePoints =
     hitTestResultsWithFeaturePoints.first  {
      let translation =
       hitTestResultWithFeaturePoints.worldTransform.translation
      addBox(x: translation.x, y: translation.y, z: translation.z)
    }
    return
  }
  node.removeFromParentNode()
}
```

Next, you'll learn to move the box around with pan gesture recognizer integration with `ARSCNView`.

# Implementing Pan Gesture Recognizer on ARSCNView

Often enough, interacting with objects require update in addition create and delete. Especially when ARKit continuously discover new feature points and understand the world better, you want to give the user the ability to move objects to new places too. You'll learn to do exactly that by giving the box the ability to move to new feature point locations.

Add the following method to ViewController:

```
@objc func didPan(withGestureRecognizer recognizer:
UIPanGestureRecognizer) {
    // 1
  switch recognizer.state {
    // 2
  case .began:
    print("Pan Began")
    // 3
  case .changed:
    print("Pan Changed")
    let tapLocation = recognizer.location(in: sceneView)
    let hitTestResults = sceneView.hitTest(tapLocation)
    guard let node = hitTestResults.first?.node,
      let hitTestResultWithFeaturePoints = sceneView.hitTest(
        tapLocation, types: .featurePoint).first else {
        return }
    let worldTransform = SCNMatrix4(
      hitTestResultWithFeaturePoints.worldTransform)
    node.setWorldTransform(worldTransform)
    // 4
  case .ended:
    print("Pan Ended")
```

```
  // 5
  default:
    break
  }
}
```

With the code you've added, you:

1. Declare a switch statement on pan gesture's state.

2. If the state of the recognizer has began, simply print "Pan Began" in the console for debugging.

3. When the pan gesture is in motion, hit test for a node and a feature point. If both objects exist, set the node's world position to the feature point's world position.

4. If the state of the recognizer has ended, simply print "Pan Began" in the console for debugging.

Next, you'll need to register a pan gesture recognizer. Add the following method to ViewController:

```
func addPanGestureToSceneView() {
  let panGestureRecognizer = UIPanGestureRecognizer(
    target: self, action: #selector(didPan(withGesture
    Recognizer:)))
  sceneView.addGestureRecognizer(panGestureRecognizer)
}
```

The method you've added registers sceneView with a pan gesture recognizer. And add the following code to viewDidLoad():

```
addPanGestureToSceneView()
```

You simply call the method to register the pan gesture onto the scene view when the view loads.

# Trying Out the Final App

Build and run your project. In addition to previous features, you should now be able to add a box onto a feature point. And you should also be able to move a box onto a new feature point.

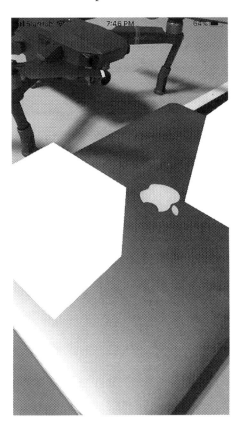

# Wrap Up

Congratulations on making it this far into the chapter. ARKit is a huge topic in itself. We have gone through a lot of the fundamentals. Yet we have only scratched the very surface of ARKit.

I hope you've enjoyed this introduction to ARKit. I can't wait to see the amazing ARKit app ideas that developers like you are going to build.

# CHAPTER 5

# Understanding and Implementing 3D Objects

Having great visual elements can give your app a unique personality. In this tutorial, we will look at 3D objects creation toolsets, online resources for 3D objects, and SceneKit supported formats and, most importantly, learn to build a very simple ARKit app using SceneKit.

Without further ado, let's cook up some 3D objects, and this is going to be fun!

## What You're Going to Learn

Alright! There is a ton of things we will walk through together. Here are the topics you will learn in this tutorial:

- A brief introduction to 3D objects creation toolsets and resources

- How to implement a single node 3D object

- How to add basic lighting

- How to implement a multiple nodes 3D object

- How to create or find the 3D Objects?

# 3D Objects Creation Toolsets

As we are going to render some 3D objects, let's first see how we can create them or find the resources.

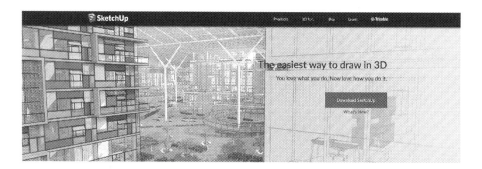

First, you can use 3D objects creation toolsets to create your 3D models from scratch. Or you can also use these toolsets to export existing 3D models in certain file formats to one which is SceneKit compatible. We will touch more on SceneKit supported format later on. If you plan to create your own 3D objects, here are some of the tools you can check out:

- Blender (www.blender.org/)

- SketchUp (www.sketchup.com/)

- Autodesk 3ds Max (www.autodesk.com/products/3ds-max/overview)

# Online Resources for 3D Objects

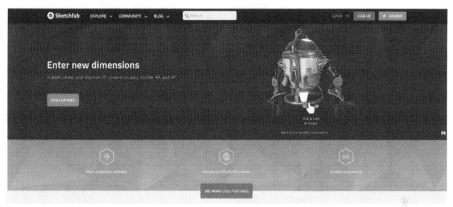

## SceneKit Supported Format

We will use SceneKit to build the ARKit app. In order to load a 3D object onto the ARKit app, Xcode needs to read your 3D object file in a SceneKit supported format. That totally makes sense.

> *SceneKit can read scene contents from a file in a supported format, or from an NSData object holding the contents of such a file.*
>
> —Apple's Documentation

In this chapter, the two SceneKit supported formats that we will look into later are **SceneKit Scene (.scn)** and **Digital Asset Exchange (.dae)**.

## Getting Started with the Starter Project

To begin with, open the **starter project** first. I've built the skeleton of the app and bundled two 3D files so that we can focus on the ARKit implementation. Once downloaded, open it in Xcode and run it for a quick test.

You should see the following on your iOS device.

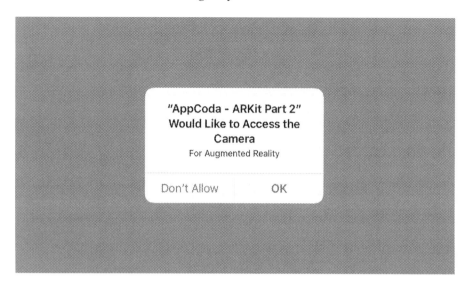

Tap OK. You should be able to see your camera's view—something like this if you happen to be coding at the Apple Store.

# Implementing a Single Node 3D Object

Awesome! Now it's time to add a single node 3D object onto our ARSCNView. Insert the following method in the `ViewController` class:

```
func addPaperPlane(x: Float = 0, y: Float = 0, z: Float
= -0.5) {
  guard let paperPlaneScene = SCNScene(named: "paperPlane.
  scn"), let paperPlaneNode = paperPlaneScene.rootNode.
  childNode(withName: "paperPlane", recursively: true) else {
  return }
  paperPlaneNode.position = SCNVector3(x, y, z)
  sceneView.scene.rootNode.addChildNode(paperPlaneNode)
}
```

In the preceding code, we first initialized and safely unwrapped a **SCNScene** object with a **paperPlane.scn** file, which is the 3D file bundled in the starter project.

Next, we initialized and safely unwrapped a **SCNNode** object with a paperPlane node name. We also set the recursive parameter to true. The recursive parameter decides whether SceneKit searches the child node subtree using a preorder traversal or not.

> *All scene content—nodes, geometries and their materials, lights, cameras, and related objects—is organized in a node hierarchy with a single common root node.*
>
> —Apple's Documentation

Once the node is initialized, we set the `paperPlaneNode`'s position to the x, y, and z arguments. The default position is the zero vector, indicating that the node is placed at the origin of the parent node's coordinate system. For the method, we set the default value of z to -0.5, indicating that the object is placed in front of the camera.

Finally, we add the paperPlaneNode to the rootNode of the sceneView.

```
override func viewDidLoad() {
  super.viewDidLoad()
  addPaperPlane()
}
```

Build and run on your device. You should see a solid white paper plane!

At the moment, the paper plane is a bit difficult to visualize. That's because of a lack of light and shadow. In the real world, we see things with lights and shadows. Lights and shadows help us visualize 3D objects.

If you open the **paperPlane.scn** file under the 3D Objects folder, you can see that the paper plane is solid white. So it doesn't have many visual depths.

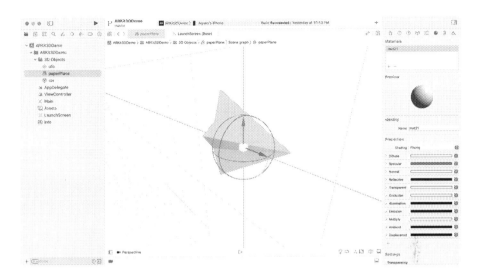

So let's add some light onto our paper plane!

# Adding Basic Lighting

There is more than one way to add lighting. For this project, we will focus on automatic lighting and automatic update lighting.

In the ViewController class, add the following method:

```
func configureLighting() {
  sceneView.autoenablesDefaultLighting = true
  sceneView.automaticallyUpdatesLighting = true
}
```

Cool. Here is what we just did:

We created a configureLighting() method.

Inside the method, we set the sceneView's autoenablesDefaultLighting property to true. If the autoenablesDefaultLighting property is set to true, SceneKit automatically adds lights to the scene. Technically, SceneKit automatically adds and places an omnidirectional light source when rendering scenes that contain no lights or only contain ambient lights.

Next, we set the sceneView's automaticallyUpdatesLighting property to true too. When the automaticallyUpdatesLighting property is set to true, the view automatically creates one or more SCNLight objects, adds them to the scene, and updates their properties to reflect estimated lighting information from the camera scene. You will want to set this value to false if you want to directly control all lighting in the SceneKit scene.

Now call the `configureLighting()` method in the `viewDidLoad()` method:

```
override func viewDidLoad() {
  super.viewDidLoad()
  configureLighting()
  addPaperPlane()
}
```

Great! Build and run on your device. You should see a paper plane with beautiful shapes, curves, and edges!

Let's have a moment of silence to fall in love with the paper plane's beautiful shapes, curves, and edges.

# Implementing a Multiple Nodes 3D Object

Now some of your 3D model files may contain multiple nodes. In such a scenario, let's consider how we can add multiple nodes of 3D objects to our ARSCNView.

Under the 3D Objects folder, there is a car.dae file. If you click the file, you will open the file in the Xcode Scene Editor. You can highlight all the nodes to see the outline of the 3D car object.

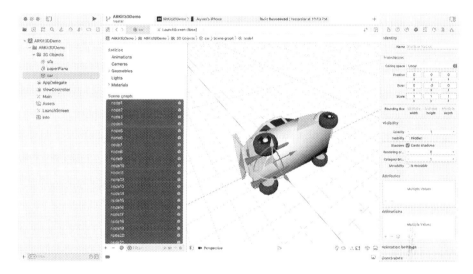

Cool. Open **ViewController**. Insert the following code under the addPaperPlane(x:y:z:) method to ViewController:

```
func addCar(x: Float = 0, y: Float = 0, z: Float = -0.5) {
  guard let carScene = SCNScene(named: "car.dae") else {
  return }
  let carNode = SCNNode()
  let carSceneChildNodes = carScene.rootNode.childNodes

  for childNode in carSceneChildNodes {
    carNode.addChildNode(childNode)
  }
```

```
  carNode.position = SCNVector3(x, y, z)
  carNode.scale = SCNVector3(0.5, 0.5, 0.5)
  sceneView.scene.rootNode.addChildNode(carNode)
}
```

Here is what we did:

- First, we safely created a SCNScene object with the car.dae file using the guard let statement. Then we initialize a SCNNode object for the car node.

- Next, we save the child nodes of the carScene's rootNode. Afterward, we loop through and add each of the car scene's child nodes to the car node.

- Then, we simply set the car node's position to the given argument values and transform the car node's x, y, and z scale value by 0.5 to shift its position.

- Finally, we add the car node to the sceneView's scene root node.

Now comment out the addPaperPlane() method and call the addCar() method in the viewDidLoad() method:

```
override func viewDidLoad() {
  super.viewDidLoad()
  configureLighting()
  //addPaperPlane()
  addCar()
}
```

Build and run the Xcode project on your device. And there should be a very cool floating car in front of you.

# Loading USDZ into Scene View

Now, you'll learn to load a popular and universal AR format (USDZ) into
ARSCNView. When you want to load a node from an external file such
as **ufo.usdz**, you can use SCNReferenceNode to do the perfect job. For
instance, if you build or integrate with a document-based app, you can
utilize SCNReferenceNode to load 3D model files saved locally, downloaded
from the cloud, transfer from other apps, etc.

---

**Note**    The file ufo.usdz can be found in and imported from the final
project's 3D Objects directory.

---

Add the following method to `ViewController`:

```
func addUFO(x: Float = 0, y: Float = -0.5, z: Float = -1) {
    // 1
  guard let ufoURL = Bundle.main.url(
    forResource: "ufo", withExtension: "usdz"),
    let ufoNode = SCNReferenceNode(url: ufoURL) else { return }
    // 2
  ufoNode.position = SCNVector3(x, y, z)
    // 3
  ufoNode.load()
    // 4
  sceneView.scene.rootNode.addChildNode(ufoNode)
}
```

Here's the breakdown:

1. You safely unwrap the ufo model's file location. This is to ensure that the file exists within the project. Then, you safely unwrap the file as a SCNReferenceNode. The file either then becomes convertible to the object type you desire or not. If yes, handle subsequent logic. Otherwise, return and do nothing.

2. You set the position of the node. Nothing special here.

3. For SCNReferenceNode, you need to load the node. Calling load() will load the node if it hasn't already. By loading the node, you set the file's content as a child of ufoNode.

4. You add the reference node onto the scene view.

Now comment out `addCar()` and call `addUFO()` in `viewDidLoad()`:

```
override func viewDidLoad() {
  super.viewDidLoad()
  configureLighting()
  //addPaperPlane()
  //addUFO() addCar()
}
```

Build and run.

It's a bird. It's a plane. It's a UFO!

P.S. the blue light in the screenshot isn't part of the USDZ model.

# Wrap Up

Congratulations on making it this far into the chapter! Hope you've enjoyed it. In the next chapter, you'll learn about plane detection.

# CHAPTER 6

# Detecting Horizontal Planes and Adding 3D Objects with Raycast in SceneKit

Augmented reality has the power to amplify the world in ways never possible before. How we interact with our world may never be the same again. With the release of iPhone X, the world is ready to embrace AR now more than ever. We are at a special time in history and just at the beginning of something **huge**. The potential of AR is endless.

## What We Are Going to Learn

In this tutorial, our focus is on horizontal planes in ARKit. We are first going to create an ocean (horizontal plane). Then, place a beautiful ship on top (3D object) of it.

© Jayven Nhan 2022
J. Nhan, *Mastering ARKit*, https://doi.org/10.1007/978-1-4842-7836-9_6

Or create a fleet of ships with lighting!

Along the way, you will learn about horizontal planes in ARKit. It is
my hope that by the end of this tutorial, you will feel more comfortable
utilizing a horizontal plane when working on your ARKit project.

# What's a Horizontal Plane?

So what exactly are we talking about when we talk about horizontal planes in ARKit? When we detect a horizontal plane in ARKit, we technically detect an ARPlaneAnchor. So what is an ARPlaneAnchor? An ARPlaneAnchor is basically an object containing information about the detected horizontal plane.

Here is a more formal description of ARPlaneAnchor from Apple:

> *Information about the position and orientation of a real-world flat surface detected in a world-tracking AR session.*

> —Apple's Documentation

# Let's Begin to Build the App

You'll use a starter project to focus on the implementation of ARKit. Open the **starter** project in Xcode to take a look. I have already created the ARSCNView in the storyboard.

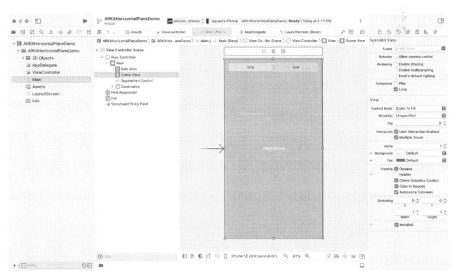

Build and run the starter project to have a quick test. You should see the following on your iOS device.

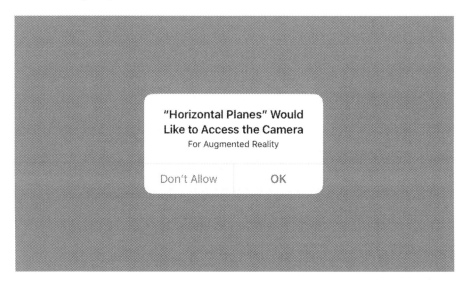

Make sure you should tap OK to grant the access to the camera. You should then see your camera's view.

# Detecting Horizontal Planes

Detecting a horizontal plane is straightforward—thanks to the "appley" Apple engineers.

Inside `ViewController`, simply add the following to the end of `setUpSceneView()`:

```
configuration.planeDetection = .horizontal
```

By setting the `planeDetection` property of `ARWorldTrackingConfiguration` to `.horizontal`, this tells ARKit to look for any horizontal plane. Once ARKit detects a horizontal plane, that horizontal plane will be added into `sceneView`'s session.

In order to detect the horizontal plane, we have to adopt the
ARSCNViewDelegate protocol. Below the ViewController class, create a
ViewController class extension to implement the protocol:

```
extension ViewController: ARSCNViewDelegate {

}
```

Now inside of the class extension, implement the
renderer(_:didAdd:for:) method:

```
func renderer(_ renderer: SCNSceneRenderer, didAdd node:
SCNNode, for anchor: ARAnchor) {

}
```

This protocol method gets called every time the scene view's session
has a new ARAnchor added. An ARAnchor is an object that represents a
physical location and orientation in a 3D space. We will use the ARAnchor
later for detecting a horizontal plane.

Next, head back to setUpSceneView(). Assign the sceneView's delegate
to your ViewController inside of setUpSceneView().

If you'd like, you can also set sceneView's debug options to show
feature points in the world. This could help you find a place with enough
feature points to detect a horizontal plane. A horizontal plane is made up
of many feature points. Once enough feature points have been detected to
recognize a horizontal surface, renderer(_:didAdd:for:) will be called.

Your setUpSceneView() method should now look like this:

```
func setUpSceneView() {
  let configuration = ARWorldTrackingConfiguration()
  configuration.planeDetection = .horizontal
```

```
  sceneView.session.run(configuration)

  sceneView.delegate = self
  sceneView.debugOptions = [ARSCNDebugOptions.showFeaturePoints]
}
```

This method gets called every time a SceneKit node's properties have been updated to match its corresponding anchor. This is where ARKit refines its estimation of the horizontal plane's position and extent.

The node argument gives us the updated position of the anchor. The anchor argument provides us with the anchor's updated width and height. With these two arguments, we can update the previously implemented SCNPlane to reflect the updated position with the updated width and height.

Next, add the following code inside renderer(_:didUpdate:for:):

```
// 1
guard let planeAnchor = anchor as? ARPlaneAnchor,
  let planeNode = node.childNodes.first,
  let plane = planeNode.geometry as? SCNPlane
  else { return }

// 2
let width = CGFloat(planeAnchor.extent.x)
let height = CGFloat(planeAnchor.extent.z)
plane.width = width
plane.height = height

// 3
let x = CGFloat(planeAnchor.center.x)
let y = CGFloat(planeAnchor.center.y)
let z = CGFloat(planeAnchor.center.z)
planeNode.position = SCNVector3(x, y, z)
```

Again, let me go through the preceding code with you:

1.  First, we safely unwrap the anchor argument as ARPlaneAnchor. Next, we safely unwrap the node's first child node. Lastly, we safely unwrap the planeNode's geometry as SCNPlane. We are simply extracting the previously implemented ARPlaneAnchor, SCNNode, and SCNPlane and updating its properties with the corresponding arguments.

2.  Here, we update the plane's width and height using the planeAnchor extent's x and z properties.

3.  At last, we update the planeNode's position to the planeAnchor's center x, y, and z coordinates.

Build and run to check out expanding horizontal plane implementation.

# Adding Objects on Horizontal Planes

Now let's add a ship on top of the horizontal plane. Inside of the starter project, I have already bundled a 3D ship object for you to use.

Insert the following method in the `ViewController` class to place a ship on top of the horizontal plane:

```
@objc func addShipToSceneView(withGestureRecognizer recognizer:
 UIGestureRecognizer) {
  let tapLocation = recognizer.location(in: sceneView)
  let hitTestResults = sceneView.hitTest(tapLocation, types:
   .existingPlaneUsingExtent)

  guard let hitTestResult = hitTestResults.first else { return }
  let translation = hitTestResult.worldTransform.translation
  let x = translation.x
  let y = translation.y
  let z = translation.z

  guard let shipScene = SCNScene(named: "ship.scn"),
    let shipNode = shipScene.rootNode.childNode(withName: "ship",
    recursively:
      false)
    else { return }

  shipNode.position = SCNVector3(x,y,z)
  sceneView.scene.rootNode.addChildNode(shipNode)
}
```

There are many familiar faces here, as explained in a previous chapter, so I will not go through the code line by line. If you want to learn more about that, check out Chapter 4, "Building Your First ARKit App with SceneKit." The only difference now is that we pass in a different argument in the types parameter to detect an existing plane anchor in the sceneView.

Before the cherry on top, add the following code:

```
func addTapGestureToSceneView() {
  let tapGestureRecognizer = UITapGestureRecognizer(target:
  self, action:
  #selector(ViewController.addShipToSceneView(withGesture
  Recognizer:)))
  sceneView.addGestureRecognizer(tapGestureRecognizer)
}
```

This method will add a tap gesture recognizer to sceneView.

For the cherry on top, call the following method inside of
viewDidLoad() to add a tap gesture recognizer to sceneView:

```
addTapGestureToSceneView()
```

If you build and run now, you should be able to detect a horizontal
plane, visualize it, and place an insanely cool ship on top.

Or a fleet of ships (with lighting).

You can enable lighting by uncommenting `configureLighting()`
inside of `viewDidLoad()`. The function is very simple with two lines of code
to enable lighting:

```
sceneView.autoenablesDefaultLighting = true
sceneView.automaticallyUpdatesLighting = true
```

# Raycasting for Physical World
# Surface Positioning

When you want to locate a point in the physical world from your device,
you can hit-test and raycast. In this section, you'll learn about the latter.
Raycast is Apple's preferred method for finding and refining positions
of real-world surfaces. The key benefit here is the continuous position
refinement of objects placed using raycast. Starting in iOS 13, projects
using `ARKit` have the capability to create raycast queries and extract
raycast results.

To begin, you'll add a make raycast query method. Add the following method to ViewController:

```
// 1
func addBoatToSceneView(location: CGPoint) {
    // 2
    guard let raycastQuery = sceneView.raycastQuery(
      from: location,
      allowing: .existingPlaneInfinite,
      alignment: .any),
        // 3
      let raycastResult = sceneView.session.raycast(
        raycastQuery).first else { return }
    // 4
    guard let boatURL = Bundle.main.url(
      forResource: "boat", withExtension: "usdz"),
      let boatReferenceNode = SCNReferenceNode(
        url: boatURL) else { return }
    boatReferenceNode.load()
    boatReferenceNode.simdPosition =
      raycastResult.worldTransform.translation
    sceneView.scene.rootNode.addChildNode(boatReferenceNode)
}
```

With the code added, you

1. Set the method to the signature to take in a CGPoint argument to decide on where to place your content onto the scene view.

2. Perform a raycast to check for anything between the ray and the surface. Specifically, the ray is cast from the tap location. And the surface of interest can extend indefinitely. It merely has to

be perpendicular to an existing surface. Finally, the target alignment dictates whether the raycast accounts for targets aligned horizontally, vertically, or in contrast to gravity.

3. From closest to farthest, raycast results are ordered by the distance between the ray and camera. If at least a successful ray is cast between the camera and a surface, you'll safely unwrap the first hit test result if there's an interception.

4. Load the boat USDZ model as a reference. Set the boat reference node position using the hit test result. Then, add the boat reference node onto the scene view.

# Refactoring for Segmented Control and Adding Additional Objects

With the additional boat, it's now necessary to have a way to incorporate it into the scene view. To achieve this, you'll make use of `ViewController`'s segmented control to choose between adding a ship or boat.

Open **Main.storyboard**. In the document outline, select **Segmented Control**. Set untick **isHidden** in the Attributes inspector to show the segmented control at runtime.

When a user taps the screen to add content onto a surface, you'll incorporate a new object based on the segmented control index.

First, replace addShipToSceneView(withGestureRecognizer:) with the following method:

```
func addShipToSceneView(location: CGPoint) {
  let hitTestResults = sceneView.hitTest(
    location, types: .existingPlaneUsingExtent)
  guard let hitTestResult = hitTestResults.first
    else { return }
  let translation = hitTestResult.worldTransform.translation
  let x = translation.x
  let y = translation.y
  let z = translation.z

  guard let shipScene = SCNScene(named: "ship.scn"),
    let shipNode = shipScene.rootNode.childNode(
      withName: "ship", recursively: false)
    else { return }

  shipNode.position = SCNVector3(x,y,z)
  sceneView.scene.rootNode.addChildNode(shipNode)
}
```

Instead of extracting the gesture's tap location, the method takes the
tap location directly from the parameter.

Second, add the following method to `ViewController`:

```
@objc func addObjectToSceneView(
  withGestureRecognizer recognizer: UITapGestureRecognizer) {
  let tapLocation = recognizer.location(in: sceneView)
  switch segmentedControl.selectedSegmentIndex {
  case 0:
    addShipToSceneView(location:  tapLocation)
  case 1:
    addBoatToSceneView(location:  tapLocation)
  default:
    break
  }
}
```

Depending on the segmented control's selected index, you'll add a
ship for 0 and add a boat for 1. You also pass in the tap location to both
contents adding methods. The tap location is utilized to either hit-test or
raycast.

Third, replace addTapGestureToSceneView() with the
following method:

```
func addTapGestureToSceneView() {
  let tapGestureRecognizer = UITapGestureRecognizer(
    target: self,
    action:  #selector(ViewController.addObjectToSceneView(
      withGestureRecognizer:)))
  sceneView.addGestureRecognizer(tapGestureRecognizer)
}
```

Here, you update the method with the latest method for adding an object to the scene view.

Build and run. Use the segmented control to choose between a ship or boat. Depending on the segmented control index, tapping on a horizontal plane in the scene view will add the chosen object.

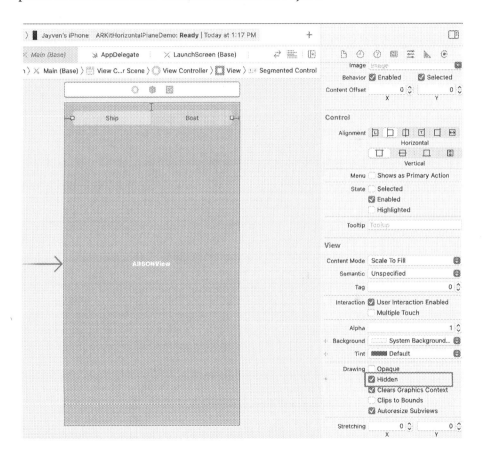

In addition to adding content using hit-testing, you've also learned how to work with raycast to locate the tap location and incorporate 3D content. Great progress!

# Up Next

I hope you have enjoyed and learned something valuable from this
chapter! Up next, you'll learn about the intricacies involved in working
with physics by launching a rocketship.

# CHAPTER 7

# Understanding Physics by Launching a Rocketship

Did that just move? Is that real? That's augmented reality. Welcome back to the fourth installment of the ARKit tutorial series. In this tutorial, we will be looking at the basics of physics inside of ARKit. We shall launch a rocketship by the end of this tutorial and then celebrate like it's the Fourth of July because we can. Let's go!

First, let's begin by opening the **starter project**. Build and run. You should be prompted to allow camera access in the app.

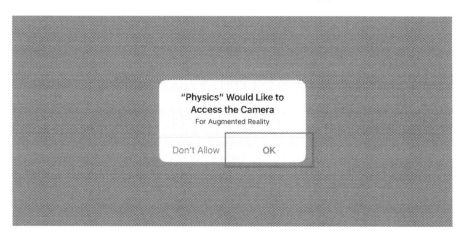

© Jayven Nhan 2022
J. Nhan, *Mastering ARKit*, https://doi.org/10.1007/978-1-4842-7836-9_7

Tap **OK**. If all goes well, you should be able to see your camera's view.

Also, just a note, this tutorial is built on top of previous knowledge from the previous plane detection discussion.

# Physics Body Explained

First things first, physics body. This is one of the fundamentals. For SceneKit to know how to simulate a SceneKit node(s) inside our app, we need to attach it to a SCNPhysicsBody. A SCNPhysicsBody is an object which adds physics simulation to a node.

SceneKit performs **physics calculations** to nodes with attached physics bodies in a scene before rendering a frame. These calculations include gravity, friction, and collisions with other bodies. You can also apply forces and impulses to a body. After these calculations, it updates the positions and orientations of the nodes and then renders the frame.

Basically, before each rendered frame, there's a physics calculation.

# Physics Body Types

To construct a physics body, you'd first need to specify the **physics body type**. A physics body determines how a physics body interacts with forces and other bodies. The three physics body types are static, dynamic, and kinematic.

## Static

You'd want to use a static physics body type for SceneKit objects like floors, walls, and terrain. A static physics body type is unaffected by forces or collisions and cannot move.

# Dynamic

You'd want to use a dynamic physics body type for SceneKit objects like a flying and fire-breathing dragon, Steph Curry shooting a basketball, or a rocketship blasting off. A dynamic physics body is a physics body that can be affected by forces and collisions.

# Kinematic

You'd want to use a kinematic physics body, say, when you create a game where you need to push a block with your finger. So you make an "invisible" block pusher, which is triggered by your finger movement. The "invisible" block is not affected by other blocks. However, the "invisible" block moves other blocks when in contact. A kinematic physics body is a physics body unaffected by forces or collisions, but it can affect other bodies when moved. Can move others, can't be moved.

# Creating a Physics Body

Let's begin by giving our detected horizontal plane a static physics body. This way, we have a solid ground for our rocketship to stand on.

Add the following method below renderer(_:didUpdate:for:) of **ViewController**:

```
func update(_ node: inout SCNNode, withGeometry geometry:
SCNGeometry, type:
  SCNPhysicsBodyType) {
    let shape = SCNPhysicsShape(geometry: geometry, options: nil)
    let physicsBody = SCNPhysicsBody(type: type, shape: shape)
    node.physicsBody = physicsBody
}
```

In this method, we created a SCNPhysicsShape object. A SCNPhysicsShape object represents the shape of a physics body. When SceneKit detects contact for the SCNPhysicsBody objects of your scene, it uses the physics shapes you defined instead of the rendered geometry of visible objects.

Next, we created a SCNPhysicsBody object by passing .static into the type parameter and our SCNPhysicsShape object into the shape parameter.

Then, we set the node's physics body to the physics body we created together.

# Attaching a Static Physics Body

We are now going to attach a static physics body to the detected plane inside of the renderer(_:didAdd:for:) method. Call the following method right before adding planeNode as the child node:

```
update(&planeNode, withGeometry: plane, type: .static)
```

After the change, your renderer(_:didAdd:for:) method should now look like this:

```
func renderer(_ renderer: SCNSceneRenderer, didAdd node:
SCNNode, for anchor:
  ARAnchor) {
    guard let planeAnchor = anchor as? ARPlaneAnchor else {
    return }

    let width = CGFloat(planeAnchor.extent.x)
    let height = CGFloat(planeAnchor.extent.z)
    let plane = SCNPlane(width: width, height: height)
    plane.materials.first?.diffuse.contents = UIColor.
    transparentWhite
```

```
let planeNode = SCNNode(geometry: plane)

let x = CGFloat(planeAnchor.center.x)
let y = CGFloat(planeAnchor.center.y)
let z = CGFloat(planeAnchor.center.z)
planeNode.position = SCNVector3(x,y,z)
planeNode.eulerAngles.x = -.pi / 2

update(&planeNode, withGeometry: plane, type: .static)

node.addChildNode(planeNode)
}
```

When our detected plane is updated with new information, it may change in geometry. Hence, we need to call the same method inside of render(_:didUpdate:for:):

```
update(&planeNode, withGeometry: plane, type: .static)
```

The render(_:didUpdate:for:) method should now look like this after the modification:

```
func renderer(_ renderer: SCNSceneRenderer, didUpdate node:
SCNNode, for
    anchor: ARAnchor) {
        guard let planeAnchor = anchor as? ARPlaneAnchor,
            var planeNode = node.childNodes.first,
            let plane = planeNode.geometry as? SCNPlane
            else { return }

        let width = CGFloat(planeAnchor.extent.x)
        let height = CGFloat(planeAnchor.extent.z)
        plane.width = width
        plane.height = height
```

```
    let x = CGFloat(planeAnchor.center.x)
    let y = CGFloat(planeAnchor.center.y)
    let z = CGFloat(planeAnchor.center.z)

    planeNode.position = SCNVector3(x, y, z)

    update(&planeNode, withGeometry: plane, type: .static)
}
```

Ground solid work!

# Attaching a Dynamic Physics Body

Now let's give our rocketship node a dynamic physics body because we want this node to be affected by forces and collisions. Declare a rocketship node name constant inside of the ViewController class:

```
let rocketshipNodeName = "rocketship"
```

Then inside the addRocketshipToSceneView(withGestureRecognizer:) method, add the following code right after adjusting the rocketship node's position:

```
let physicsBody = SCNPhysicsBody(type: .dynamic, shape: nil)
rocketshipNode.physicsBody = physicsBody
rocketshipNode.name = rocketshipNodeName
```

We gave our rocketshipNode a static physics body and a name. We'll see the name be used to identify the rocketshipNode later on. Build and run. And you should be able to see something like this.

# Applying Force

We are now going to apply force onto our rocketship.

Before we do that, we need a way of triggering the action. We can do this with the help of a UISwipeGestureRecognizer. First, add the following method below the addRocketshipToSceneView(withGestureRecognizer:) method:

```
func getRocketshipNode(from swipeLocation: CGPoint) -> SCNNode? {
    let hitTestResults = sceneView.hitTest(swipeLocation)
    guard let parentNode = hitTestResults.first?.node.parent,
        parentNode.name == rocketshipNodeName
        else { return nil }

    return parentNode
}
```

This method will help us get the rocketship node from the swipe location of the swipe gesture. You may be wondering why we safely unwrapped the parent node. The reason is the returned node from the hit test result could be any one of the five nodes that make up the rocketship.

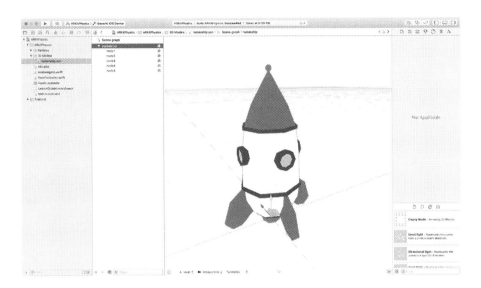

Right below the previous method, add the following method:

```
@objc func applyForceToRocketship(withGestureRecognizer
recognizer:
  UIGestureRecognizer) {
    // 1
    guard recognizer.state == .ended else { return }
    // 2
    let swipeLocation = recognizer.location(in: sceneView)
    // 3
    guard let rocketshipNode = getRocketshipNode(from:
    swipeLocation),
      let physicsBody = rocketshipNode.physicsBody
      else { return }
    // 4
    let direction = SCNVector3(0, 3, 0)
    physicsBody.applyForce(direction, asImpulse: true)
}
```

From the preceding code, we

1. Made sure the swipe gesture state is ended.

2. Get hit test results from the swipe location.

3. See if the swipe gesture was acted on the rocketship.

4. Apply a force in the y-direction to the parent node's physics body. If you notice, we also set the impulse argument to true. This applies an instantaneous change in momentum and accelerates the physics body immediately. Basically, this option allows you to simulate an instantaneous effect like a projectile launch when set to true.

Great! Build and run. Swipe up on the rocketship. And you should be able to apply a force onto your rocketship!

# Adding SceneKit Particle System and Changing Physics Properties

The starter project comes with a reactor SceneKit particle system under the "Particles" folder.

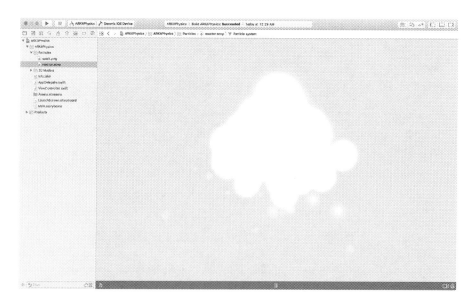

In this tutorial, we will not go over how to create a SceneKit particle system. We will go over how to add a SceneKit particle system onto a node and some of its physics properties.

Open up `ViewController`. Declare the following variable inside of the `ViewController` class:

```
var planeNodes = [SCNNode]()
```

Inside of the `renderer(_:didAdd:for:)` method, add the following as the method's last line of code:

```
planeNodes.append(planeNode)
```

Simply, when a new plane is detected, we append it onto our plane nodes array. We are referencing the plane nodes for the reactor SceneKit particle system's collider nodes property later on.

Right below the `renderer(_:didAdd:for:)` method, add the following delegate method:

```
func renderer(_ renderer: SCNSceneRenderer, didRemove node:
SCNNode, for anchor: ARAnchor) {
    guard anchor is ARPlaneAnchor,
        let planeNode = node.childNodes.first
        else { return }
    planeNodes = planeNodes.filter { $0 != planeNode }
}
```

This delegate method gets called when a SceneKit node corresponding to a removed AR anchor has been removed from the scene. At this time, we will filter the plane nodes array to only the ones that do not equal to the removed plane node.

Next, add the following method right below the applyForceToRocket ship(withGestureRecognizer:) method:

```
@objc func launchRocketship(withGestureRecognizer recognizer:
    UIGestureRecognizer) {
    // 1
    guard recognizer.state == .ended else { return }
    // 2
    let swipeLocation = recognizer.location(in: sceneView)
    guard let rocketshipNode = getRocketshipNode(from:
    swipeLocation),
        let physicsBody = rocketshipNode.physicsBody,
        let reactorParticleSystem = SCNParticleSystem(named:
        "reactor", inDirectory: nil),
        let engineNode = rocketshipNode.childNode(withName:
        "node2", recursively:
          false)
        else { return }
    // 3
    physicsBody.isAffectedByGravity = false
    physicsBody.damping = 0
    // 4
    reactorParticleSystem.colliderNodes = planeNodes
    // 5
    engineNode.addParticleSystem(reactorParticleSystem)
    // 6
    let action = SCNAction.moveBy(x: 0, y: 0.3, z: 0,
    duration: 3)
    action.timingMode = .easeInEaseOut
    rocketshipNode.runAction(action)
}
```

In the preceding code, we

1. Made sure the swipe gesture state is ended.

2. Safely unwrapped the rocketship node and its physics body like before. Also, we safely unwrapped the reactor SceneKit particle system and the engine node. We want to add the reactor SceneKit particle system onto the rocketship's engine—hence, the interest in the engine node.

3. Set the physics body's `isAffectedByGravity` property to false, and its effect is as it sounds. Gravity will no longer affect the rocketship node. We also set the damping property to zero. The damping property simulates the effect of fluid friction or air resistance on a body. Setting it to zero will result in zero impact from fluid friction or air resistance on the rocketship node's physics body.

4. Set the reactor particle system to collide with the plane nodes. This will make the particles from the particle system bounce off the detected planes when in contact instead of flying right through them.

5. Add the reactor particle system onto the engine node.

6. Move the rocketship node up by 0.3 meters with ease in and ease out animation effect.

# Adding Swipe Gestures

Before we can apply force and launch our rocketship, we need to add swipe gesture recognizers onto our scene view. Add the following below addTapGestureToSceneView():

```
func addSwipeGesturesToSceneView() {
    let swipeUpGestureRecognizer = UISwipeGestureRecognizer(
    target: self,
      action:
      #selector(ViewController.applyForceToRocketship(
      withGestureRecognizer:)))
    swipeUpGestureRecognizer.direction = .up
    sceneView.addGestureRecognizer(swipeUpGestureRecognizer)

    let swipeDownGestureRecognizer = UISwipeGestureRecognizer(
    target: self, action:   #selector(ViewController.launch
    Rocketship(withGestureRecognizer:)))
    swipeDownGestureRecognizer.direction = .down
    sceneView.addGestureRecognizer(swipeDownGestureRecognizer)
}
```

A swipe up gesture will apply force onto the rocketship node. A swipe down gesture will launch the rocketship. Nice!

Last but not least, call the method inside of viewDidLoad():

```
addSwipeGesturesToSceneView()
```

That's it!

# Showtime

Congratulations, it's showtime. Swipe down on the rocketship and see what you get!

And try to swipe down and then up. Off the rocketship goes!

# Implementing Custom Object Collision Detection Logic

By setting physics bodies onto rocketship nodes and planes, the objects know how to interact with each other like in the real world. However, the fine control over how collisions work doesn't stop there. In this section, you'll learn about category, collision, and contact test bitmasks.

## Category Bitmasks

A category bitmask represents an object category with UInt32—meaning a scene is capable of handling up to 32 different category bitmasks. A physics body can have multiple category bitmasks. For example, a rocketship can belong to high heat conductivity and player-controlled categories. By setting these categories, you give the physics body an identity. With the identity, you can dictate the business logic for the collision between various physics bodies.

At the moment, placing two rocketships on top of each other causes one to collide with the other. In the scenario where you want the rocketship to only collide with the plane, you'll want to give each rocketship a category bitmask and a collision bitmask. You'll learn more about collision bitmask next.

## Collision Bitmasks

A collision bitmask defines which physics bodies a physics body should come into contact with. If you want a rocketship to collide with another rocketship, then set each rocketship's collision bitmask to rocketship. If you want your rocketship to collide with an additional physics body like the plane, you can rocketship node collision bitmasks to include rocketship and plane. Any other bitmasks that come into contact with the rocketship physics body are undetected. And the scene's object physics behaviors will act accordingly.

With category and collision bitmasks on a physics body, you can already have finer control over the collisions that happen in a scene. The more nuanced control over object collision doesn't stop there. When two physics bodies come into contact with each other, what do you want to do? Next, you'll learn about contact test bitmasks as a bridge for handling custom collision business logic.

## Contact Test Bitmasks

A contact test bitmask defines which collision causes an intersection notification. You can have two rocketship physics bodies collide with each other and wish to or not wish to know about it. To obligate physics bodies to notify collisions within a scene, you set the collision test mask on the physics bodies. The notification will come in the form of a protocol method. The scene's enclosing object (i.e., UIViewController) will need to conform to SCNPhysicsContactDelegate.

You've grasped the ideas behind category, collision, and contact test bitmasks. Next, you'll put knowledge into practical use by implementing various bitmasks in the sample project.

## Implementing the Solution

First, you'll define category bitmasks with an enum. Add the following value type to ViewController:

```
enum CollisionBody: Int {
    case plane = 1
    case rocket = 2
}
```

For the custom collision logic that you're about to implement, the value type's job is to create code clarity and reusability.

Second, you'll create two methods to set bitmasks for respective objects. Add the following methods to `ViewController`:

```
// 1
func setRocketCollisionBitmask(onNode node: SCNNode) {
    node.physicsBody?.categoryBitMask = CollisionBody.rocket.
    rawValue
    node.physicsBody?.collisionBitMask = CollisionBody.plane.
    rawValue
    node.physicsBody?.contactTestBitMask = CollisionBody.plane.
    rawValue
}
// 2
func setPlaneCollisionBitmask(onNode node: SCNNode) {
    node.physicsBody?.categoryBitMask = CollisionBody.plane.
    rawValue
    node.physicsBody?.collisionBitMask = CollisionBody.rocket.
    rawValue
    node.physicsBody?.contactTestBitMask = CollisionBody.
    rocket.rawValue
}
```

Here's a breakdown of the newly added code:

1.   Categorize the node's physics body as a rocket.
     Set the node's physics body to collide with plane
     physics body. Set the node's physics body to notify
     collision with plane physics body.

2. Categorize the node's physics body as a `plane`.
   Set the node's physics body to collide with `rocket`
   physics body. Set the node's physics body to notify
   collision with `rocket` physics body.

Third, you're going to use the methods you've just created to integrate
with the scene's objects.

Fourth, in `addRocketshipToSceneView(withGestureRecognizer:)`
and below `rocketshipNode.name = rocketshipNodeName`, add the
following line of code:

```
setRocketCollisionBitmask(onNode:  rocketshipNode)
```

Before a rocketship is added to the scene view, you'll set the
collision bitmasks.

Fifth, in `update(_:withGeometry:type:)` and below `node.`
`physicsBody = physicsBody`, add the following line of code:

```
setPlaneCollisionBitmask(onNode:  node)
```

Anytime a new horizontal plane is detected or an existing horizontal
plane is updated with a new physics body, you'll set the node's collision
bitmasks.

Sixth, add the following extension code block to the end of
**ViewController**:

```
// MARK: - SCNPhysicsContactDelegate
// 1
extension ViewController: SCNPhysicsContactDelegate {
    // 2
    func physicsWorld(_ world: SCNPhysicsWorld, didBegin contact:
      SCNPhysicsContact) {
```

```
        // 3
        guard (contact.nodeA.physicsBody?.categoryBitMask ==
            CollisionBody.plane.rawValue
                && contact.nodeB.physicsBody?.
                categoryBitMask ==
                    CollisionBody.rocket.rawValue)
                || (contact.nodeA.physicsBody?.
                categoryBitMask ==
                    CollisionBody.rocket.rawValue
                        && contact.nodeB.physicsBody?.
                        categoryBitMask ==
                            CollisionBody.plane.rawValue)
        else { return }
        // 4
        guard isFirstRocketLanded else { return }
        isFirstRocketLanded = false
        // 5
        for planeNode in planeNodes {
            planeNode.geometry?.firstMaterial?.diffuse.contents   =
                UIColor.transparentOrange
        }
    }
}
```

Here's the code breakdown:

1.   Make `ViewController` adopt
     `SCNPhysicsContactDelegate`.

2.   Implement the protocol method for handling
     physics body contact. This method notifies
     the delegate of the first contact between two
     physics bodies.

3. Compare the category bitmasks between two physics bodies. Ensure that the collision is between a plane category bitmask and a rocketship category bitmask. It can be a plane colliding into a rocketship. Or it can be a rocketship colliding into a plane. If either of the statement is true, proceed onto the remaining method's business logic. Otherwise, return.

4. Use a guard statement to ensure that the remaining business logic follows through if it is the first rocket landing on top of the plane. If so, proceed and update the first rocket landed state. Otherwise, return.

5. Update all the existing planes' materials to transparent orange.

Finally, to put the icing on the cake, add the following code to the end of setUpSceneView():

```
// 1
sceneView.scene.physicsWorld.contactDelegate = self
// 2
sceneView.debugOptions = [.showPhysicsShapes]
```

You've made two changes to the scene view:

1. Set the physics contact delegate to ViewController. This means that ViewController will be notified about physics body collision events.

2. For visualization of physics body shapes, you add it as a debug option onto the scene view.

Build and run.

You'll be able to see the physics shape of your nodes.

Once a rocketship lands on a plane, the color of existing planes changes to transparent orange.

When you place rocketships on top of each other, they will no longer collide between rocketships. Instead, rocketships will only collide with the planes.

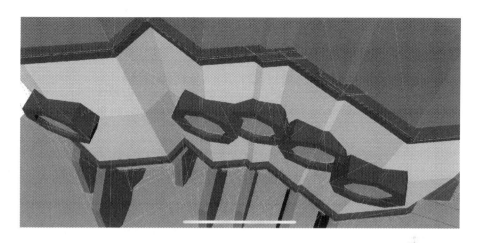

You've learned so much about physics! Now, the virtual world is your oyster!

# CHAPTER 8

# Light Estimation and Environment Texturing

Once upon a time, a rock skid made a spark, and humankind learned to create fire. This is the fifth installment of our ARKit series. Today, we will walk you through how to implement light estimation in augmented reality with ARKit.

Light estimation enhances your graphics' blending with the real world in AR—with shading algorithms utilization. When your app renders graphics, you can use the rendering information and shading algorithms to match your camera's captured real-world lighting conditions with your scene graphics.

I hope that you'll enjoy this ARKit chapter. And hopefully, this ARKit chapter can also spark up an amazing idea like that rock.

Now let's begin.

## What You'll Implement and Learn

In building out this tutorial's ARKit light estimation project, we will do the following:

- Place a sphere node on top of a detected horizontal plane.

- Illuminate the sphere node with a light node.

© Jayven Nhan 2022
J. Nhan, *Mastering ARKit*, https://doi.org/10.1007/978-1-4842-7836-9_8

- Test out the intensity and temperature light properties.

- Update and implement UIs.

- Finally, implement light estimation inside a SceneKit's scene rendering method.

# Getting Started

First, open the **starter project**. I have already built the UI of the app and created the action method of the buttons.

Build and run. You should be prompted to allow camera access in the app. Tap OK to allow camera access in your app.

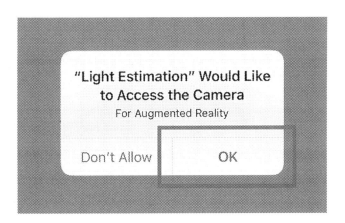

# Creating a Sphere Node

First, we will start by creating a sphere in augmented reality. Open up the ViewController file in Xcode. Replace the code inside getSphereNode (withPosition:height:) with the following:

```
let sphere = SCNSphere(radius: 0.1)
let sphereNode = SCNNode(geometry: sphere)
sphereNode.simdPosition = position
sphereNode.position.y += Float(sphere.radius) + height

return sphereNode
```

The getSphereNode(withPosition:height:) method does the following:

- Take in a position parameter.

- Create a sphere geometry with a 0.1 CGFloat radius.

- Create a sphere node with the sphere geometry we created earlier.

- Set the sphere node's position to the position argument value.

- Add the sphere's radius value onto the sphere node's y-position value so that the sphere is right on top of detected horizontal surfaces.

- Increase the sphere node's y-position by one. This way, the sphere node will sit 1 meter above detected horizontal surfaces.

- Return the sphere node.

In brief, this method creates a sphere and place it on top of a detected horizontal plane.

# Adding Light Node

Next, we are going to add a light source (i.e., SCNLight) to illuminate the scene. Replace the code inside getLightNode() with the following:

```
let light = SCNLight()
light.type = .omni
light.intensity = 0
light.temperature = 0

let lightNode = SCNNode()
lightNode.light = light
lightNode.position = SCNVector3(0,1,0)

return lightNode
```

The way to illuminate a scene is by attaching lights to SCNNode objects using their light property. This is what this method is about. Let me explain what the getLightNode( ) method does in detail:

- First, we create a SceneKit light object (i.e., SCNLight) with its type set to omni. An omni light type illuminates a scene from a point in all directions. There are other light types, including directional, spot, and ambient.

- Next, we set the light object's intensity and temperature property value to zero.

- To use the light object to illuminate the scene, we create a light node object and set the light source to the node's light property.

- We also set the light node object's y-position to 1 meter above its parent node.

Now, let's add the following code to addLightNodeTo(_:):

```
let lightNode = getLightNode()
node.addChildNode(lightNode)
lightNodes.append(lightNode)
detectedHorizontalPlane = true
```

The preceding code does the following:

- Get a sphere node with the plane anchor center position.

- Add a light node onto the sphere node.

- Set the mapped anchor node as the sphere node's parent node.

- Set detected horizontal plane variable to true.

# Testing Light Properties

Now, let's test out the effects ambient intensity and color temperature has on rendered graphics. Before that, update the ambientIntensitySliderValueDidChange(_:) method like this:

```
@IBAction func ambientIntensitySliderValueDidChange(_ sender:
UISlider) {
    DispatchQueue.main.async {
        let ambientIntensity = sender.value
        self.ambientIntensityLabel.text = "Ambient Intensity:
        \(ambientIntensity)"

        guard !self.lightEstimationSwitch.isOn else { return }
        for lightNode in self.lightNodes {
            guard let light = lightNode.light else { continue }
            light.intensity = CGFloat(ambientIntensity)
        }
    }
}
```

The preceding code runs on the main thread and altogether sets the light nodes' light intensity property value to the slider's sender value. Also, update the ambientColorTemperatureSliderValueDidChange(_:) method like this:

```
@IBAction func ambientColorTemperatureSliderValueDidChange(_
sender: UISlider)
    {
    DispatchQueue.main.async {
        let ambientColorTemperature =
            self.ambientColorTemperatureSlider.value
```

```
self.ambientColorTemperatureLabel.text  =
"Ambient Color Temperature: \(ambientColorTemperature)"

guard !self.lightEstimationSwitch.isOn else { return }
for lightNode in self.lightNodes {
    guard let light = lightNode.light else { continue }
    light.temperature = CGFloat(ambientColor
    Temperature)
}
}
}
```

The preceding code runs on the main thread and altogether sets the light nodes' light temperature property value to the slider's sender value.

Cool! Let's build and run the project. Point the device's camera to a horizontal surface. Upon horizontal plane detection, you should be able to see a floating sphere. Feel free to play with the sliders to get a feel for the light's intensity and color temperature properties.

# Showing/Hiding the Light Estimation Switch

For now, the ambient intensity and color temperature controls are always displayed. But for the light estimation switch, it is hidden by default. What I want to do is to display the controls when a horizontal plane is detected. Therefore, update the detectedHorizontalPlane property's didSet method like this:

```
var detectedHorizontalPlane = false {
    didSet {
        DispatchQueue.main.async {
            self.mainStackView.isHidden =
                !self.detectedHorizontalPlane
```

```
        self.instructionLabel.isHidden =
            self.detectedHorizontalPlane
        self.lightEstimationStackView.isHidden  =
            !self.detectedHorizontalPlane
    }
  }
}
```

This light estimation stack view contains a UISwitch object as well as a UILabel object. We set the light estimation stack view to show when detectedHorizontalPlane has been set to true.

# Working with the Light Estimation Switch

Now we are going to implement the light estimation switch. Add the following inside the lightEstimationSwitchValueDidChange(_:) method:

```
ambientIntensitySliderValueDidChange(
    ambientIntensitySlider)
ambientColorTemperatureSliderValueDidChange(
    ambientColorTemperatureSlider)
```

On light estimation switch value change, we update the light nodes' light intensity and temperature property value to their respective slider value.

# Implementing Light Estimation

Okay, what's left is the light estimation implementation. First things first, why light estimation? As I mentioned at the very beginning of this tutorial, light estimation enhances your graphics' blending with AR's real world.

You want to make those graphics match the real-world lighting conditions. For instance, if you dim your room's lights, you want to reflect the light condition on the virtual object to make it more realistic.

You can get the estimated scene lighting information from the captured video frame. Now add the following method inside the ViewController class:

```
func updateLightNodesLightEstimation() {
    DispatchQueue.main.async {
        guard  self.lightEstimationSwitch.isOn,
            let lightEstimate = self.sceneView
                .session.currentFrame?.lightEstimate
            else { return }

        let ambientIntensity =
            lightEstimate.ambientIntensity
        let ambientColorTemperature =
            lightEstimate.ambientColorTemperature

        for lightNode in self.lightNodes {
            guard let light = lightNode.light else { continue }
            light.intensity = ambientIntensity
            light.temperature = ambientColorTemperature
        }
    }
}
```

The updateLightNodesLightEstimation() method runs on the main thread and does the following:

- Make sure the light estimation switch's state is on.

- Safely unwrap the current scene view sessions frame's light estimate.

- Extract the unwrapped light estimate's ambient intensity and ambient color temperature property values.

- Loop through the light nodes.

- Safely unwrap the light node's light property.

- Set the light's intensity property to the ambient intensity constant.

- Set the light's temperature property to the ambient color temperature constant.

Next, call the following method inside the `renderer(_:updateAtTime:)` method:

`updateLightNodesLightEstimation()`

The `renderer(_:updateAtTime:)` method gets called exactly once per frame in SceneKit before any animation, action evaluation, or physics simulation. Light estimation is to be constantly applied to our scene. Hence, the `updateLightNodesLightEstimation()` method is called inside of the `renderer(_:updateAtTime:)` method.

As with all UI updates, it is best practice to do the UI updates on the main thread. We call the `updateLightNodesLightEstimation()` method inside the asynchronous method.

# Trying Out the App Demo

That's it! Now it's time to try out the complete demo. Build and run the project. Upon a horizontal plane detection, you can switch the light estimation switch on and see light estimation in effect.

143

You can try the light estimation by switching your lights on/off.

With great control of the environment lighting, you'll now move into reading about environment probe anchors for realistic reflectivity.

# Environment Texturing

Introduced at WWDC18, ARKit 2 and SceneKit can use environment texturing features for realistic reflections.

Setting your scene to include environment texturing adds realism to your augmented reality experience. By incorporating environment texturing, the virtual world blends that much more into the physical world. As if some of the high-quality 3D content aren't real, adding the surface reflectiveness based on the environment steps up the 3D content realism.

Environment texture is about adapting an object's material to its surrounding. Like having a steel ball vs. a rubber ball, the steel ball should have high reflectivity. Meanwhile, the rubber ball has close to none.

Environment texturing takes camera imagery as input, accounts for surfaces and lights, and uses image-based algorithms to produce realistic virtual objects. There are two ways for you to configure environment texturing, automatically or manually.

# Physically Based Lighting Model, Metalness, and Roughness

Like almost anything, there are two sides to a coin. Automatic environment texturing gets you about 80% of what you'd want from the feature with little work. You'll check out automatic environment texturing now.

In `setUpSceneView()`, add the following line of code below `configuration.planeDetection = .horizontal`:

```
configuration.environmentTexturing = .automatic
```

It's good to be aware that for devices running on iOS 13 and above, `wantsHDREnvironmentTextures` is `true` by default. This implies a high-quality environment texturing for your scene.

At the moment, nothing changes because the sphere material's lighting model is constant. To see reflectiveness, you'll need to set the lighting model to be physically based. On top of that, you'll also need to set the material's metalness and roughness.

Metalness, as the name suggests, defines how dielectric or metallic a material appears on a surface. The property takes a value between 0 and 1. Higher value means more metal-like. This property takes effect only when the material's lighting model name is set to physically based. Metalness helps decide how lights bounce off the material surface.

Roughness, on the other hand, defines how shiny a material gets to be. The property takes a value between 0 and 1. Higher values mean a more rough material. A rougher material clouds the reflectiveness of the surrounding, whereas a smoother material increases reflectiveness.

To set up the sphere material, add the following property to ViewController:

```
let sphereMaterial: SCNMaterial = {
    let material = SCNMaterial()
        material.lightingModel = .physicallyBased
    material.metalness.contents = 0
    material.roughness.contents = 0
    return material
}()
```

You define the sphere material with a physically based lighting model to reflect off the surrounding environment surfaces. Also, you set the initial metalness and roughness of the material to 0.

Now, in getSphereNode(withPosition:height:), add the following line of code below let sphere = SCNSphere(radius: 0.1):

```
sphere.firstMaterial = sphereMaterial
```

You set the sphere material to the property you've defined earlier.

Next, add the following code to roughnessSliderValueDidChange(_:):

```
let roughness = sender.value
DispatchQueue.main.async {
    self.roughnessLabel.text =
    "Roughness: \(roughness)"
    self.sphereMaterial
        .roughness.contents = roughness
}
```

You update the roughness label and the sphere material's roughness.

Then, add the following code to
metalnessSliderValueDidChange(_:):

```
let metalness = sender.value
DispatchQueue.main.async {
    self.metalnessLabel.text =
    "Metalness: \(metalness)"
    self.sphereMaterial
        .metalness.contents = metalness
}
```

You update the metalness label and the sphere material's metalness.

Finally, to show roughness and metalness labels and sliders, open
**Main.storyboard**. In the document outline, select **Environment Stack
View**. Then in the Attributes inspector, untick **Hidden** to show the
stack view.

Build and run. Tap on the screen to place spheres. Then, play around
with the material roughness and metalness.

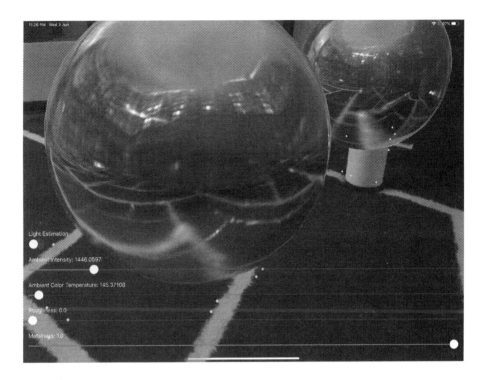

You can see the environment texturing feature takes precedence. On a smooth and metallic surface, you can see the surrounding reflect on the sphere clearly.

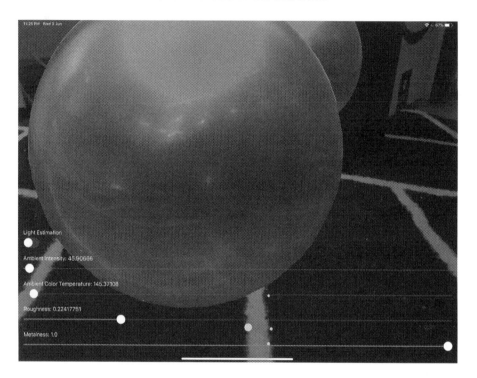

On a rougher metallic surface, you can see the surrounding reflect on the sphere to be more clouded.

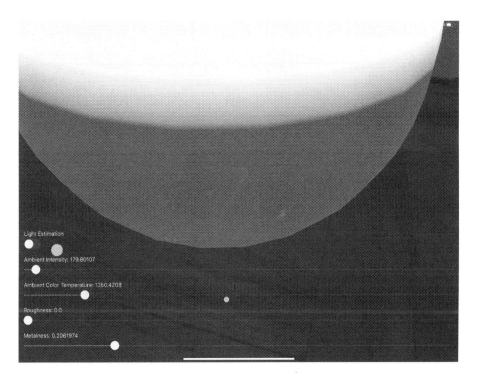

The more dielectric a surface becomes, the less light the material should pick up. And the effect takes precedence in the form of less reflectiveness.

In a darker lighting environment, the sphere's surface reflection also accounts for the lighting environment. This adds realism to the virtual objects.

And you've completed this chapter! I hope you have enjoyed and learned something valuable from this chapter.

# CHAPTER 9

# 2D Image Recognition and Filter Modification

Welcome to Chapter 9. In this chapter, we are going to talk about image recognition in augmented reality. Starting from iOS 11.3, ARKit has the capability to recognize 2D images. If you are interested in learning about building apps that recognize 2D images with ARKit, this chapter is written for you.

> *Many AR experiences can be enhanced by using known features of the user's environment to trigger the appearance of virtual content. For example, a museum app might show a virtual curator when the user points their device at a painting, or a board game might place virtual pieces when the player points their device at a game board. In iOS 11.3 and later, you can add such features to your AR experience by enabling image recognition in ARKit: Your app provides known 2D images, and ARKit tells you when and where those images are detected during an AR session.*
>
> —Apple's Documentation

© Jayven Nhan 2022
J. Nhan, *Mastering ARKit*, https://doi.org/10.1007/978-1-4842-7836-9_9

# What You'll Build

We shall build an ARKit image recognition app. At any time the app detects a recognizable image, it shall run an animation sequence that shows the detected image's location and size in the world. On top of that, the app will have a label that reflects the detected image's name. If you don't know what I mean, the following image will give you a better idea.

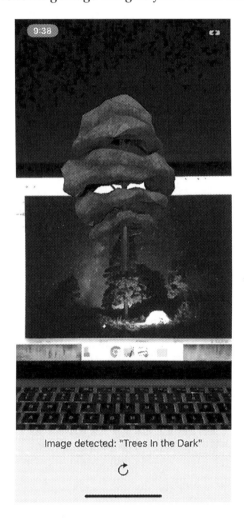

# Getting Started

First, begin by opening the **starter project**. The starter project has pre-built UI elements and action methods. This way, we can focus on the core elements of ARKit's image recognition.

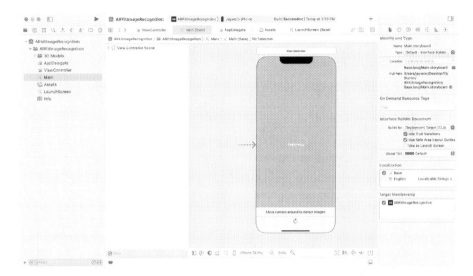

Once you have downloaded the starter project, build and run it on your iOS device. You should be prompted to allow camera access in the app. Tap OK to allow camera access in your app.

Nice. Now let's jump into preparing images for ARKit image recognition.

# Enabling Image Recognition in ARKit

In order for ARKit to recognize images, you will first need to provide two things:

1.  The images that are to be recognized by your app

2.  The physical size of the images

Let's begin with the first step by providing the images themselves. Inside the starter project, click the **Assets.xcassets** group. Afterward, you should be able to see the **AR Resources** group. Click that group. There should be three images within that group.

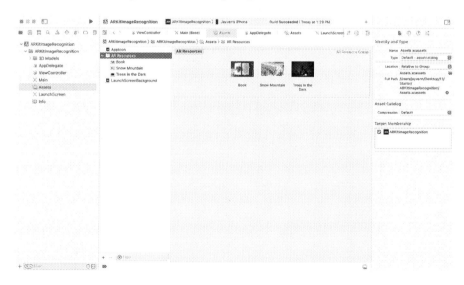

You can also drag your own images into this group. But make sure to give the image a descriptive name as well.

As mentioned earlier, by having the image file itself within your project is only the first step in preparing for ARKit image recognition. In addition, you'll also need to provide the physical image size.

Let's move on to the next section to talk about the physical image size.

# Physical Image Size

ARKit needs to know the physical image size in the world to determine the distance of the image from the camera. Entering an incorrect physical image size will result in an ARImageAnchor that has the wrong distance from the camera.

Remember to provide the physical image size every time you add a new image for ARKit to recognize. The values should reflect the image size when measured in the world. For example, the "Book" image has the following physical size.

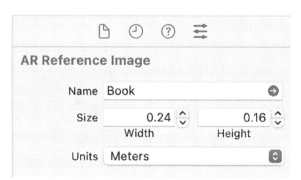

This is the physical image size property for when the image file is opened in Preview on a 15.4 inch MacBook Pro display. You can set physical image size properties accordingly in the image's attributes inspector.

# Image Properties

The image recognition capability of ARKit may vary with the images' properties. Take a look at the images inside the **AR Resources** group. You'll see that the "Book" image has two quality estimation warnings. Pay attention to this when you add reference images. Image detection works best when the image has high contrast.

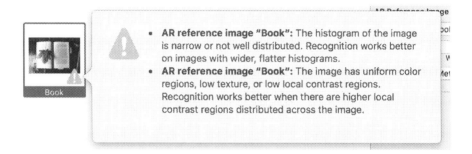

The "Snow Mountain" and "Trees In The Dark" images have no yellow warnings. This means ARKit considers these images are easily recognizable.

Snow Mountain                    Trees In the Dark

Despite the yellow warnings or not, it is still best to test out the images you plan to use in the world. And then, you can see it yourself in which images are easily recognizable.

Next, we are getting our hands dirty with some code.

# Setting Configuration for Image Recognition

We will set our scene view's configuration to detect the **AR Resources** group's reference images. The configuration will have to reset tracking and remove existing anchors run options. After running the scene view session with the configuration, we update the label's text with App usage instruction.

Open **ViewController**. Insert the following method to ViewController:

```
func resetTrackingConfiguration() {
    guard let referenceImages = ARReferenceImage
        .referenceImages(inGroupNamed: "AR Resources",
                        bundle: nil)
        else { return }
    let configuration = ARWorldTrackingConfiguration()
    configuration.detectionImages = referenceImages
    let options: ARSession.RunOptions =
        [.resetTracking, .removeExistingAnchors]
    sceneView.session.run(configuration, options: options)
    DispatchQueue.main.async {
        self.label.text = "Move camera around to detect images"
    }
}
```

Next, call `resetTrackingConfiguration()` inside of `viewWillAppear(_:)` and `resetButtonDidTouch(_:)`.

# Recognizing Images with ARImageAnchor

We are now going to overlay a transparent white plane onto newly detected images. The plane will reflect the newly detected reference image's shape, size, and the distance the image is from the device's camera. The plane overlay UI will appear when a new node is mapped to the given anchor.

---

**Note**    The anchor is of type ARImageAnchor inside the renderer*(_:didAdd:for:) method.*

---

Update the `renderer(_:didAdd:for:)` method like this:

```
func renderer(_ renderer: SCNSceneRenderer,
            didAdd node: SCNNode,
            for anchor: ARAnchor) {
    guard let imageAnchor = anchor as? ARImageAnchor else {
    return }
    let referenceImage = imageAnchor.referenceImage
    let imageName = referenceImage.name ?? "no name"

    let planeNode = getPlaneNode(
        withReferenceImage:  imageAnchor.referenceImage)
    planeNode.opacity = 0.20
    planeNode.eulerAngles.x = -.pi / 2
```

```
    planeNode.runAction(fadeAction)
}
```

The plane node is set to run a `SCNAction` sequence that it runs a fade in and fade out animation.

Now that we have the plane node and the detected image's name, we will add the plane node to the node parameter and set the label's text to show the recognized image's name. Insert the following code right after `planeNode.runAction(fadeAction)`:

```
node.addChildNode(planeNode)
DispatchQueue.main.async {
    self.label.text = "Image detected: \"\(imageName)\""
}
```

Great! You've got yourself a newly built ARKit image recognition app.

## Testing the Demo App

For the demo, you can print out a physical image copy for each of the **AR Resources** group's images. Or you can test it out by opening up the image file in Preview.

Let's transition to the next round and overlay 3D objects on detected images.

# Overlaying 3D Objects on Detected Images

Now, we have visualized the detected image's size and location in the world. Let's overlay 3D objects on detected images.

First, replace the code inside `renderer(_:didAdd:for:)` with the following:

```
DispatchQueue.main.async {
    guard let imageAnchor = anchor as? ARImageAnchor,
        let imageName = imageAnchor.referenceImage.name else
        { return }
    let overlayNode = self.getNode(
        withImageName: imageName)
    overlayNode.opacity = 0
    overlayNode.position.y = 0.2
    overlayNode.runAction(self.fadeAndSpinAction)
    node.addChildNode(overlayNode)
    self.label.text = "Image detected: \"\(imageName)\""
}
```

Upon image detection, you should now be able to see a SceneKit node run a fade and spin animation sequence away from your detected image and toward you.

# Dynamically Create ARReferenceImage Programmatically

When it comes to content, you won't always have everything you need at your disposal. Content can be dynamic. For instance, some apps can make use of downloading an image from the Internet. Then, use the image to turn it into ARReferenceImage where ARKit can recognize and perform virtual changes on the image. You'll look into this next.

You'll use a cute cat image provided by Mikhail Vasilyev on Unsplash.

First, add the following property to ViewController to store any cat reference images:

```
var catReferenceImages: Set<ARReferenceImage> = []
```

Since you only care for distinct and want to exclude duplicate reference images, you initialize an empty reference image set. You'll store images that are downloaded and converted into this property. Then, when it's time to configure ARKit for image detection, you'll refer back to the property.

Second, add the following method to ViewController:

```
// 1
func makeReferenceImageFromImage(_ image: UIImage) {
    // 2
    guard let cgImage = image.cgImage else { return }
    // 3
```

165

```
let referenceImage = ARReferenceImage(
    cgImage, orientation: .up,
    physicalWidth: CGFloat(
    cgImage.width / 1000))
// 4
referenceImage.name = "cat"
// 5
  catReferenceImages.insert(referenceImage)
// 6
debugPrint("Did insert cat reference image.")
// 7
resetTrackingConfiguration()
}
```

Here's the code breakdown:

1. The method signature takes in a UIImage for constructing an augmented reality reference image.

2. Ensure that the image passed into the parameter has a cgImage. Otherwise, return. CG stands for Core Graphics. A CGImage is a bitmap of an image. In other words, it's a grid that describes the pixel of the image.

3. Initialize a reference image from the safely unwrapped CGImage. The second parameter is of type CGImagePropertyOrientation. CGImagePropertyOrientation describes the image's orientation. If you are creating a photo editing app, you can use this property to rotate the photo to the correct orientation. If the physical world's image is rotated or vice versa, you can set this property accordingly. You also set the reference image's

physical width to the image's width divided by a
thousand. You can play around with the number—
just know that 1 CGFloat equals 1 meter in the
physical world.

4.  Give the reference image a name to reference the cat
    node in getNode(withImageName:) for animation.

5.  Insert the newly created reference image into the cat
    reference images set.

6.  Without creating additional user interfaces, simply
    print to the console that you've made it to insert a
    reference image.

7.  Afterward, reset the tracking configuration. This
    way, the newly created reference image is part of the
    augmented reality tracking configuration.

Third, for downloading an image, add the following method to
ViewController:

```
func downloadImageWithURL(_ url: URL) {
    // 1
    URLSession.shared.dataTask(with: url) {
      (data, response, error) in
      // 2
      if let error = error {
          print("Error:", error.localizedDescription)
          return
      }
      // 3
      guard let data = data,
          let image = UIImage(data: data)
          else { return }
```

```
    // 4
    self.makeReferenceImageFromImage(image)
  }.resume()
}
```

With the added method, you

1. Start a task to begin a task to download data using the provided URL in the parameter.

2. Check for networking error. If there exists one, then print the error's description for debugging before executing the return statement.

3. Safely unwrap data and turn the data into an image. Otherwise, execute the return statement.

4. With a successfully parsed image on hand, pass the image to the reference image-maker.

Fourth, add the following code to the end of `viewDidLoad()`:

```
guard let catImageUrl = URL(
    string: "https://bit.ly/2XB83sl")
    else { return }
downloadImageWithURL(catImageUrl)
```

Here, you simply give instructions to download the safely unwrapped cat image URL.

Fifth, you need to update the augmented reality world tracking configuration to include any cat reference image set. Replace the following code:

```
configuration.detectionImages = referenceImages
```

With:

```
let detectionImages = referenceImages.union(
    catReferenceImages)
configuration.detectionImages = detectionImages
```

Here, you combine the two sets to generate a sequence of unique reference images. The new sequence includes the locally stored and any downloaded images. Then, set the new sequence to the augmented reality world tracking configuration to look out for and recognize the image.

Build and run.

You can use the following link to bring up the image:

```
https://bit.ly/2XB83sl
```

After the image has downloaded, the console will print the statement you've set earlier in the debug console. And, upon image detection of the cat, you'll see the label update to say cat.

Congratulations on making it to the end of this chapter! You've opened great opportunities to amplify photo experiences in the physical world.

# CHAPTER 10

# Saving and Restoring World Mapping Data to Create a Persistence AR Experience

Starting from iOS 12, ARKit has the capability to persist in world mapping data. In the past, you can't save the AR world mapping data. iOS 12 has given developers the power to create a persistent AR experience. If you are interested in learning about building apps that persist world mapping data in augmented reality, this tutorial is written for you.

Here is what you are going to build.

© Jayven Nhan 2022
J. Nhan, *Mastering ARKit*, https://doi.org/10.1007/978-1-4842-7836-9_10

As you can see from the video, what I mean by persisting world mapping data is that you can save the AR world map and restore the mapping data later, even if the app is terminated. This has been one of the deficiencies in iOS 11. Now you can always allow users to return to the previous AR experience by saving the world mapping data.

# Getting Started

First, begin by opening the starter project. The starter project has pre-built UI elements and action methods. This way, we can focus on the core elements of working with ARKit's world map persistence.

Build and run the project on your device. You should be prompted
to allow camera access in the app. Tap **OK** to allow camera access in
your app.

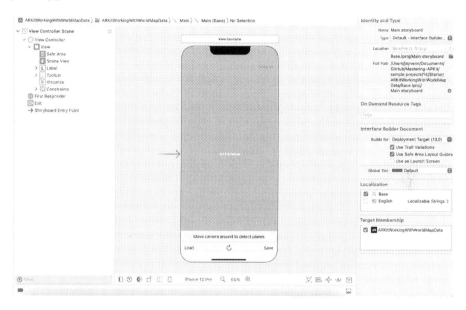

Nice. Now let's talk about what an `ARWorldMap` object is and how we are
going to work with it for ARKit world mapping data.

# Working with ARWorldMap

An ARWorldMap object contains a snapshot of all the spatial mapping
information that ARKit uses to locate the user's device in real-world space.

An `ARWorldMap` object works a lot like it sounds. It represents a mapped
out space in the physical world. When you work with an `ARWorldMap`, you
have the ability to archive an `ARWorldMap` object into a `Data` object and save
it in your device's local directory. Afterward, you go into your device's local
directory of where you saved the world map Data object for unarchiving.

To restore the map, you set your world tracking configuration's initial world map to the saved `ARWorldMap` object.

That's how we work with the `ARWorldMap` object. Now, let's implement the demo.

# Setting Up the World Map Local Document Directory

First, declare a variable of type URL which gives us the document directory path for writing and reading the world map data. Add the property to the `ViewController` class:

```
var worldMapURL: URL = {
    do {
        return try FileManager.default.url(
           for: .documentDirectory,
           in: .userDomainMask,
           appropriateFor: nil,
           create: true)
           .appendingPathComponent("worldMapURL")
    } catch {
      fatalError("Error getting world map URL from document
      directory.")
    }
}()
```

With the world map URL in place, let's create a world map data archiver method and write it to our local document directory.

# Archiving an AR World Map as Data

You are now going to create an archiver method to save your ARWorldMap object. Insert the following code in the ViewController class:

```
func archive(worldMap: ARWorldMap) throws {
    let data = try NSKeyedArchiver.archivedData(
        withRootObject: worldMap, requiringSecureCoding: true)
    try data.write(to: self.worldMapURL, options: [.atomic])
}
```

After archiving the world map as a Data object, we write the data object to the local directory. We use the .atomic option since this guarantees the file to either complete writing onto your device or not. The method has the throws statement in the signature. This is because it is possible for writing data to a device's document directory to throw an error, whether it'd be out of space or for any other reasons.

With the world map archiver method well on its way, let's actually archive the world map from the scene view.

# Saving an AR World Map Data into Your Document Directory

To get the current session's world map, Apple has given us a convenient method to help us do so. Update the saveBarButtonItemDidTouch(_:) method like this:

```
@IBAction func saveBarButtonItemDidTouch(_ sender:
UIBarButtonItem) {
    sceneView.session.getCurrentWorldMap { (worldMap, error) in
```

```
guard let worldMap = worldMap else {
    return self.setLabel(text: "Error getting current
    world map.")
}

do {
    try self.archive(worldMap: worldMap)
    DispatchQueue.main.async {
        self.setLabel(text: "World map is saved.")
    }
} catch {
    fatalError("Error saving world map: \(error.
    localizedDescription)")
}
}
}
```

Our scene view's session contains a method to get the current world map conveniently. Inside of the getCurrentWorldMap closure, we safely unwrap the returned optional ARWorldMap object. In the case where the ARWorldMap object ceases to exist, we will simply return and set the label text with an error message.

After we have safely unwrapped an ARWorldMap object, we declare a do-catch statement. If the code throws an error in the do clause, we will handle the error in the catch clause. At this point, we stop the code execution and print an error message to debug the issue.

Build and run the app. Scan your environment and tap on your device to add sphere(s) into your scene. Upon tapping the **Save** button, make sure that your label reads, "World map is saved." Now your current AR world map is saved.

# Loading an AR World Map Data from Your Document Directory

With saving an ARWorldMap object out of the way, it is time that we create a method to unarchive the ARWorldMap data from the document directory and load it onto our scene.

Before we can unarchive the world map data, we would need to successfully get the world map data from a previously saved document directory.

Add the following method to your ViewController class:

```
func retrieveWorldMapData(from url: URL) -> Data? {
    do {
        return try Data(contentsOf: self.worldMapURL)
    } catch {
        self.setLabel(text: "Error retrieving world map data.")
        return nil
    }
}
```

The preceding code declares a do-catch statement to try to retrieve a Data object from the world map URL. In the case where the code lands in the catch clause, we simply set the label with an error text message.

Now that we have a method that will help us get our data from the document directory with a world map URL, it's time for us to try and unarchive the returned Data object into an ARWorldMap object.

First, add the following method to your ViewController class:

```
func unarchive(worldMapData data: Data) -> ARWorldMap? {
    guard let unarchievedObject = try?
        NSKeyedUnarchiver.unarchivedObject(
```

```
        ofClass: ARWorldMap.self, from: data),
    let worldMap = unarchievedObject else { return nil }
  return worldMap
}
```

We use the NSKeyedUnarchiver to try and unarchive the Data object passed into the unarchive(worldMapData:) method. If the unarchiving process is a success and the unarchived ARWorldMap object does not equal to nil, we return the safely unwrapped ARWorldMap object.

Now that we have the unarchiver method in place, let's update the loadBarButtonItemDidTouch(_:) method with the following code:

```
@IBAction func loadBarButtonItemDidTouch(
  _ sender: UIBarButtonItem) {
  guard let worldMapData = retrieveWorldMapData(
    from: worldMapURL),
    let worldMap = unarchive(
        worldMapData: worldMapData) else { return }
  resetTrackingConfiguration(with:  worldMap)
}
```

Now, whenever we tap on the **Load button**, we call up the retrieveWorldMapData(_:) method to retrieve the world map data from the given URL. If the retrieval is successful, we then unarchive the world map data into an ARWorldMap object. After that, we call the resetTracki ngConfiguration(with:) method with the loaded data to restore the AR world map.

# Setting the Scene View Configuration's Initial World Map

Add the following code to `resetTrackingConfiguration(with:)` right after declaring the options constant:

```
if let worldMap = worldMap {
    configuration.initialWorldMap = worldMap
    setLabel(text: "Found saved world map.")
} else {
    setLabel(text: "Move camera around to map your surrounding
    space.")
}
```

The preceding code sets the scene view configuration's initial world map to the world map parameter. We then update the label text to say that a world map is found. Otherwise, we set the label text to instruct the users to move the camera around to map their surrounding space.

Party time, demo time.

# Persistence AR Demo

In the demo, the user tapped the screen to add a sphere node onto the scene view. Then, the user hit the save button to archive the scene view's current world map. Since the archive process is a success, the label updates with the text saying, "World map is saved." After tapping the load button, the saved world map is successfully loaded onto the scene view.

Interesting, right?

# Visualizing a World Map in 3D Space with ARPointCloud

You've learned how to save and load world maps. You've learned how to customize world tracking configuration with an initial world map. Using the raw feature point data from a world map, you'll create a 3D space in SCNScene to visualize them.

With a world map, you have raw feature points. These feature points are contained in a property called ARPointCloud. This point cloud property is the yellow dots that you see when you set a scene view to run with show feature points in the debug options. Each point contains a coordinate and an identifier.

Open **Main.storyboard**. Select **Visualize** from the document outline.
Then, in the Attributes inspector, untick the **hidden** property.

Now, the visualize button will show when you build and run your
project. You'll use the button to present VisualizationViewController.
The view controller is responsible for managing and creating raw feature
points visualization from a world map. Next, you'll set up the internals of
the view controller.

Besides feature points, to include objects such as balls you placed on the map, you'll draw out anchors from ARWorldMap. You extract the position and name of each anchor. Then, you can go to town with the visualization. Since the process is almost identical, you'll skip adding other objects to focus on feature points. Time to jump in!

Open **VisualizationViewController**. Add the following properties:

```
private let worldMap: ARWorldMap
private let sceneView = SCNView()
private let scene = SCNScene()

private let cameraNode: SCNNode = {
   let cameraNode = SCNNode()
   cameraNode.camera = SCNCamera()
   cameraNode.position = SCNVector3(
      x: 0, y: 0, z: 10)
   return cameraNode
}()

private let omniLightNode: SCNNode = {
   let lightNode = SCNNode()
   lightNode.light = SCNLight()
   lightNode.light?.type = .omni
   lightNode.position = SCNVector3(
      x: 0, y: 10, z: 10)
   return lightNode
}()

private let sphereNode: SCNNode = {
   let sphere = SCNSphere(radius: 0.01)
   let material = SCNMaterial()
   material.metalness.contents = 0
   material.roughness.contents = 0
```

```
    material.lightingModel = .blinn
    sphere.firstMaterial?.diffuse.contents =
        UIColor.systemYellow
    let sphereNode = SCNNode(geometry: sphere)
    return sphereNode
}()
```

Here, you declare the properties that every
`VisualizationViewController` holds. One of them is a world map. The
rest relates to `SceneKit` and setting up the world map visualization in a
3D space.

You'll see a Swift compiler error for initializing `worldMap`. You'll handle
the initialization of this property now.

Next, add the following initializer methods to
`VisualizationViewController`:

```
init(worldMap: ARWorldMap) {
    self.worldMap = worldMap
    super.init(nibName: nil, bundle: nil)
}

required init?(coder: NSCoder) {
    fatalError("init(coder:) has not been implemented")
}
```

You've created an initializer for the view controller. For objects that
initialize `VisualizationViewController` programmatically, juxtapose with
interface builder, they will have to pass in an `ARWorldMap` using dependency
injection. Because the view controller isn't meant to be initialized from the
interface builder, the interface builder initializer returns the fatal error.

The error message is that the interface builder's initializer isn't
implemented. If you want to use the interface builder and without
dependency injection, there are various ways of achieving this like
property injection. That's a digressing topic for another day.

183

Now, you'll need to set up the scene for the view controller.

Add the following scene setup method to
VisualizationViewController:

```
private func setupSceneView() {
    // 1
    sceneView.translatesAutoresizingMaskIntoConstraints = false
    view.addSubview(sceneView)
    NSLayoutConstraint.activate(
        [sceneView.leadingAnchor.constraint(equalTo: view.
        leadingAnchor),
         sceneView.rightAnchor.constraint(equalTo: view.
         rightAnchor),
         sceneView.topAnchor.constraint(equalTo: view.topAnchor),
         sceneView.bottomAnchor.constraint(equalTo: view.
         bottomAnchor)]
)
    // 2
    scene.rootNode.addChildNode(omniLightNode)
    scene.rootNode.addChildNode(cameraNode)
    // 3
    sceneView.scene = scene
    sceneView.autoenablesDefaultLighting = true
        sceneView.backgroundColor = .systemBackground
    sceneView.allowsCameraControl = true
}
```

Here's a breakdown of the code:

1.  You apply Auto Layout constraints on the
    scene view.

184

2.  Add the light and camera nodes with predisposed
    properties from the initializers.

3.  Set the scene view's scene, automatic lighting
    configuration, and background color. Also, you
    allow the user to control the scene's camera with
    touch gestures.

Then, call the method at the end of `viewDidLoad()`:

```
setupSceneView()
```

As soon as the view loads, you'll set up the scene view. Next, you'll
create the method to clone the sphere node you added earlier to
`VisualizationViewController` for each feature point. Add the following
method to `VisualizationViewController`:

```
private func visualizeWorldMap() {
    // 1
    for point in worldMap.rawFeaturePoints.points {
        // 2
        sphereNode.position = SCNVector3(
            point.x, point.y, point.z)
        // 3
        sceneView.scene?.rootNode.addChildNode(
            sphereNode.clone())
    }
}
```

With the code you've added, you

1.  Iterate through the 3D coordinate of the world
    map's raw feature points. You'll use the coordinates
    to position the sphere nodes that'll represent the
    feature points.

185

2. Set the sphere node's position from the current
   point's x-, y-, and z-positions.

3. Add a cloned sphere node version. You do this
   to create a new instance of the node instead of a
   reference.

Then, call the method at the end of `viewDidAppear()`:

```
visualizeWorldMap()
```

Once your view appears, you'll execute the method to
visualize `ARWorldMap` in a `SCNView`. Before you can present
`VisualizationViewController` by tapping on the **Visualize** button, you'll
need to give it the instruction.

Open `ViewController`. Add the following block of code to
`visualizeButtonDidTouchUpInside(_:)`:

```
guard let worldMapData = retrieveWorldMapData(from:
worldMapURL),
    let worldMap = unarchive(worldMapData: worldMapData) else {
    return }
let visualizationViewController =
    VisualizationViewController(worldMap: worldMap)
let navigationController = UINavigationController(
    rootViewController: visualizationViewController)
navigationController.modalPresentationStyle = .fullScreen
DispatchQueue.main.async { [weak self] in
    self?.present(navigationController, animated: true)
}
```

Similar to when loading a saved world map, you safely unarchive
and extract a world map using the world map URL, which correlates
to the world map saved directory. Afterward, you initialize a
`VisualizationViewController` with the world map property using

dependency injection as designed earlier. Place the view controller into a navigation controller. Set the navigation controller to present itself full screen modally. Then, present the navigation controller running on the main queue.

Great!

Build and run.

Move the device around to capture feature points. Tap the **save** button to save the feature points. Then, tap the **Visualize** button to bring up VisualizationViewController.

Depending on your capture feature points, you'll see something like this.

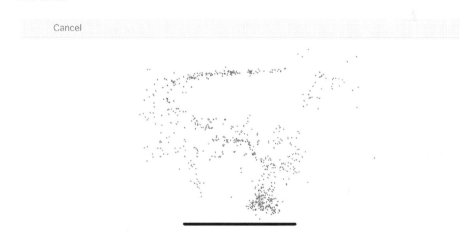

You can pan, zoom, and drag to move the camera around.

# Conclusion

Congratulations on completing the chapter! World map is an incredible invention for saving and loading augmented reality experience. Plus, you've learned to visualize a world map in a 3D space. There's so much you can with this knowledge. It's up to you to put them to great use, get creative, and have fun!

# CHAPTER 11

# Advancing App with Real-Time Image Analysis, Machine Learning, and Vision

Machine learning adds another dimension to what's possible with augmented reality. Augmented reality can open up another completely different world when combined with machine learning. Not only can you bring the world recognition capabilities from augmented reality, but you can also have a world intelligently adapt for your purpose/need in real time.

Want to check if the lost dog belongs to your friend? Or if a product is genuine?

Want to know a word definition without taking out your phone effortlessly? Or the right bolt for the correct socket?

How about controlling a robot with your hand motion? Like something that comes out of an *Iron Man* movie—except you can build it yourself.

Without further ado, I invite you to join me in another thrilling AR chapter!

© Jayven Nhan 2022
J. Nhan, *Mastering ARKit*, https://doi.org/10.1007/978-1-4842-7836-9_11

# Getting Started

Open the **starter project**. The starter project has pre-built UI elements and action methods. This way, you can focus on the core elements of working with real-time Vision and Core ML in ARKit.

The starter project includes an open source ML model. The model is named **Gesture** in the project. You will use this model to identify hand gestures through the camera lens.

Here are the conditions we want to implement in our app. If the gesture model identifies

- An open hand with 70+ percent confidence, move the toy robot forward at 5 cm/s.

- A close hand (fist) with 70+ percent confidence, move the toy robot backward at 3 cm/s.

- Anything else, nothing happens to the robot.

Okay, let's control the robot using hand gesture recognition. Get ready, Jarvis!

# Creating an Image Analysis Request for Your Core ML Model

Real-time video analysis was science fiction a century ago. Yet that capability lives in your pocket today. Using Vision in conjunction with Core ML models, you can leverage computer vision algorithms to classify elements of input images and video frames. Vision allows you to detect still images and video. With ARKit, it makes sense to classify elements in video frames and benefit from the real-time feedback. So that's the role of Vision. It provides the algorithms to act on input images and video frames.

Core ML models help you make educated predictions for the users based on the model's empirical evidence. You can leverage machine learning models in two primary forms on iOS. You either use a Core ML model for continuous refinement or static. A continuously refined model learns user behaviors as he/she provides data to the app—thus making better predictions for the specific user over time and data provided. A static machine learning model utilizes data entirely from the developer. Based on the problem your app is solving, you'll choose the better fitting solution. The former simply needs you to feed data to an existing data while the latter doesn't.

Core ML provides the brain. `Vision` provides the bridge for the brain to interact with your app.

You'll now begin to set up the core components for image analysis. This includes creating a vision machine learning request. Within the request, you'll set the working machine learning model and request's action handler. For example, you can instruct what to do after.

Open **ViewController**. Under `// MARK: - Vision Request.`

Add the following properties to `ViewController`:

```
// 1
private lazy var visionCoreMLRequest: VNCoreMLRequest = {
    // 2
    do {
        let mlModel = try MLModel(contentsOf: Gesture.
        urlOfModelInThisBundle)
        let visionModel = try VNCoreMLModel(for: mlModel)
        let request = VNCoreMLRequest(model: visionModel) {
        request, error in
            self.handleObservationClassification(request: request,
            error: error)
        }
```

```
      // 3
      request.imageCropAndScaleOption = .centerCrop
      return request
      // 4
  } catch {
    fatalError("Error: \(error.localizedDescription)")
  }
}()
```

Here's the property's breakdown. You

1. Lazy load your vision Core ML request to only create the property when needed instead of at the initialization stage.

2. Load the machine learning model with a do-catch statement. Since it's possible to load your machine learning model unsuccessfully, you're prepared to handle the error.

3. Crop the center of the image in the request. The input image can come in various dimensions depending on internal and external layout changes. Your user uses various devices that come in various resolutions. Also, your users can go into a split view. And you can deliberately change the frame of your augmented reality scene. The center crop is one of the scaling options. It keeps the image's aspect ratio to fit the shorter side of the image. Then, it uses the ratio to center the resulting image. This scaling method is preferred for machine learning models built to recognize equal length and width bounding boxes.

4. Stop the app execution and print the error
   description when the project is incapable of loading
   the gesture machine learning model.

Under `// MARK: - Vision Request`, add the following code to
`handleObservationClassification(request:error:)`:

```
// 1
guard let observations = request.results
        as? [VNClassificationObservation],
      let observation = observations.first(
        where: { $0.confidence > 0.8 })
else { return }
// 2
let identifier = observation.identifier
let confidence = observation.confidence
// 3
var text = "Show your hand."
if identifier.lowercased().contains("five") {
   text = "\(confidence) open hand."
} else if identifier.lowercased().contains("fist") {
   text = "\(confidence) closed fist."
}
DispatchQueue.main.async {
   self.label.text = text
}
```

Here's the breakdown of the added code:

1. Safely cast the request results as an array of
   `VNClassificationObservation`. Each observation
   result is a classification model containing an
   identifier and a confidence score. The observation

is a derivative of your Core ML model. Then, you draw out the first observation with an observation confidence of 80% or higher. Otherwise, you will return from the method.

2. For reusability, extract the observation identifier and confidence properties into constants.

3. Based on the identifier, update the user about the confidence score and classification. Or simply instruct the user to show his/her hand. You'll inform the user via a label. The update will run on the main queue.

You've done the groundwork for creating an image analysis request for your Core ML model. Next, you'll learn to put the request to work during frame classification.

# Classifying Camera's Pixel Buffer from Video Frame

As mentioned earlier, Vision helps you classify your frame. One of the prerequisites for the frame classification is

Add the following property to ViewController:

```
private var cvPixelBuffer: CVPixelBuffer?
```

You'll use the property to reference a captured image from an ARFrame for image analysis. This is also the same property that you'll use to handle vision requests.

Under // MARK: - Computed Properties, add the following computed property to ViewController:

```
private var requestHandler: VNImageRequestHandler? {
```

```
// 1
guard let pixelBuffer = cvPixelBuffer,
      let orientation = CGImagePropertyOrientation(
        rawValue: UInt32(UIDevice.current.orientation.
        rawValue))
else { return nil }
// 2
return VNImageRequestHandler(cvPixelBuffer: pixelBuffer,
                            orientation: orientation)
}
```

Here's a breakdown of the computed property:

1. Ensure that a pixel buffer is loaded into
   cvPixelBuffer and that you can initialize an image
   property orientation. CGImagePropertyOrientation
   is a value type to indicate the orientation of your
   image. By setting the correct image orientation,
   the machine learning model will usually have
   greater classification confidence. This is because
   of the data fed. The idea here is analogous to how
   FaceID works.

2. Return an image request handler by passing in
   the two safely unwrapped properties. This image
   request handler object is used by Vision to classify
   an image.

With the image request handler intact, you'll move on to using the
computed property for frame classification.

Add the following method to ViewController:

```
// 1
private func classifyFrame(_ frame: ARFrame) {
```

```
// 2
cvPixelBuffer = frame.capturedImage
// 3
DispatchQueue.global(qos: .background).async { [weak
self] in
   guard let self = self else { return }
   // 4
   do {
      defer {
         self.cvPixelBuffer = nil
      }
      try self.requestHandler?.perform(
         [self.visionCoreMLRequest])
   } catch {
      print("Error:", error.localizedDescription)
   }
}
}
```

Here's a breakdown of the method:

1.  The method takes in an ARFrame. This frame will
    derive from your scene's ARSession.

2.  Update the current pixel buffer using the frame's
    captured image. The frame's captured image is
    in the format of CVPixelBuffer. The pixel buffer
    is a collection of pixels stored in the device's
    main memory.

3.  Run the classification on the background thread
    for smooth user experience and to not block the
    main thread.

4. Use a do-catch statement to perform a request that
   can throw an error safely. Upon completing the
   request, you'll set the pixel buffer to nil to load pixel
   buffers one by one. When an ongoing request is
   occurring, no other pixel buffer should be requested
   to perform classification.

Now, you'll need to pass in the frame explicitly.

Inside ARSessionDelegate extension block, implement the following
protocol method:

```
func session(_ session: ARSession, didUpdate frame: ARFrame) {
    guard cvPixelBuffer == nil else { return }
    classifyFrame(frame)
}
```

To prevent overrunning the user's device memory with frame
classification request, you decide only to make a frame classification when
no pixel is queued. Only then, you will proceed with frame classification.
As you can imagine, for devices running 60 or 120 frames per second,
running an immense quantity of classifications on every frame is a sure
way to turning your device into a toaster and unnecessarily drain the
device's energy.

You can space out the in-between time for classifications even further.
You can add custom logic to create a buffer of at least 1 second, 3 seconds,
etc. I do think that you'll need to look at the use case and balance between
energy utilization and requesting for frame classification.

You've ensured pixel buffers are processed one at a time. Afterward,
you call the frame classification method to apply machine learning to the
current frame. Next, you'll implement controlling toy robot by analyzing
hand gestures.

# Controlling Toy Robot with Hand Gesture Analysis

Now, you'll implement the logic to handle when your toy robot moves, how your toy robot moves, etc.

Under `// MARK: - Toy Robot`, add the following method:

```
// 1
private func moveToyRobot(isForward: Bool) {
    // 2
    guard !isAnimating else { return }
    isAnimating = true
    // 3
    let z: CGFloat = isForward ? 0.05 : -0.03
    let moveAction = SCNAction.moveBy(
        x: 0, y: 0, z: z, duration: 1)
    toyRobotNode.runAction(moveAction) {
        // 4
        self.isAnimating = false
    }
}
```

Here's the code breakdown:

1. The method takes in a Boolean which to decide the toy robot's forward or backward movement.

2. Ensure that the toy robot has completed its animation before queuing up another animation.

3. When you instruct the toy robot to move forward, it will move forward at 5 cm/s. On the contrary, instructing the toy robot to move backward will move it back at 3 cm/s. The direction is relative to where the toy robot is facing on a horizontal plane.

4. Upon the robot's move action completion, set the animation Boolean to `false`. This indicates that the toy robot is no longer in the middle of a move animation. And the toy robot is ready for the next move animation.

Now, you'll incorporate the toy robot movement logic to the observation classification handler. In `handleObservationClassification` `(request:error:)`, add the following line of code under `if identifier.` `lowercased().contains("five") {`:

```
self.moveToyRobot(isForward: true)
```

Then, inside the same method, add the following line of code under `}` `else if identifier.lowercased().contains("fist") {`:

```
self.moveToyRobot(isForward: false)
```

After finding a classification observation with a confidence greater than 80%, you'll decide whether the toy robot moves. You command the app to execute on the toy robot's movement on two conditions. The toy robot moves forward when the identifier contains the word "five." And the toy robot moves backward when the identifier includes the word "fist."

Next, you'll place the toy robot upon plane detection.

# Adding Toy Robot upon Plane Detection

Once the app detects a horizontal plane, you'll place the toy robot on that plane.

First, add the following property to `ViewController`:

```
private let toyRobotNode: SCNReferenceNode = {
    let resourceName = "toy_robot_vintage"
    guard let url = Bundle.main.url(
```

```
        forResource: resourceName, withExtension: "usdz"),
      let referenceNode = SCNReferenceNode(url: url)
   else { fatalError("Failed to load \(resourceName).") }
   referenceNode.load()
   return referenceNode
}()
```

Here, you initialize the toy robot node.

Second, under // MARK: - ARSCNViewDelegate, add the following extension block:

```
// 1
extension ViewController: ARSCNViewDelegate {
   // 2
   func session(_ session: ARSession, didAdd anchors:
   [ARAnchor]) {
      for anchor in anchors {
         // 3
         guard !isToyRobotAdded,
            anchor is ARPlaneAnchor else { continue }
         isToyRobotAdded = true
         // 4
         label.isHidden = false
         // 5
         toyRobotNode.simdTransform = anchor.transform
         // 6
         DispatchQueue.main.async {
            self.sceneView.scene.rootNode.addChildNode(
               self.toyRobotNode)
         }
      }
   }
}
```

Here, you

1. Make `ViewController` adopt `ARSCNViewDelegate` to gain access to the protocol method that fires when a new anchor is added onto the scene.

2. Implement the protocol method that triggers new anchor detection from the scene.

3. Ensure that only one toy robot will be added to the scene. Plus, you ensure that the anchor added is a plane anchor.

4. Show the label. The label's text will instruct the user to show his/her hand or details the observation classification.

5. Position and rotate the toy robot with respect to the plane anchor.

6. Add the toy robot node onto the scene.

There you have it. You've learned to advance app with real-time image analysis, machine learning, and vision. It's showtime.

# Showtime

Build and run.

Show an open hand.

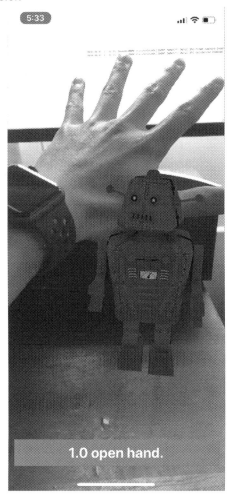

You should see the toy robot move forward.

Show a closed hand.

You should see the toy robot move backward.

Augmented reality opens a new dimension of possibilities. Machine learning dramatically broadens the dimension of possibilities. The sky is the limit.

**CHAPTER 12**

# Crafting 3D Assets

Fire-spitting dragons, flesh-hungry great white sharks, and a real-size dinosaur! Scary stuff… Fun stuff!

3D assets can be super-detailed. You can have a 3D model that shows every pore of a person's face.

Photo by <a href="https://unsplash.com/@houcinencibphotography?
utm_source=unsplash&utm_medium=referral&utm_conte
nt=creditCopyText">Houcine Ncib</a> on <a href="https://
unsplash.com/s/photos/person-face?utm_source=unsplash&utm_
medium=referral&utm_content=creditCopyText ">Unsplash</a>

And, on the contrary, you can also have less detailed 3D models. For example, there are polygonal 3D models.

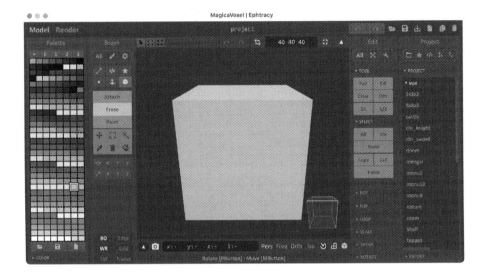

Both have their beauty and uniqueness in a 3D world.

It's like comparing *PlayStation 5* graphics with a *Nintendo Switch* graphics. Triple-A graphical intensive games like *God of War* has pixel details that make a model looks much closer to life-like. While games on the *Nintendo Switch* do not have the most graphically intensive games, there are exclusive Nintendo titles that sell like hot cakes because of "fun."

Fun is subjective, and this is more opinion than fact. Video games are not just about pushing pixels and achieving photo-realism. Other factors like immersion, music, sound effects, ambiance, storytelling, art style, and social factors all contribute to a gaming experience. Hence, games like *Super Smash Bros Ultimate, Animal Crossing,* or *Metroid Dread* have sold more copies and won over the hearts of genres than a plethora of Xbox and PlayStation titles.

Detail graphics can create immersive world-like experiences. However, it doesn't always equate to a delightful experience.

There are many ways to go about creating 3D assets for iOS augmented reality. You've been introduced to how to obtain 3D assets in Chapter 5, "Understanding and Implementing 3D Objects." Now, it's time for you to learn to create your own!

Take out the *Valyrian steel* from the oven. Let's start crafting, Craftsman!

Psst, we're going to build a tower defense game in a bit. Let's build a tower.

# Crafting a Tower in SpriteKit

SpriteKit is Apple's 2D graphics framework. Using SpriteKit with SceneKit, you can create intriguing assets where you have 2D assets in a 3D world.

You can turn a 2D asset into a 3D asset and have it behave like a 3D object. Imagine a piece of paper. Although it's flat and looks two-dimensional, it's a three-dimensional object. A similar philosophy follows.

You'll have a better idea later when you see your assets in augmented reality action! For now, we'll focus on creating assets using different Apple's proprietary graphics tools beginning with SpriteKit.

Open **Xcode**. Create a new iOS app **project**.

Create a new **SpriteKit Scene**.

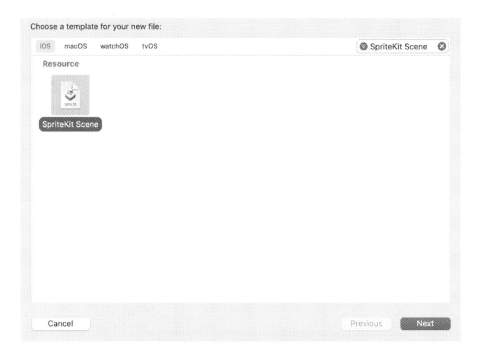

Name the file **Tower.sks**.

With the file opened in the Editor, you should see this.

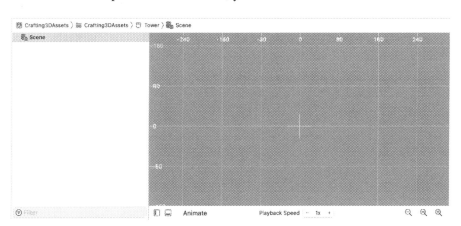

Open the **Object library**. Type **Empty**.

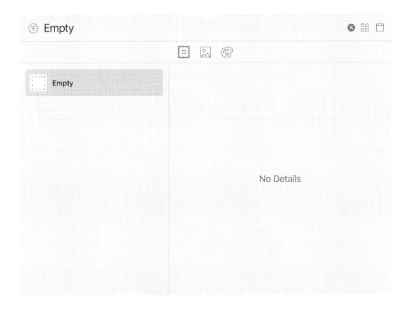

Drag **Empty** into the SpriteKit scene.

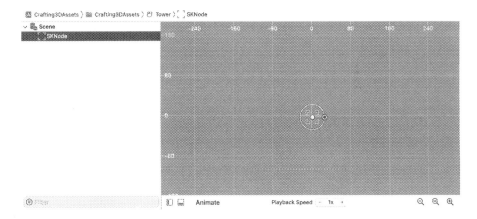

You've added an empty node onto the scene.

Select **SKNode** from the **Scene Graph View**.

Over the Attributes inspector, set the name to **Tower** and position to **(0, 0)**.

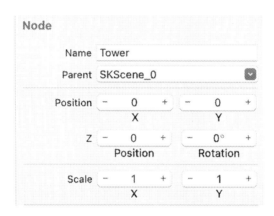

Drag in four **Shape Node (Square)** under **Tower** in the **Scene Graph View**. Like this.

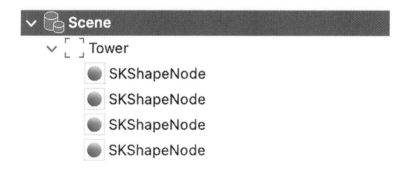

Rename the shape nodes to

- CenterRectangle

- TopRectangle

- HealthBar

- BottomRectangle

Like this.

Select the following nodes:

- CenterRectangle

- TopRectangle

- BottomRectangle

Set their **Fill Color** to **Window Frame Text Color**.

Select **HealthBar**. Set **Fill Color** to **System Green Color**.

211

Next, give the following nodes with their respective position (x, y) and scale (x, y):

- CenterRectangle—(0, 0) and (4, 8)

- TopRectangle—(0, 500) and (6, 2)

- HealthBar—(0, 0) and (2, 6)

- BottomRectangle—(0, -500) and (6, 2)

You should see this in the Editor.

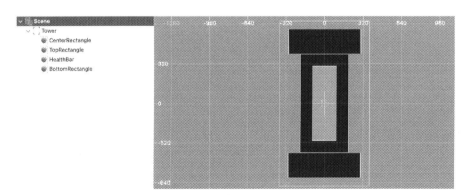

There you go with your tower!

# Crafting a Fireball in SceneKit

Now, it's your time to create your 3D fireball projectile.

Create a new **SceneKit Scene File**.

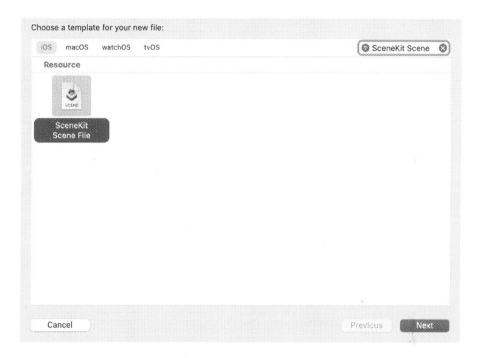

Name the file **Fireball.scn**.

Open the **Scene Graph View**. You should see this.

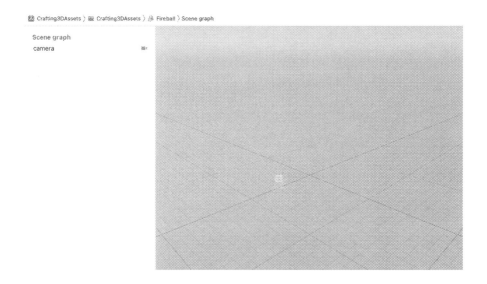

Remove the **camera** node.

Drag an **empty** node onto the scene. Set the node name to **fireball**.

Drag a **sphere** node onto the scene. Drag **sphere** under the fireball.
This makes the sphere node a child node of the fireball node.

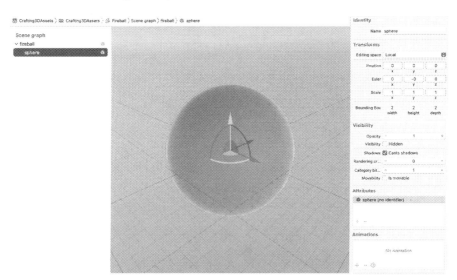

To make the fireball more interesting, drag two **torus nodes** under fireball to make them the child nodes.

On the second torus node, set its z Euler angle to **90**.

Now, you have this.

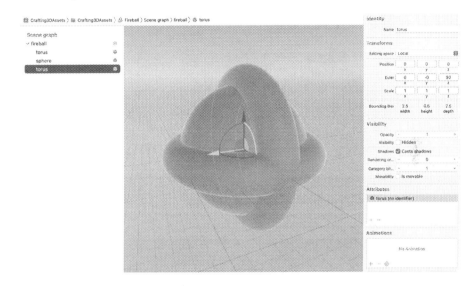

Now, the fireball looks a bit pale. We'll spice it up!

Select **sphere**. Click **Material inspector**.

In the Diffuse section, click the **drop-down menu**. Select **Colors…**.

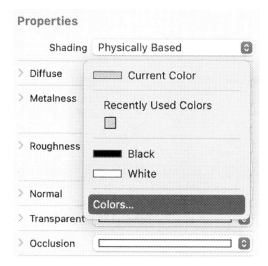

Select the **Color Sliders** tab. You should see a drop-down menu right underneath the tab.

Click the **drop-down menu**. Select **RGB Sliders**. Set the Hex Color # to **E74C3C**.

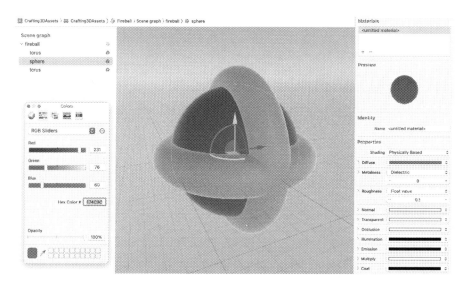

Set both of the torus diffuse color to **E74C3C** as well.

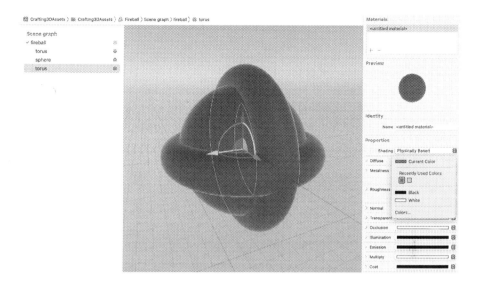

Nice fireball! The flame can come later with the usage of particle systems. For now, we only need to worry about the projectile solid itself.

# Crafting a Troop in Reality Composer

The most highly recommended way to create content for your iOS augmented reality experience is to use Reality Composer. And that's exactly what you're going to learn to do right now!

Create a new **Reality Composer Project**.

217

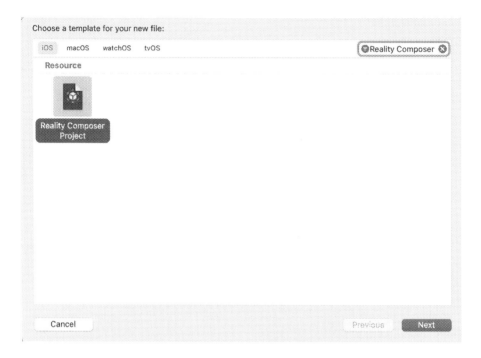

Name the file **Troop.rcproject**.

With the file opened in the Editor, you should see this.

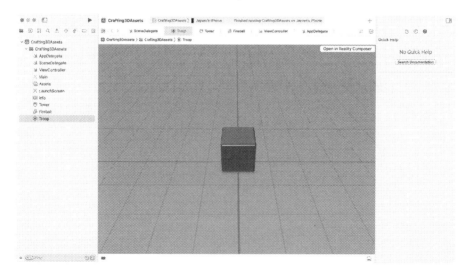

Click **Open in Reality Composer**.

You should see this.

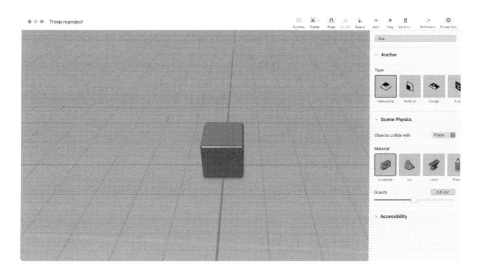

Here, you have a canvas that's similar to that of a SceneKit file. However, the user interface is much friendlier and built with 3D content and augmented reality in mind. Even the object files you'll see are in USDZ (file format made for augmented reality experiences).

Reality Composer is useful for having an existing 3D model in USDZ format and building on top of that format. In regard to the physical structure of virtual objects, you won't be making material changes to an existing object in Reality Composer. However, you can customize the object with exception to the primitive shapes like cube, cylinder, sphere, etc.

Select the **cube**. Press **delete**.

Click the + button to open the content library.

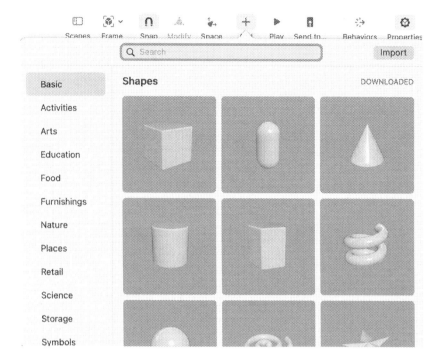

Reality Composer comes with downloadable objects from Apple's library.

Select **Activities** from the side panel. Double-click the **black horse**.

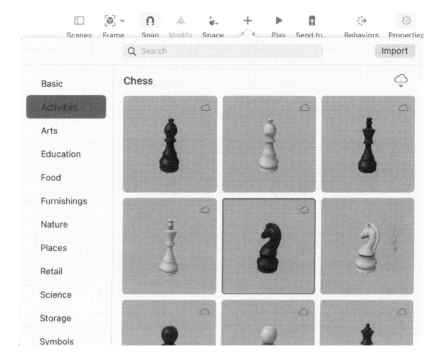

The object will begin to download from the Internet.

---

**Note**   For future Reality Composer projects, the chances are that you'll encounter projects where an asset isn't preloaded. Consequently, one of the first few places to diagnose the problem is the content library and downloading the relevant content.

---

Once the content is loaded, you should see this.

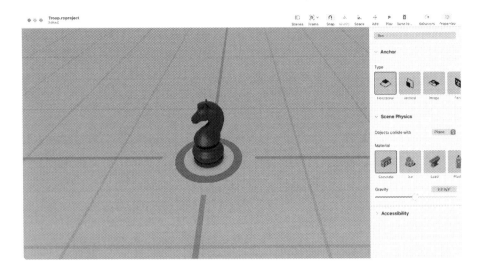

Select the **black horse**.

In the object settings pane, click **Iconic** under the Style section.

Here, you can select the style for your object. Realistic, as the name suggests, is a render that is close to a real object you'll find in the real world. Stylized is one that is colored a certain way by the creator. With iconic, you can select the material coating on the object.

Under the Material section, scroll until you see Gold and **select** on it.

Afterward, you should see this.

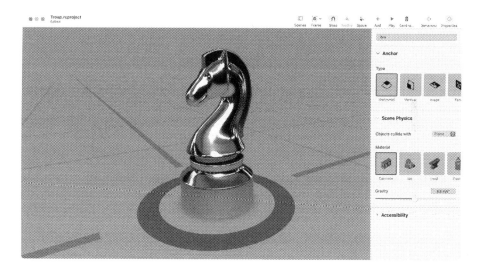

Now, it's time to give the scene a more descriptive name for clarity. In the top-right section, click the **Scenes** button to toggle the scene panel.

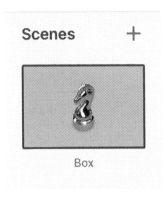

Click the **Box** scene. Then, in the properties pane, rename Box to
**Gold Horse**.

We'd later want to have another troop attacking from the other side on
a game. Let's go ahead and create another scene.

Click the + button next to scenes.

It'll ask you to choose an anchor for your content. With horizontal
selected, click next.

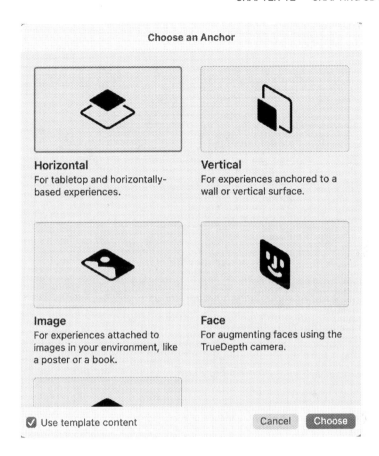

Rename the scene as **Black Rook**.

Select and delete the **cube** and the **text**.

Open the **content library**. Search for **Rook**.

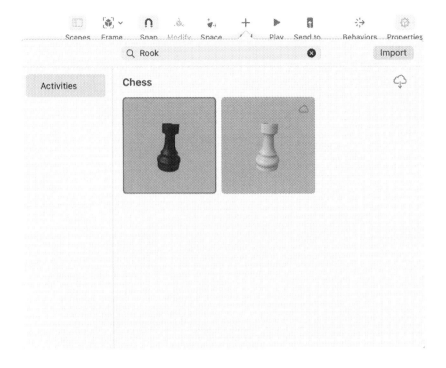

Double-click the **black rook**.

After the asset is loaded, you should see this.

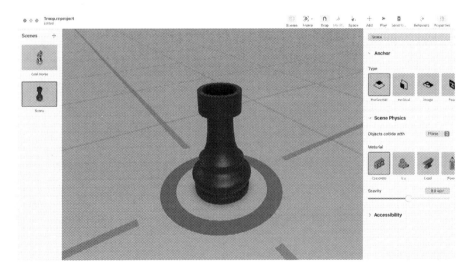

To make the content even more interesting, we'll have the rook sit on a star. Like a nimbus cloud from *Dragon Ball*.

Open the **content library**. Search for **Star**.

Double-click the **Star**.

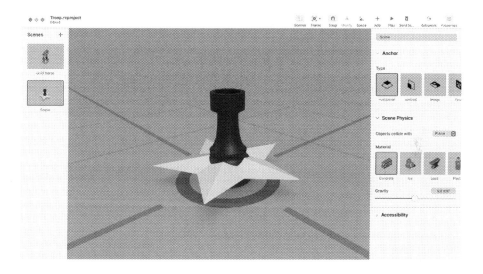

Select the **star**.

Set the position to **(X: 0, Y: 1.11 cm, Z: 0)**.

Set the diameter to **10**. Set the thickness to **35**. Set the inset to **0.5**. To reiterate, you alter the physical form of basic objects like the star you are working with.

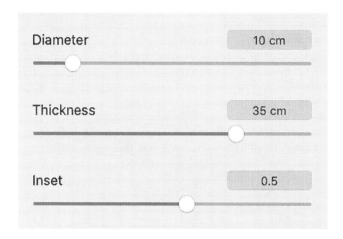

Here we make updates to the user interface properties to the star regarding its diameter, thickness, and inset.

Change the material color to **black**.

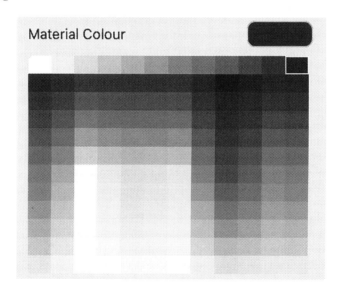

Then, select the **black rook**. Set its style to **Iconic**.

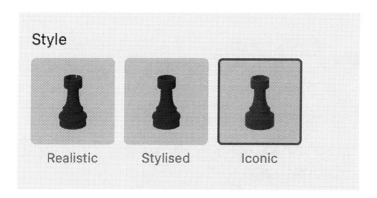

And set its material color to **dark gray** second to the right of the panel of colors.

And set its y-position to **1**.

You should have something that looks like this in the Editor.

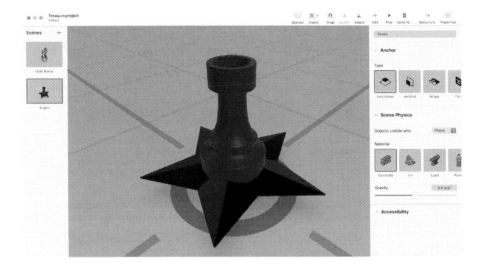

We always spice things up. One of the greatest challenges beyond creating 3D content for augmented reality experiences is creating animations and doing it with ease. We will rotate the star under the rook.

Click **Behaviors** at the top-right corner.

Click the + button to the right of behaviors.

**Scroll down** on the pop-up. Select **custom**.

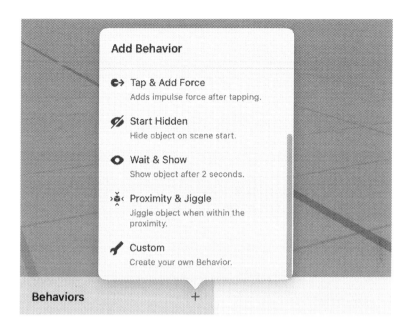

Click **Add a Trigger to this Behavior**.

Select **Scene Start**.

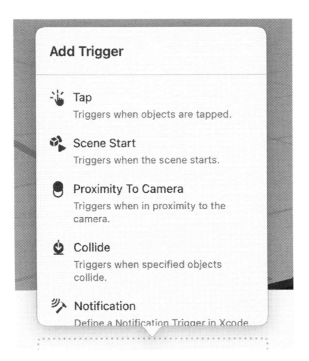

Click **Add an Action to this sequence**.

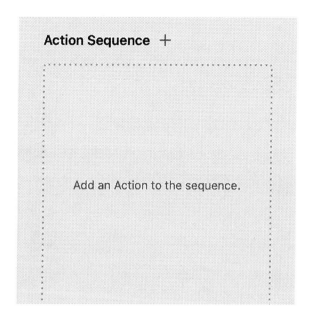

Select **Move, Rotate, Scale By**.

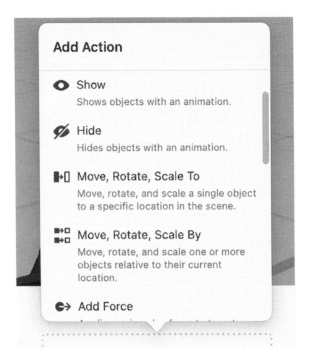

Afterward, Reality Composer will ask you to attach an object to the action sequence. Select the **star**.

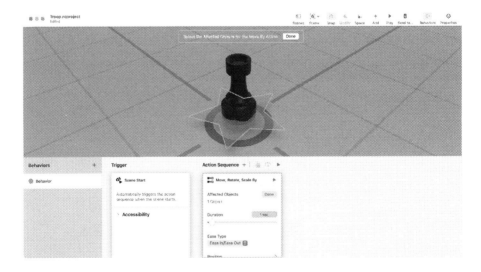

Set duration to **4** and ease type to **none**.

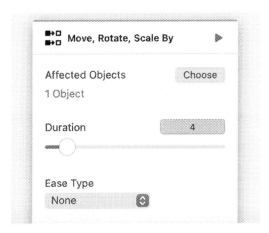

Scroll down. Click the **reset** button next to Position—to make sure the x, y, and z are at 0.

Then, set the y rotation to **90**.

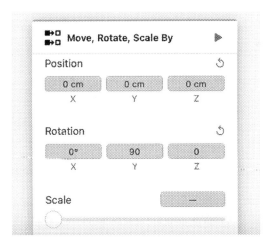

Finally, toggle **looping** to have the action sequence loop forever.

You can press the **play** button to see the animation in action.

It'll look something like this with a focus on the star.

Alternatively, you could also click the **Play** button at the navigation bar.

And you'll be able to see the animation without the star in highlight.

It's a rook that sits on a star. Cool!

Using basic object shapes, you can mix and match to create an object of your liking. If given the option to choose between SceneKit and Reality Composer, it's recommended to choose Reality Composer for its close integration with the Metal framework at export. Thanks to the lower-level framework optimization, it gives your app the more optimal augmented reality experience performance.

That's it! Feel free to play around and mix and match to see what you come up with any of Apple's graphics creation tools earlier.

# More Tools

At the time of writing this chapter, there were many discussions and considerations as to whether or not the book should include another/a couple more chapters to cover 3D creation tool(s) outside Apple's first-party tools environment.

With the complex 3D creation tools, there exists a high learning curve. Getting set up and getting used to the controls/navigations may have some people tear their hairs out.

If you look to create 3D assets outside Apple's first-party tools environment, you can check out

1. Blender

2. Maya

3. Adobe Project Aero

# Conclusion

In this chapter, you've learned how to create 2D SpriteKit, 3D SceneKit, and 3D RealityKit composer models that can be integrated in an ARKit project. On top of that, you've learned to customize the appearances, create relationships between nodes, and integrate action sequence to the crafted 3D assets.

Congratulations on making it to the end of the chapter. Gear up for another adventure!

# CHAPTER 13

# Creating Immersive Audio Experiences

Immersion gives people chills. Sometimes, it puts people on the edge of heart attacks because an app is so real.

Immersion is about putting the users in the driver's seat and letting the eyes experience a world as if it's real.

It's like going to the movies to watch a scary movie. The brain can logically fathom what the eyes see isn't going to harm the person. Yet humans react to the **perception** of realism regardless of realism.

© Jayven Nhan 2022
J. Nhan, *Mastering ARKit*, https://doi.org/10.1007/978-1-4842-7836-9_13

Beyond visual realism, another aspect that can make or break an immersive augmented reality experience is **sound**. In this chapter, you'll learn how to create a spatially aware audio experience. You're going to learn to develop sound immersive augmented reality experiences!

Here's what you'll build to implement spatial sound awareness:

- Add a lion model onto the ARSceneView upon horizontal plane detection.

- Create a 3D spatial-aware audio source.

- Implement mono over the stereo audio channel.

Without further ado, let's begin.

# Implementing Spatial Sound Awareness

To let SceneKit decide the position of an audio source, you'll need to create a sound source.

Open **ViewController**. Add the following property to ViewController:

```
private let audioSource: SCNAudioSource = {
    // 1
    let fileName = "lion-stereo.mp3"
    guard let audioSource = SCNAudioSource(fileNamed: fileName)
        else { fatalError("\(fileName) can not be found.") }
    // 2
    audioSource.loops = true
    // 3
    audioSource.load()
    // 4
    return audioSource
}()
```

With the preceding code, you

1. Make sure that the audio source with the `fileName` can be found in the project. If not, then throw a `fatalError` with an error message.

2. Want the sound of the track to repeat—hence setting `loops` to `true`.

3. Load the `audioSource` so that the audio source is ready to play. If not, you could experience delays.

4. Return the configured `SCNAudioSource` object.

You've added a `SCNAudioSource` property with an audio source containing an audio track of a lion. The audio source gives your AR experience 3D spatial sound awareness.

When you add the audio source onto a node, SceneKit will know how to play audio based on the user's device position in a 3D space.

Next, add the following method to `ViewController`:

```
private func addAudioSource() {
    // 1
    lionNode.removeAllAudioPlayers()
    // 2
    lionNode.addAudioPlayer(
        SCNAudioPlayer(source: audioSource))
}
```

With the preceding code, you

1. Remove any `SCNAudioPlayer` object attached to the `lionNode`.

2. Add a `SCNAudioPlayer` with its audio source coming from the `audioSource` you recently configured.

Afterward, add the following extension to the end of the file:

```
// MARK: - ARSCNViewDelegate
extension ViewController: ARSCNViewDelegate {

}
```

In the preceding ARSCNViewDelegate extension group, you're going to configure ARSession's fail conditions, add the lionNode, and configure lionNode's audio player.

Add the following method inside the ARSCNViewDelegate extension group:

```
func session(_ session: ARSession, didFailWithError error: Error) {
    resetTrackingConfiguration()
}
```

The preceding code simply resets the tracking configuration when a session fails for any reason.

Next, add the following method inside the ARSCNViewDelegate extension group:

```
func renderer(_ renderer: SCNSceneRenderer,
              didAdd node: SCNNode,
              for anchor: ARAnchor) {
    guard anchor is ARPlaneAnchor else { return }
    node.addChildNode(lionNode)
    addAudioSource()
    turnOffPlaneDetectionTracking()
}
```

Whenever an ARAnchor is added onto the sceneView, renderer(_:didAdd:for:) gets called. Inside renderer(_:didAdd:for:), we make sure that the anchor is an ARPlaneAnchor. When the anchor is an

ARPlaneAnchor, ARKit has detected a horizontal plane in the ARSession based on the project's configurations.

Now, you need to set the delegate ARSCNViewDelegate. Add the following code to setupSceneView():

```
sceneView.delegate = self
```

The preceding code sets the ARSCNViewDelegate to ViewController. Great, you're ready to test out the AR experience!

For a more obvious environment-aware audio experience in a 3D space, connect your earphones to your device.

Build and run. Detect a horizontal plane. Upon plane detection, you should be able to find yourself looking at a lion model. You should also be able to hear the sound of a growling lion.

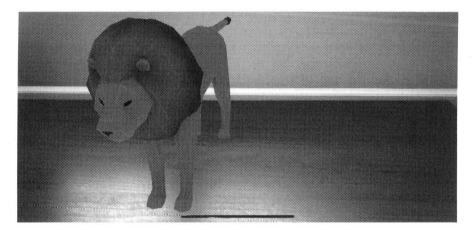

At the moment, the audio source's spatial awareness isn't particularly obvious. Stereo audio sources tend to produce low-quality 3D audio effects. To best implement SceneKit's node-based audio API to associate environmental sounds, it is best to use audio tracks with mono audio channels.

Replace the following line of code:

```
let fileName = "lion-stereo.mp3"
```

With the following:

```
let fileName = "lion-mono.mp3"
```

Build and run. Detect a horizontal plane. This time, the audio contrasts and adjusts its volume based on the position difference between the device and the lion model.

As you move closer or further away from the lion, you should be able to differentiate where the audio is coming from with respect to the device. A similar effect occurs when you move to the lion's left or right; you can imagine how fun and realistic an AR action, horror, or any game that utilizes sound in a 3D space can be.

This is great! You've learned to create an AR experience with spatial sound awareness.

# Stereo to Mono Audio Channels Conversion Tools

Most of the audio tracks you find will come in the form of a stereo audio channel. As mentioned earlier, SceneKit works best to create a spatially aware audio experience with audio tracks of mono audio channels. There are applications to convert stereo audio tracks to mono audio tracks such as Audacity.

You can also use the following website to convert a stereo audio track to a mono audio track:

- .online-convert.com/convert-to-mp3

You've traveled through the jungle, seen a lion, and heard it roar. And you've made it out alive! You are something else. Get ready, mate. There's more coming your way.

# CHAPTER 14

# Working with SpriteKit and ARKit

ARKit interacts with the physical world. With augmented reality experiences taking place in a 3D space, it's often easy to forget/neglect that 2D content also plays a role in the 3D world.

This means that in addition to 3D content, you can create and let the users interact with 2D content using SpriteKit and ARKit. This is exactly what you're going to learn about today.

You'll be building out a **Unicorn Tapper** game. The objective of the game is to last as long as possible without the unicorns count reaching 10. Unicorns will spawn randomly around the user between every 1 and 2 seconds. As soon as the game starts, so does the game timer.

© Jayven Nhan 2022
J. Nhan, *Mastering ARKit*, https://doi.org/10.1007/978-1-4842-7836-9_14

When a user taps on a unicorn, the unicorn fades away. The unicorns count decrement. If a user mistakenly taps a unicorn or taps into space, a new unicorn spawns where the user taps. The unicorns count also increment.

It's a simple, a bit physical, and surprisingly fun game. Enough talk for now, let's get the sweat on! Finger sweats first.

# Getting Started

Open the **starter project**.

Look around the project files. The majority of the existing code is simply setting up the view's UIs and world tracking configurations with ARKit.

Here's **Main.storyboard**.

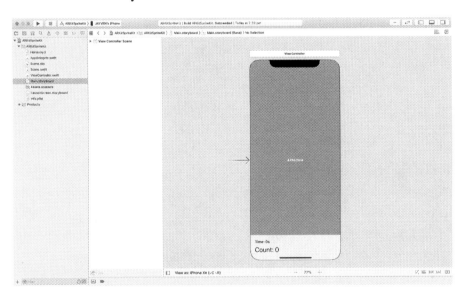

You will build on top of the views above.

The first thing you'll do to set up this game with a custom SKScene.

# Working with SKScene

## What Is SKScene?

Like SceneKit's scene, SpriteKit has its own scene property as well. SKScene helps you bring 2D content to the user. SKScene displays SpriteKit content.

The way in which you'll use SKScene will be to configure for the game logic. Also, you will use SKScene to coordinate value changes with ViewController.

## Setting Up a Custom SKScene

Later, you'll be having unicorn spawning around the user. Right now, you're about to create a custom protocol to let the delegate know about when the unicorn node is tapped.

Open **Scene**. Add the following protocol above Scene:

```
protocol SceneGestureDelegate: AnyObject {
    func didTouchObjectNode()
}
```

Add the protocol name suggests. Its job is intended to notify the delegate gesture triggers. The delegator will notify the delegate when the user touches on an object node. For the project, it'll be when the user taps on the unicorn node.

Next, add the following property to Scene:

```
weak var gestureDelegate: SceneGestureDelegate?
```

Adding this property allows Scene to set a delegate.

Nice job on the prep work! Let's move on to randomly generating unicorns around the user.

# Randomly Placing 2D Object in 3D Space

To randomly place a basic 2D object in a 3D space, there are essentially three steps:

1. Randomly generate a 3D coordinate.

2. Generate an anchor with randomized coordinates onto the scene.

3. Create a SpriteKit node using the randomized coordinates anchor.

Let's jump over to step 1!

To begin, you'll create an extension to make the degrees of a full circle conveniently accessible in the scene.

Add the following Float extension code block below Scene:

```
fileprivate extension Float {
    static var fullCircle: Float {
        return .pi * 2
    }
}
```

The Float extension above makes itself accessible only to the custom scene. Now, you can get the degrees of a circle within the scene by calling Float. fullCircle.

Time to move on to step 2. You'll add the code to randomly generate an anchor's x, y, and z coordinate values. Afterward, add the anchor onto your custom SKScene.

Add the following method to Scene:

```
private func addRandomPositionAnchor() {
    guard let sceneView = self.view as? ARSKView else { return }
    // 1
    let xAngle: Float = .fullCircle * .random(in: 0...1)
    let xRotation = simd_float4x4(SCNMatrix4MakeRotation(xAngle,
    1, 0, 0))
    // 2
    let yAngle: Float = .fullCircle * .random(in: 0...1)
    let yRotation = simd_float4x4(SCNMatrix4MakeRotation(yAngle,
    0, 1, 0))
    // 3
    let rotation = simd_mul(xRotation, yRotation)
    // 4
    var translation = matrix_identity_float4x4
    translation.columns.3.z = -1 - .random(in: 0...1)
    // 5
    let transform = simd_mul(rotation, translation)
    // 6
    let anchor = ARAnchor(transform: transform)
    // 7
    sceneView.session.add(anchor: anchor)
}
```

With the preceding code, here's what you did:

1.  Make random rotation between 0 and 360 degrees
    for the x-axis.

2.  Make random rotation between 0 and 360 degrees
    for the y-axis.

3.  Combine the x and y rotations into a single
    rotation matrix.

4.  Make a translation matrix with the z-position be
    between -1 and -2 meters. In other words, randomly
    position a node between 1 and 2 meters away from
    the device's camera.

5.  Combine the rotation matrix with the translation
    matrix to create a new transformation
    matrix. This will be the node anchor's final
    transformation matrix.

6.  Initialize an anchor using the final
    transformation matrix.

7.  Add the anchor onto the session.

Next, you'll create the logic for when a player taps and misses the
unicorn node.

# Positioning a SpriteKit Node on Tap

Placing a SpriteKit node onto a scene essentially needs you to do what
you just did. Except, you'll use the camera transform's translation and
some complementary logic. The complementary logic includes combining
the camera transform's translation and the positioning translation
matrixes.

Afterward, you'll have a matrix to create an anchor exactly 0.2 meters
from the camera's front. With the created anchor, you add the anchor onto
the scene.

Add the following method to Scene:

```
private func addAnchorToSceneView(_ sceneView: ARSKView, in
frame: ARFrame) {
    // 1
    var translation = matrix_identity_float4x4
    // 2
    translation.columns.3.z = -0.2
    // 3
    let transform = simd_mul(frame.camera.transform,
                             translation)
    // 3
    let anchor = ARAnchor(transform: transform)
    // 4
    sceneView.session.add(anchor: anchor)
}
```

With the preceding code, you

1. Initialize an identity 4 × 4 matrix which composes of zeroes to represent an origin.

2. Change the matrix's third row and the third column to -0.2. This is to create an anchor 0.2 meters away from the camera.

3. Using the translation matrix you've created, combine it with the frame camera's transform for a new anchor.

4. Create a new anchor with the combined translation matrixes.

5. Add the new anchor onto the scene view's session.

You've created the business logic to put an anchor onto the scene based on the game logic intentions. Now, you'll need to call these methods in conformance to the game interaction logic.

# Detecting Change in Time in SKScene

Now, you'll implement a timer that spawns a unicorn a repeated schedule until the game is over. The timer schedules a repeated addRandomPositionAnchor() method call every 1–2 seconds. Once the game is over, the timer will stop making calls to addRandomPositionAnchor().

Add the following properties to Scene:

```
// 1
private var initialTimeInterval: TimeInterval = 0
```

```
// 2
var isGameOver = false
```

With the preceding properties, you

1.  Create a TimeInterval property to keep track of a change in time. When it's initialized, it'll be the initial time of the scene.

2.  Add a property to indicate whether the game is over or running. It will start as running, as indicated by false at initialization.

Add the following method override in Scene:

```
// 1
override func update(_ currentTime: TimeInterval) {
```

```
// 2
guard !isGameOver,
    currentTime > initialTimeInterval else { return }
// 3
initialTimeInterval = currentTime + TimeInterval(Float.
random(in: 1...2))
// 4
addRandomPositionAnchor()
}
```

Here's the breakdown of the code you added:

1. update(_:) is called every frame. You'll place the game logic here.

2. The first condition you check prior to doing anything is whether the game is over or not with isGameOver. The second condition is to ensure the scene's total time pass is greater than the initial game time.

3. When the two conditions pass, update the initial time to a time that's 1–2 seconds from the current scene time.

4. Before ending on the current frame, call addRandomPositionAnchor().

You have the game logic for randomly adding an anchor around the player's camera position. Next, you'll implement the logic to handle adding an anchor based on the player's tap position. In addition, handle when the user taps on an existing node on the scene.

# Detecting Touches in SKScene

You'll add a sequence action for when you tap an existing node. The existing node will be the unicorn node, which you'll later place onto the scene.

Add the following property to Scene:

```
private let sequenceAction: SKAction = {
    .sequence([.playSoundFileNamed("Horse.mp3",
                                   waitForCompletion: false),
              .fadeOut(withDuration: 0.3),
              .removeFromParent()])
}()
```

With the code you added, your action consists of

1. Playing a soundtrack

2. Fading out the node in 0.3 seconds

3. Removing the node from its parent node

Now, you'll detect touches on the scene and implement the appropriate game logic.

Add the following method to Scene:

```
override func touchesBegan(_ touches: Set<UITouch>, with event:
UIEvent?) {
    super.touchesBegan(touches, with: event)
    // 1
    guard let sceneView = view as? ARSKView,
        let currentFrame = sceneView.session.currentFrame,
        let touch = touches.first else { return }
    // 2
    let touchLocation = touch.location(in: self)
```

```
// 3
guard let node = nodes(at: touchLocation).first else {
    return addAnchorToSceneView(sceneView, in: currentFrame)
}
// 4
gestureDelegate?.didTouchObjectNode()
// 5
node.run(sequenceAction)
}
```

With the code added and when the scene detects touches on the screen, you

1. Safely unwrap the scene view as ARSKView, the scene view session's current frame, and the first touch detected on the scene, and return when the values aren't safely unwrapped.

2. Get the touch location in CGPoint. This represents where the user taps on the device's screen.

3. Using the device's screen tap location, safely unwrap the first node that's tapped. When the value isn't safely unwrapped, add an anchor relative to where the user taps.

4. Let the delegate know that a node is tapped.

5. Run the SKAction you initialized earlier on the node.

Upon tapping an existing node on the scene, the node will play sound, fade out, and remove itself from its parent node.

You've created most of the core game logic. Now, you'll need to hook the Scene to the ViewController.

# Setting Up SKScene with View Controller

Open **ViewController**.

Add the following property:

```
private lazy var scene: Scene = {
    guard let scene = SKScene(fileNamed: "Scene") as? Scene
        else { fatalError() }
    return scene
}()
```

You lazy load a scene for a later use case and safely unwrap a scene file named Scene as type Scene.

To run the scene within sceneView, add the following method:

```
private func presentScene() {
    sceneView.presentScene(scene)
}
```

Then, **call** presentScene() in viewDidLoad().

Next, you'll update the labels' texts when the node count and game time get set.

Add the following properties:

```
private var nodesCount: Int = 0 {
    didSet {
        countLabel.text = "Count: \(nodesCount)"
    }
}
```

```
private var seconds: Double = 0 {
    didSet {
        let roundedSeconds = Double(round(1000*seconds)/1000)
        timeLabel.text = "Time: \(roundedSeconds)s"
    }
}
```

The properties' names and setter methods are rather self-explanatory. You update countLabel.text when the nodesCount value has been set. The timeLabel.text displays a rounded Double when the seconds value has been set.

Next, you'll set up the time label's timer.

# Setting Up the Time Label's Timer

The time label indicates how long the user has lasted in the game. You'll implement the logic for the time label.

Add the following property to ViewController:

```
private var timer = Timer()
```

Here, you initialize a Timer. It does nothing at this point. But you'll use timer to reference within ViewController. This way, you can update the timer to take different actions at different times in the game.

Add the following method to ViewController:

```
@objc func updateSeconds() {
    seconds += 0.1
    guard nodesCount >= 10 else { return }
    scene.isGameOver = true
    scene.gestureDelegate = nil
```

```
    sceneView.delegate = nil
    timer.invalidate()
    countLabel.text = "Game Over"
}
```

The method you've added does the following:

1.  Increment seconds by 0.1.

2.  Ensure the nodesCount is at least 10 with a guard
    statement. Continue the subsequent logic when
    nodesCount hits 10.

3.  Let the scene know that the game is over at this point.

4.  Set the sceneView and scene delegates to nil. So the
    player's touch gestures and the associate logics no
    longer apply. This includes introducing a new node
    on miss tap and updating the countLabel. You'll keep
    the scene's node action sequence on tap untouched.

5.  Stop the time label's timer.

6.  Indicate that the game is over at this point with
    countLabel.

Now, you'll create the timer to run on a scheduled interval.
Add the following method to ViewController:

```
private func setupTimer() {
    timer = Timer.scheduledTimer(timeInterval: 0.1,
                                 target: self,
                                 selector:
                                 #selector(updateSeconds),
                                 userInfo: nil,
                                 repeats: true)
}
```

The method sets timer to call updateSeconds() on a 0.1 seconds interval. To make the timer take effect, **call** setupTimer() in viewDidLoad(). Next, you'll generate the unicorn SpriteKit node.

# Creating the SpriteKit Node

You'll now create and configure the unicorn SpriteKit. Add the following extension block below ViewController:

```
// MARK: - SpriteKit Node
fileprivate extension ViewController {
    private func makeLabelNode() -> SKLabelNode {
        // 1
        let labelNode = SKLabelNode(text: "🦄")
        // 2
        labelNode.fontSize = 80
        // 3
        labelNode.horizontalAlignmentMode = .center
        labelNode.verticalAlignmentMode = .center
        // 4
        return labelNode
    }
}
```

With the code added, you

1.  Initialize a SKLabelNode with a unicorn emoji.

2.  Set the label's font size.

3. Center align the label node horizontally and vertically. This makes the label node point toward the camera node perpendicularly on the x- and y-axes, resulting in an always upright-facing unicorn.

4. Finally, return the final label node for the method.

Next, you'll implement `ViewController` conform to `ARSKViewDelegate`.

# Working with ARSKViewDelegate

Add the following extension block below `ViewController`:

```
// MARK: - ARSKViewDelegate
extension ViewController: ARSKViewDelegate {
    func view(_ view: ARSKView, nodeFor anchor: ARAnchor) ->
    SKNode? {
        nodesCount += 1
        return makeLabelNode()
    }
}
```

When a newly added anchor is from the random position or miss tap, you increment `nodeCount` and generate the unicorn `SpriteKit` node.

Next, you'll conform `ViewController` to `SceneGestureDelegate`.

# Working with SceneGestureDelegate

Add the following extension block below `ViewController`:

```
// MARK: - SceneGestureDelegate
extension ViewController: SceneGestureDelegate {
    func didTouchObjectNode() {
        nodesCount -= 1
    }
}
```

With the code added, you decrement `nodesCount` when `sceneView` indicates that you've touched on an object node. In this scenario, it would be whenever the player touches a unicorn `SpriteKit` node.

# Setting the Delegates

Finally, to set `ViewController` as the delegates, replace the `scene` property with the following:

```
private lazy var scene: Scene = {
    guard let scene = SKScene(fileNamed: "Scene") as? Scene else
      { fatalError() }
    scene.gestureDelegate = self
    return scene
}()
```

And add the following code to `setupSceneView()`:

```
sceneView.delegate = self
```

`ViewController` will now register the delegate methods from the scene and scene view.

# Running the Game

Build and run. Go ahead and enjoy the game you've built. I sure enjoyed this game more than I thought I would!

Tap on the unicorn nodes. They will play a horse neigh sound and fade away from the scene. Try and last as long as you could in the game.

Once the nodes count hits 10, you'll see the countLabel text indicates that the game is over.

Let's see if you can reach 60 seconds. It's not easy I tell you, but it's super fun!

The best part would probably be playing this game in public. People may think you're out of this world!

# Conclusion

In this chapter, you've learned how to add 2D content alongside 3D content using ARKit. Amazing! You can now delight your users with interactive 2D content using SpriteKit and ARKit. The **Unicorn Tapper** game you've built shows the sweet science of 2D content in a 3D world.

# CHAPTER 15

# Building Shared Experiences with Multipeer Connectivity

Adding the multiuser capability into an augmented reality experience can be a game-changer for your app. It instantly unlocks a new plane of possibilities by incorporating inputs from more people. Building shared experiences in augmented reality is one of the most significant challenges augmented reality developers are going to face. The amount of variabilities involved is tremendous. Your code base will look bloated if you are to build the multiuser experience from scratch on your own. Thank you, WWDC19!

In WWDC19, Apple has added many new capabilities to ARKit. One of the capabilities is building collaborative experiences in ARKit.

In this chapter, you'll learn about the following augmented reality shared experiences topics:

- Implementing `ARCoachingOverlayView`

- Configuring and incorporating `MultipeerSession`

- Configuring and incorporating `MCPeerID`

- Discovering and joining nearby peers with `MCSession` integration

- Implementing a nearby service browser

© Jayven Nhan 2022
J. Nhan, *Mastering ARKit*, https://doi.org/10.1007/978-1-4842-7836-9_15

- Implementing a nearby service advertiser
- Observing ARSession changes using the key-value observing pattern
- Parsing and handling participant anchors
- Visualizing multipeer virtual content
- Encoding and decoding collaboration data
- Merging world maps

By the end of this chapter, you'd know how to create a multiuser augmented reality app with ARKit.

---

**Note**    To see the full shared experiences features in motion, you'll need two devices.

---

# Getting Started

Open the **starter project**. Feel free to play around with the project to get a feel for it.

The first mission is to set up the tracking configurations for ARKit to understand that you want to enable collaborations. Similar to previous chapters, you'll set a property of an ARWorldTrackingConfiguration.

Open **ViewController**. Add the following property to ViewController:

```
private let worldTrackingConfiguration:
ARWorldTrackingConfiguration = {
    let worldTrackingConfiguration =
    ARWorldTrackingConfiguration()
    worldTrackingConfiguration.isCollaborationEnabled = true
```

```
worldTrackingConfiguration.environmentTexturing =
.automatic
return worldTrackingConfiguration
}()
```

Here, you let ARKit know that you will make use of collaboration data. Therefore, ARSession should expect to send collaboration data to your peers via session(_:didOutputCollaborationData:) and receive data from your peers via ARSession.update(with:). More on these protocol methods later.

Next, you'll build a quick, effective, and standardized onboarding experience using ARCoachingOverlayView.

# Implementing ARCoachingOverlayView

When searching for a plane in augmented reality, one of the greatest design challenges is to onboard the user smoothly. Fortunately, Apple has provided a standard onboarding experience for devices running on iOS 13 and above. Starting with iOS 13, you can utilize ARCoachingOverlayView.

ARCoachingOverlayView is a standard user onboarding view where you can find in Apple's augmented reality apps. Apple has made this view available with a list of APIs. Hence, you don't need to reinvent the onboarding wheel. And the users don't need to learn a new way of onboarding for different apps. It is a win-win situation for developers and users.

To begin implementing ARCoachingOverlayView, add the following property to ViewController:

```
private lazy var coachingOverlayView: ARCoachingOverlayView = {
    let coachingOverlayView = ARCoachingOverlayView()
    coachingOverlayView.session = arView.session
    coachingOverlayView.delegate = self
    coachingOverlayView.goal = .tracking
```

```
coachingOverlayView.
translatesAutoresizingMaskIntoConstraints = false
return coachingOverlayView
}()
```

With the code you've added, you

- Assign coachingOverlayView to arView.session. In other words, you let coachingOverlayView know which augmented reality view it should bind onto to handle tracking instructions.

- Set ARCoachingOverlayViewDelegate to ViewController.

- Set the goal of the coaching overlay to ARCoachingOverlayView.Goal.tracking. You can set a different goal to instruct the coaching overlay view to showcase different tracking instructions.

- Turn off autoresizing masks on coachingOverlayView to enable Auto Layout.

At the moment, you should see a Swift compiler error. That's because ViewController has yet to conform to ARCoachingOverlayViewDelegate. You'll do that next.

Under // MARK: - ARCoachingOverlayViewDelegate, add the following code:

```
extension ViewController: ARCoachingOverlayViewDelegate {
    // 1
    func coachingOverlayViewWillActivate(
        _ coachingOverlayView: ARCoachingOverlayView) {
      resetButton.isHidden = true
      linkButton.isHidden = true
```

```
    peersButton.isHidden = true
  }
  // 2
  func coachingOverlayViewDidDeactivate(
    _ coachingOverlayView: ARCoachingOverlayView) {
    resetButton.isHidden = false
  }
  // 3
  func coachingOverlayViewDidRequestSessionReset(
    _ coachingOverlayView: ARCoachingOverlayView) {
    resetTrackingConfiguration()
  }
}
```

Here's a breakdown of the preceding code:

1. When the coaching layer view activates, `coachingOverlayViewWillActivate(_:)` fires. In preparation for the onboarding process, you can hide any user interfaces that you want.

2. Once the coaching layer view deactivates, the onboard coaching dismisses. Here, you show user interfaces that you want once the coaching is over.

3. This is an optional protocol method. When unimplemented, the overlay runs current `ARSession` configuration with `ARSessionRunOptionResetTracking` and `ARSessionRunOptionRemoveExistingAnchors`. If you want to control the relocalization state manually, implement this method and you can run a different set of configurations and/or options.

Next, you need to add coachingOverlayView as a subview of arView. Add the following code to setupCoachingOverlayView():

```
arView.addSubview(coachingOverlayView)
NSLayoutConstraint.activate([
    coachingOverlayView.leadingAnchor.constraint(
        equalTo: arView.leadingAnchor),
    coachingOverlayView.trailingAnchor.constraint(
        equalTo: arView.trailingAnchor),
    coachingOverlayView.topAnchor.constraint(
        equalTo: arView.topAnchor),
    coachingOverlayView.bottomAnchor.constraint(
        equalTo: arView.bottomAnchor)
])
```

Before you can see the coaching overlay activation, you'll need to run ARWorldTrackingConfiguration first. In viewDidAppear(_:), add the following code to reset tracking configuration:

```
resetTrackingConfiguration()
```

Then, add the following code to resetTrackingConfiguration():

```
arView.session.run(worldTrackingConfiguration,
                   options: [.removeExistingAnchors])
```

Build and run. You should be able to see ARCoachingOverlayView's coaching.

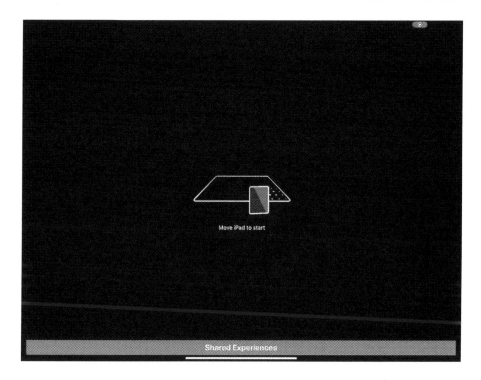

At any moment, you can activate the coaching overlay again by covering the camera lens.

Next, you'll look into multipeer connectivity.

# Setting Up MultipeerConnectivity

MultipeerConnectivity is a framework for discovery and connectivity with nearby devices. For data transmission and synchronization, the framework utilizes infrastructure Wi-Fi networks, peer-to-peer Wi-Fi, and Bluetooth personal area networks. In this section, you'll work with the following objects from the framework:

- **MCSession**: A session to handle connectivity between peers. Whether your peers are joining, maintaining, or leaving, this object is responsible for managing the events.

- **MCNearbyServiceAdvertiser**: A signal from the device to other devices regarding the type of session it is willing to join. Specified inside the app using the advertiser object.

- **MCAdvertiserAssistant**: Functions like `MCNearbyServiceAdvertiser`, but it has the option to present a standard user interface for handling invitations.

- **MCNearbyServiceBrowser**: A browser that searches nearby devices using infrastructure Wi-Fi, peer-to-peer Wi-Fi, and Bluetooth.

- **MCBrowserViewController**: Presents a standard user interface to initialize a browser and search for your peers' devices.

- **MCPeerID**: A unique identifier representing a peer in a session. Each device running on a particular app that joins a session will have a unique identifier. This object identifies your own device and your peers' devices.

You'll see a Swift compiler error when adding the snippet of codes. You'll fix them along the way in the coming instructions.

First, you'll create a custom object to encapsulate `MultipeerConnectivity` operations. Create a new file called **MultipeerSession**. Add the following code to the file:

```
// 1
import MultipeerConnectivity
// 2
final class MultipeerSession: NSObject {
    // MARK: - Value Types
```

```
// 3
typealias PeerDataHandler = (Data, MCPeerID) -> Void
typealias PeerMoveHandler = (MCPeerID) -> Void
typealias PeerDiscoverHandler = (MCPeerID) -> Bool
// MARK: - Properties
// 4
static let serviceType = "ar-collab"
// 5
private let receiveData: PeerDataHandler
private let joinPeer: PeerMoveHandler
private let leavePeer: PeerMoveHandler
private let discoverPeer: PeerDiscoverHandler
// 6
private let myPeerID = MCPeerID(
    displayName: UIDevice.current.name)
```
}

You've set up `MultipeerSession` by

1. Importing `MultipeerConnectivity`

2. Creating a `final` object

3. Declaring custom value type

4. Declaring static service type that you'll use broadcast to nearby devices over your Wi-Fi infrastructure

5. Declaring that the object will have these custom handlers (later, you'll pass these custom handlers from `ViewController`)

6. Initializing your peer identifier with a display name coming from your current device's name

Next, add the following properties to `MultipeerSession`:

```
// 1
private lazy var session: MCSession = {
   let session = MCSession(
      peer: myPeerID,
      securityIdentity: nil,
      encryptionPreference: .required)
    session.delegate = self
    return session
}()
// 2
private lazy var nearbyServiceAdvertiser:
MCNearbyServiceAdvertiser = {
   let nearbyServiceAdvertiser = MCNearbyServiceAdvertiser(
      peer: myPeerID,
      discoveryInfo: nil,
      serviceType: MultipeerSession.serviceType)
    nearbyServiceAdvertiser.delegate = self
    return nearbyServiceAdvertiser
}()
// 3
private lazy var nearbyServiceBrowser:
MCNearbyServiceBrowser = {
   let nearbyServiceBrowser = MCNearbyServiceBrowser(
      peer: myPeerID,
      serviceType: MultipeerSession.serviceType)
    nearbyServiceBrowser.delegate = self
    return nearbyServiceBrowser
}()
// MARK: - Computed Properties
```

```
// 4
var connectedPeers: [MCPeerID] {
  session.connectedPeers
}
```

Here's a breakdown of the preceding code:

1. Lazy load an encrypted MCSession with your personal MCPeerID. Then, set MCSessionDelegate to MultipeerSession.

2. Lazy load a service advertiser with your personal MCPeerID, broadcasting to invite other peers looking for the same service type to join. Then, set MCSessionDelegate to MultipeerSession.

3. Lazy load a service browser with your personal MCPeerID, searching for invitations into the same service type.

4. Declare a computed property to access the current session's connected peers easily.

You'll see a Swift compiler error when adding the snippet of codes. You'll fix them along the way in the coming instructions.

Now, you'll set up the class initializers. Add the following code to MultipeerSession:

```
// 1
init(receiveData: @escaping PeerDataHandler,
     joinPeer: @escaping PeerMoveHandler,
     leavePeer: @escaping PeerMoveHandler,
     discoverPeer: @escaping PeerDiscoverHandler) {
  self.receiveData = receiveData
  self.joinPeer = joinPeer
  self.leavePeer = leavePeer
```

```
    self.discoverPeer = discoverPeer
    super.init()
    // 2
    nearbyServiceAdvertiser.startAdvertisingPeer()
    // 3
    nearbyServiceBrowser.startBrowsingForPeers()
}
```

In the initializer, you

1. Pass arguments and set the parameters as `MultipeerSession`'s properties.

2. Start the nearby service advertiser to begin inviting peers.

3. Start the nearby service browser to begin searching for invitations.

Next, you'll conform `MultipeerSession` to `MCSessionDelegate` for handling your `MCSession`.

## Handling MCSessionDelegate

During your collaboration session, many events take precedence, such as the states of your peers changing or there's incoming data from your peers. To handle these events, you adopt an object to `MCSessionDelegate` and conform to the protocol.

Below the class declaration of `MultipeerSession`, add the following extension:

```
// MARK: - MCSessionDelegate
extension MultipeerSession: MCSessionDelegate {
    // 1
    func session(
```

```
    _ session: MCSession,
    peer peerID: MCPeerID,
    didChange state: MCSessionState) {
    switch state {
    case .connected:
      joinPeer(peerID)
    case .notConnected:
      leavePeer(peerID)
    default:
      break
    }
  }
  // 2
  func session(_ session: MCSession,
            didReceive data: Data,
            fromPeer peerID: MCPeerID) {
    receiveData(data, peerID)
  }
}
```

Here's a breakdown of the preceding code:

1. When a peer connects to your session, call
   `MultipeerSession.getter:leavePeer`. When
   a peer disconnects from your session, call
   `MultipeerSession.getter:leavePeer`.

2. When your session receives data, call
   `MultipeerSession.getter:receiveData`.

Inside the same extension code block, add the remaining required
protocol methods:

```
func session(
    _ session: MCSession,
    didReceive stream: InputStream,
    withName streamName: String,
    fromPeer peerID: MCPeerID) {
}

func session(
    _ session: MCSession,
    didStartReceivingResourceWithName resourceName: String,
    fromPeer peerID: MCPeerID, with progress: Progress) {
}

func session(
    _ session: MCSession,
    didFinishReceivingResourceWithName resourceName: String,
    fromPeer peerID: MCPeerID,
    at localURL: URL?,
    withError error: Error?) {
}
```

There's nothing more you need to do. You won't handle input streams or resources from your peers. These are the required protocol methods. Hence, you've implemented them in your class.

Next, you'll conform MultipeerSession to MCNearbyServiceBrowserDelegate for handling your MCNearbyServiceBrowser events.

## Handling MCNearbyServiceBrowserDelegate

Earlier, you've initialized MCNearbyServiceBrowser to look for nearby devices with the same service type to connect them to your session. Also, you've set nearbyServiceBrowser's delegate to MultipeerSession.

Now, you'll decide how you want to handle the discovery of a peer by making MultipeerSession adopt MCNearbyServiceBrowserDelegate.

In **Multipeer**, add the following extension to the end of the file:

```
// MARK: - MCNearbyServiceBrowserDelegate
extension MultipeerSession: MCNearbyServiceBrowserDelegate {
    // 1
    func browser(_ browser: MCNearbyServiceBrowser,
                 foundPeer peerID: MCPeerID,
                 withDiscoveryInfo info: [String: String]?) {
        guard discoverPeer(peerID) else { return }
        browser.invitePeer(peerID, to: session,
                           withContext: nil,
                           timeout: 10)
    }
    // 2
    func browser(_ browser: MCNearbyServiceBrowser,
                 lostPeer peerID: MCPeerID) {
    }
}
```

Here's a breakdown of the preceding code:

1. When your browser has found a nearby advertising peer, you check if the peer has already been discovered. You'll guard the remaining code with MultipeerSession.getter:discoverPeer. Later, you'll implement a limit to the number of available peers.

2. You've added this protocol method for protocol conformance. When a peer is no longer on the advertising radar, you're not going to implement any custom logic here.

Next, you'll conform `MultipeerSession` to
`MCNearbyServiceAdvertiserDelegate` for handling your
`MCNearbyServiceAdvertiser` events.

# Handling MCNearbyServiceAdvertiserDelegate

The `MCNearbyServiceAdvertiser` advertises to nearby peers with
a specified service type describing the app's networking protocol.
After indicating your availability to your peers, it's time to handle
invitations. You can decide to accept or not accept a peer's invitation. To
implement the logic, you'll begin by conforming `MultipeerSession` to
`MCNearbyServiceAdvertiserDelegate`. Then, you'll use the completion
handler inside one of the protocol methods.

Now, you'll decide what to do when you receive an invitation from
your peer.

In **Multipeer**, add the following extension to the end of the file:

```
// MARK: - MCNearbyServiceAdvertiserDelegate
extension MultipeerSession: MCNearbyServiceAdvertiserDelegate {
    func advertiser(_ advertiser: MCNearbyServiceAdvertiser,
                    didReceiveInvitationFromPeer peerID:
                    MCPeerID,
                    withContext context: Data?,
                    invitationHandler: @escaping
                    (Bool, MCSession?) -> Void) {
        invitationHandler(true, session)
    }
}
```

When a peer invites you to join a session, you'll automatically accept the
invitation. Here, you can use the information given in arguments to present
custom logics like offering a user interface for invitation acceptance.

Next, you'll incorporate `MultipeerSession` in `ViewController`.

# Setting Up ViewController for MultipeerConnectivity

There is still much work to be done before reaching your desired destination. Making multiuser in augmented reality isn't the most straightforward job, but it sure is fulfilling to see your ideas blossom. You're about halfway there!

Open **ViewController**. To begin incorporating multipeer connectivity, add the following properties to ViewController:

```
// 1
private let anchorName = "Anchor for cube placement."
// 2
private var sessionIDObservation: NSKeyValueObservation?
// 3
private var multipeerSession: MultipeerSession?
// 4
private var peerSessionMap: [MCPeerID: String] = [:]
```

These properties serve as references, specifically for

1. Creating and identifying a specific anchor type

2. Observing changes in ARSessionID

3. Passing data between MultipeerSession and ViewController

4. Storing and retrieving peer identifiers that are part of your MCSession

The next step to take is to set up MultipeerSession within ViewController. Add the following code to setupMultipeerSession():

```
multipeerSession = MultipeerSession(
   receiveData: receiveData,
   joinPeer: joinPeer,
   leavePeer: leavePeer,
   discoverPeer: discoverPeer)
```

Here, you pass in the respective methods to initialize MultipeerSession. When initialized, MultipeerSession will have access to those methods and can use them within its class. This is a bridge between the two objects.

Next, you're going to notify your peers of changes to ARSession using key-value observing.

## Sending Data in MCSession

To notify your peers with new data, you need a data transfer solution. MCSession has a method to help you accomplish that.

In **MultipeerSession**, add the following method:

```
// MARK: - Data Transmission
func sendPeersData(_ data: Data, dataMode:
MCSessionSendDataMode) {
    // 1
   guard !connectedPeers.isEmpty else { return }
    // 2
   do {
       // 3
     try session.send(data, toPeers: connectedPeers,
                     with: dataMode)
   } catch {
       // 4
     print(error.localizedDescription)
   }
}
```

With the code you've added, here's the breakdown:

1.  Check that your MCSession has peer connections established. Otherwise, the guard statement will void further method logic.

2.  Since it's possible for MCSession.
    send(_:toPeers:with:) to throw an error, you'll utilize Swift's first-class support for runtime error handling with a do-catch statement.

3.  Instruct session to send data to your connected peers. With data mode, it decides on the data's reliability. Reliable data ensures in-order data delivery, whereas unreliable data is sent without queuing, and the delivery isn't guaranteed.

4.  When the do-catch statement catches an error, you'll print the error's localized description to the console.

You may wonder about the right timing and location for calling this method. In the next section, you'll look at the first scenario for sending data to peers.

# Key-Value Observing (KVO)

When a MCPeerID changes, you'd want to notify your peers about the changes. This way, everyone in the session knows which anchors ultimately belong to which user.

In **ViewController**, add the following code to setupKVO():

```
// 1
sessionIDObservation = observe(
   \.arView.session.identifier,
   options: [.new]) { _, change in
```

```
// 2
  guard let newValue = change.newValue,
    let multipeerSession = self.multipeerSession
    else { return }
print("SESSION ID: \(newValue)")
// 3
  self.sendARSessionIDTo(
    peers: multipeerSession.connectedPeers)
}
```

Here, you're doing the following:

1. Assign `sessionIDObservation` to observe for new `arView.session.identifier`.

2. Upon receiving a new `ARSession` identifier, you'll safely unwrap the new session identifier. Then, print the session identifier into the console for debugging.

3. Call `sendARSessionIDTo(peers:)` to notify yours and your peers' `ARSession` of a new `ARSession`.

You'll continue to the multipeer session next. Specifically, it'll be on the topic of encoding collaboration data.

# Encoding Collaboration Data

`ARSession` generates world tracking collaboration data. Two devices can have two different sets of world map data. `ARKit` needs to merge the various world maps.

Before `ARKit` can display shared anchors and device locations, it has to first become successful in merging the world maps. For the world maps combining to occur, users will have to feed `ARKit` common areas in their respective devices.

With collaboration enabled, ARKit calls session(_:didOutputColla borationData:) to provide collaboration between peers. You'll need to provide additional client code to send collaboration data over the air.

Under // MARK: - Collaboration, add the following code:

```
extension ViewController {
    // 1
    func session(
        _ session: ARSession,
        didOutputCollaborationData data: ARSession.
        CollaborationData) {
        // 2
        guard let multipeerSession = multipeerSession,
            !multipeerSession.connectedPeers.isEmpty,
            // 3
            let encodedData = try? NSKeyedArchiver.archivedData(
                withRootObject: data,
                requiringSecureCoding: true) else { return }
        // 4
        multipeerSession.sendPeersData(
            encodedData,
            dataMode: data.priority == .critical
                ? .reliable
                : .unreliable)
    }
}
```

With the code you've added, you

1. Implement the session(_:didOutputCollaboratio nData:) from ARSessionDelegate.

2. Safely unwrap multipeerSession and void further action if there are no peers connected to your MCSession.

3. Use NSKeyedArchiver to encode collaboration data from ARSession. Whenever possible and for improved security, you should require secure coding. This ensures the encoded object conforms to NSSecureCoding and that the data can be decoded in the future.

4. Invoke multipeerSession to send the safely unwrapped encoded collaboration data to peers. If the data is critical, then the data mode should guarantee order and delivery. For optional data, unlike the latter, send the data immediately without queueing or delivery guarantee.

# Receiving Peer Data

Contrary to sending data where you've archived data, you'll unarchive the data upon receiving it. In addition, you'll keep track of your peers using a hash map.

In **ViewController**, add the following code to receiveData(_:from:):

```
let sessionIDStr = "ARSessionID:"
// 1
if let collaborationData =
    try? NSKeyedUnarchiver.unarchivedObject(
        ofClass: ARSession.CollaborationData.self,
        from: data) {
    return arView.session.update(with: collaborationData)
}
// 2
guard let command = String(data: data, encoding: .utf8),
    command.starts(with: sessionIDStr),
    let oldSessionID = peerSessionMap[peer] else { return }
```

```
// 3
let newSessionID = String(
   command[command.index(command.startIndex,
                         offsetBy: sessionIDStr.count)...])
// 4
removeAllAnchorsFromARSessionWithID(oldSessionID)
// 5
peerSessionMap[peer] = newSessionID
```

Here's what you've done:

1. Try unarchiving the parameter data as a collaboration data type. If successful, update your ARSession with the unarchived collaboration data.

2. Check if the data from the command begins with sessionIDStr and the peer exists in the hash map. Otherwise, return.

3. Take the peer's new session ID.

4. Remove anchors with the old session ID.

5. Keep a reference to the peer's new session identifier.

Next, you'll implement virtual content with different anchor types.

# Making Virtual Content with AnchorEntity

There are various ways to add virtual content onto an augmented reality scene. By using RealityKit, you can add virtual content onto an ARScene with AnchorEntity. You're going to create a metallic red sphere next.

In **ViewController**, add the following method inside ARSessionDelegate extension block:

```
// 1
private func makeSphereAnchorEntity(
   from anchor: ARAnchor,
   color: UIColor = .systemRed) -> AnchorEntity {
```

```
// 2
let sphereRadius: Float = 0.04
let sphereEntity = ModelEntity(
   mesh: MeshResource.generateSphere(radius: sphereRadius),
   materials: [
       SimpleMaterial(
           color: color, isMetallic: true)
])
sphereEntity.collision = CollisionComponent(
   shapes: [.generateSphere(radius: sphereRadius)])
sphereEntity.position = [0, sphereRadius, 0]
// 3
let anchorEntity = AnchorEntity(anchor: anchor)
anchorEntity.addChild(sphereEntity)
return anchorEntity
}
```

With what you've added, you

1. Take an anchor to transform the anchor into an entity anchor for ARScene. In the method signature, you set a default parameter value of systemRed for the sphere's color.

2. Set the shape, size, and material for the sphere.

3. Initialize an anchor entity and add the sphere entity as its child. Then, return the resulting anchor entity.

You now have a sphere anchor entity maker. You're going to use this helper method soon.

Now, you'll implement the logic for when a user taps on their screen to interact with the augmented reality world. In **ViewController**, add the following code to didTap(withGestureRecognizer:):

```
// 1
let tapLocation = recognizer.location(in: arView)
// 2
let raycastResults = arView.raycast(
    from: tapLocation,
    allowing: .estimatedPlane,
    alignment: .horizontal)
// 3
guard let firstRaycastResult = raycastResults.first else {
return }
// 4
let anchor = ARAnchor(name: anchorName,
                      transform: firstRaycastResult.
                      worldTransform)
arView.session.add(anchor: anchor)
```

Here's a breakdown of the code you've just added:

1.  Get the tap position based on the user's tap on the screen relative to arView.

2.  By using ARKit's preferred method for finding real-world surface positions, the system can continuously improve virtual content positioning over time. The feature points you get are based on the user's tap location. It will include feature points around the target ray sitting on a horizontal plane.

3.  Ensure there's a raycast result from raycastResults.

4.  Generate an anchor based on the raycast's position in the world and add it onto your ARView.

Next, you'll work with participant anchors.

# Working with ARParticipantAnchor

Once ARKit merges your peers' world, the system also knows each user's respective locations relative to the shared world map. Each user's device location can be found in ARParticipantAnchor.

Add the following code to session(_:didAdd:):

```
anchors.forEach {
  // 1
  if let participantAnchor = $0 as? ARParticipantAnchor {
    linkButton.isHidden = true
    peersButton.isHidden = false
    arView.scene.addAnchor(
      makeSphereAnchorEntity(from: participantAnchor))
  // 2
  } else if $0.name == anchorName {
    arView.scene.addAnchor(
      makeSphereAnchorEntity(from: $0))
  }
}
```

Here's a breakdown of the added code:

1.  If the anchor belongs to a participant or one of your peers, you'll hide linkButton and show peersButton, a simple user interface to visualize the connectivity state. You'll also make a sphere model entity from the anchor with a system blue color. Afterward, append the anchor onto arView.

2.  If the anchor belongs to you, as determined by the current anchor's name, then you'll make a sphere model entity from the anchor. Afterward, append the anchor onto arView.

You'll go into completing the peers' discovery integration next.

# Discovering Peers

Earlier in `MultipeerSession`, you delegated the decision for letting in a peer to a closure in the initializer. Now, you'll pass in the method to handle the logic.

In **ViewController**, replace the code inside of `discoverPeer(_:)` with the following:

```
guard let multipeerSession = multipeerSession,
    multipeerSession.connectedPeers.count <= 1
    else { return false }
return true
```

With the code added, you've set a max capacity for your `MCSession`. You've instructed the method to allow newly discovered peers to join if your session has one or less peers. You can decide on the number of connected peers permitted based on your app's content.

You'll go into completing joining new peers next.

# Joining Peers

Once a peer joins, you'll update your user interface to reflect a new state. Also, you'll update the session with the peer's identifier and let the connected peers know about the newly joined peer.

In **ViewController**, add the following code to `joinPeer(_:)`:

```
DispatchQueue.main.async { [weak self] in
    self?.linkButton.isHidden = false
}
sendARSessionIDTo(peers: [peer])
```

You set your user interface's appearance update on the main queue for the uninterrupted user experience. In addition, you call `sendARSessionIDTo(peers:)` to notify `MCSession`'s connected users of a new peer. You'll need to add some code to `sendARSessionIDTo(peers:)` in order to complete the operation.

289

Add the following code to sendARSessionIDTo(peers:):

```
let command = "ARSessionID:\(arView.session.identifier.uuidString)"
guard let multipeerSession = multipeerSession,
    let data = command.data(using: .utf8) else { return }
multipeerSession.sendPeersData(data, dataMode: .reliable)
```

Here, you're sending a specific command about a newly added peer to connected peers in your MCSession.

Last but not least, you'll go into handling leaving peers.

## Leaving Peers

Last but not least, you'll handle peers who are leaving from your session. When a peer leaves, you'll remove the anchors that belong to him or her. You'll handle that using a hash map and standard library operations.

In **ViewController**, add the following code to removeAllAnchorsFromARSessionWithID(_:):

```
guard let frame = arView.session.currentFrame else { return }
frame.anchors.forEach {
    guard let sessionIdentifier = $0.sessionIdentifier,
        sessionIdentifier.uuidString == identifier else { return }
    arView.session.remove(anchor: $0)
}
```

Using the anchor identifier passed from the parameter, you remove anchors belonging to it from your ARSession.

In **ViewController**, add the following code to leavePeer(_:):

```
// 1
guard let sessionID = peerSessionMap[peer] else { return }
// 2
peersButton.isHidden = true
```

```
// 3
removeAllAnchorsFromARSessionWithID(sessionID)
// 4
peerSessionMap.removeValue(forKey: peer)
```

Here's a breakdown of the code:

1. Safely unwrap a value from `peerSessionMap` using `peer` as the key.

2. Once your peer leaves, update the user interface.

3. Remove anchors belonging to your peer.

4. Remove your peer from `peerSessionMap`.

Build and run the project on two devices. Place the devices next to each other. Wait for the connectivity signal to show, then hide. When the peers icon shows, the two devices are linked up to the session!

You and your friends can share virtual content in an augmented reality experience. You can also see your friend's device position indicated by a sphere by their device. And you can tap the reset button on either device to see the respective anchors removed.

---

**Tip**   If you see *Error getting pose for participant anchor: CMMapNotAvailable* in the console, it means ARKit is figuring out how to mesh the two world maps. You can assist the framework by moving around more to feed ARKit more data.

---

# Where to Go from Here?

You've learned how to create a shared experience in augmented reality using ARKit and MultipeerConnectivity. You've unlocked the capability to have more people join your app. Come to think of it; you've built an app that's quite rare. I can't wait to see the shared augmented reality experiences that you build!

# CHAPTER 16

# Face Tracking

The TrueDepth front-facing camera is the most potent in augmented reality. The camera has an infrared emitter capable of projecting over 30,000 invisible dots to create your face's face mesh and infrared image representation. Apple's state-of-the-art TrueDepth camera system is capable of mapping the geometry of your face accurately. You'll delve into how you can make the most out of the TrueDepth front-facing camera with `ARKit`.

---

**Note**  To run and experience the full features in this chapter, you'll need an iOS device with TrueDepth camera support.

---

In this chapter, you'll learn about the following face tracking topics:

- Integrating transform

- Retrieving facial textures

- Implementing 3D overlay

- Blending shapes

By the end of this chapter, you'd understand how to create your own face tracking augmented reality app.

© Jayven Nhan 2022
J. Nhan, *Mastering ARKit*, https://doi.org/10.1007/978-1-4842-7836-9_16

# Getting Started

Open the **starter project**. Feel free to play around with the project to get a feel for it.

First things first, set up the augmented reality tracking configuration to track face.

Open **ViewController**. Add the following property to ViewController:

```
private let faceTrackingConfiguration:
ARFaceTrackingConfiguration = {
    let faceTrackingConfiguration =
    ARFaceTrackingConfiguration()
    faceTrackingConfiguration.isLightEstimationEnabled = true
    return faceTrackingConfiguration
}()
```

You've created a property that utilizes the front-facing camera to track the face. Once ARKit detects a face, it will add an ARFaceAnchor to the augmented reality session. Using ARFaceAnchor, you can retrieve geometry information regarding the user's face. More on this later. Plus, you've enabled light estimation for added realism to your app.

Your second objective now is to get your ARView to run the configuration. Add the following code to resetTrackingConfiguration():

```
arView.session.run(
    faceTrackingConfiguration,
    options: [.removeExistingAnchors, .resetTracking])
```

With the code you've added, you set your augmented reality session to run the face tracking configuration you configured earlier. And you tell the session to remove anchors that are previously added if it's an ongoing session. Also, reset the tracking to forget about existing tracking information.

resetTrackingConfiguration() gets called at viewDidAppear(_:) and resetButtonDidTouchUpInside(_:), when the view appears and when your user clicks the reset button.

Your third objective is to set your ARView's session to ViewController. Add the following code to setupARView():

arView.session.delegate = self

ViewController has already conformed to ARSessionDelegate. The code you've just added ensures ARView's events are directed toward ViewController. ARSessionDelegate methods will allow you to extract your face geometry information.

Next, you'll learn to generate eyeballs and plug them on your eyes.

# Preparing Your Model Entity for ARFaceAnchor

To implement your model entity, you'll utilize an anchor to position it. The beauty of anchors is that the 3D content follows you when you move your head, eyes, eyebrows, etc.

Under // MARK: - Model Entity, add the following helper method:

```
private func makeSphereModelEntity(
    radius: Float,
    color: UIColor = .customOrange) -> ModelEntity {
    let sphereEntity = ModelEntity(
        mesh: MeshResource.generateSphere(radius: radius),
        materials: [
            SimpleMaterial(
                color: color, isMetallic: false)
    ])
    return sphereEntity
}
```

295

You'll use this helper method to help you generate a sphere model entity using `RealityKit`.

When you create your eyeballs, you'll want to keep a reference of the left and right eyeballs. This way, when you need to, you can use the referenced properties to make an update. Add the following properties to `ViewController`:

```
private var leftEyeModelEntity: ModelEntity?
private var rightEyeModelEntity: ModelEntity?
```

Now that you have a place to reference your left and right eye model entities, it's time to create a helper for your eyeballs.

Next, add the following code under `// MARK: - Anchor Entity`:

```
// 1
private func makeEyeballAnchorEntity(
    from faceAnchor: ARFaceAnchor,
    isLeftEye: Bool = true) -> AnchorEntity {
        // 2
    let sphereRadius: Float = 0.04
    let sphereEntity = makeSphereModelEntity(radius:
    sphereRadius)
    sphereEntity.setTransformMatrix(
        isLeftEye
          ? faceAnchor.leftEyeTransform
          : faceAnchor.rightEyeTransform,
        relativeTo: nil)
        // 3
    let boxEntity = makeBoxModelEntity(size: 0.03)
    boxEntity.position.z = sphereRadius
    sphereEntity.addChild(boxEntity)
        // 4
    if isLeftEye {
        leftEyeModelEntity = sphereEntity
```

```
} else {
    rightEyeModelEntity = sphereEntity
}
    // 5
let anchorEntity = AnchorEntity(anchor: faceAnchor)
anchorEntity.addChild(sphereEntity)
return anchorEntity
}
```

Here's a breakdown of the code:

1. In the method signature, you take in `ARFaceAnchor`
   to extract facial structure and anchoring
   information. In addition, the method takes an
   `isLeftEye` argument to generate and reference
   eyeball using a different set of properties from
   `ARFaceAnchor`.

2. Use the sphere model entity helper method to
   generate a sphere. Afterward, set the sphere's
   transform to either the face anchor's left or right eye
   transform based on `isLeftEye`.

3. Because using just a sphere makes recognizing
   where the eyes are looking difficult, you'll create a
   box entity to represent the retina. You'll position the
   box toward the camera by `sphereRadius`. Then, add
   the box entity as a child of the sphere entity.

4. Set the sphere entity to `leftEyeModelEntity` or
   `rightEyeModelEntity` depending on the current eye
   configuration.

5. Return an anchor entity with a sphere entity as
   the child.

# Adding Your Anchor Entity onto ARFaceAnchor

You've prepared your helper methods. Now, you'll need to implement the eyeball anchor entity you've generated onto the face anchor.

Add the following code to session(_:didAdd:):

```
// 1
for case let faceAnchor as ARFaceAnchor in anchors {
    // 2
    let leftEyeAnchorEntity = makeEyeballAnchorEntity(
        from: faceAnchor)
    let rightEyeAnchorEntity = makeEyeballAnchorEntity(
        from: faceAnchor, isLeftEye: false)
    // 3
    arView.scene.addAnchor(leftEyeAnchorEntity)
    arView.scene.addAnchor(rightEyeAnchorEntity)
}
```

Once ARKit detects a new anchor, it'll send the event's information to session(_:didAdd:). Using the parameters, you

1. Extract ARAnchors that can be unwrapped as ARFaceAnchor.

2. Generate the left and right eye anchor entities.

3. Add the generated anchor entities onto the ARView scene.

## Updating Anchor Entity from New ARFaceAnchor

There's a contingency here. What if you want your eyeballs to roll around? Well, that sounds like fun, so you'll implement eye-rolling feature next!

Add the following code to session(_:didUpdate:):

```
for case let faceAnchor as ARFaceAnchor in anchors {
    leftEyeModelEntity?.transform = Transform(
        matrix: faceAnchor.leftEyeTransform)
    rightEyeModelEntity?.transform = Transform(
        matrix: faceAnchor.rightEyeTransform)
}
```

Build and run.

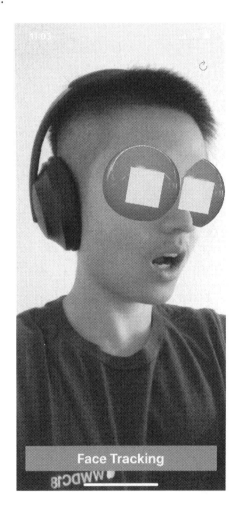

# Incorporating RealityKit Animoji in ARView

RealityComposer is built ground-up for creating 3D content for augmented reality. It boasts the tight integration with ARKit. It's like cooking a fresh omelet. From the time the omelet is perfectly cooked, the omelet goes on your plate and into your mouth. There's no packaging the omelet into a lunch box or leaving the omelet in the open air. If the omelet's intention is freshness, RealityKit's intention is to integrate beautifully with ARKit.

Open **ViewController**. Add the following constants to ViewController:

```
private let steelHead: Face.SteelHead
private let leftEyeEntity: Entity
private let rightEyeEntity: Entity
private let mouthEntity: Entity
private let mouthEntityTransformOrigin: Transform
```

Next, add the following code under // MARK: - Initializers:

```
required init?(coder: NSCoder) {
    guard let smileyFace = try? Face.loadSteelHead(),
        let leftEyeEntity = smileyFace.findEntity(named: "leftEye"),
        let rightEyeEntity = smileyFace.findEntity(named:
        "rightEye"),
        let mouthEntity = smileyFace.findEntity(named:
        "mouth") else {
        fatalError("Unable to load completely load Face.Smiley
        components.")
    }
    mouthEntityTransformOrigin = mouthEntity.transform
    self.smileyFace = smileyFace
    self.leftEyeEntity = leftEyeEntity
    self.rightEyeEntity = rightEyeEntity
```

```
    self.mouthEntity = mouthEntity
    super.init(coder: coder)
}
```

Replace the code within session(_:didAdd:) for the following code:

```
for case let faceAnchor as ARFaceAnchor in anchors {
    let anchorEntity = AnchorEntity(anchor: faceAnchor)
    anchorEntity.addChild(steelHead)
    arView.scene.addAnchor(anchorEntity)
}
```

Here, you add an anchor entity onto ARView's session. The anchor entity contains steelHead as its child.

# Setting Up RealityKit Action Handlers

When action completes, you can use a completion handler to connect subsequent events. Conveniently, you can set up the completion handlers for continuity flow.

Add the following code to setupSmileyFaceActionHandlers():

```
steelHead.actions.bearSoundHasEnded.onAction = {
    [weak self] _ in
    self?.isPlayingSound = false
}
steelHead.actions.jiggleHatHasEnded.onAction = {
    [weak self] _ in
    self?.isPlayingEyebrowsAnimation = false
}
```

Here, you're updating sound and animation playing states.

Note that setupSmileyFaceActionHandlers() is already called for you at the end of viewDidLoad().

# Updating Your Animoji

You can detect the movement of different face components like the jaw, tongue, eyebrows, etc. To detect the location of a face part on an ARFaceAnchor, you use the blend shape coefficient, which ranges from 0 to 1. 0 is the natural position of your face part where it's at rest. 1 is ARKit's expectation of the maximum movement of a face part. For example, if your jaw is closed, then the blend shape coefficient is 0. When your jaw is stretched open, the blend shape coefficient is 1.

To update your Animoji, add the following method to ViewController:

```
private func updateSteelHead(from faceAnchor: ARFaceAnchor) {
    let blendShapes = faceAnchor.blendShapes
    // 1
    if let jawOpen = blendShapes[.jawOpen] {
        // 2
        mouthEntity.transform.translation.z =
            mouthEntityTransformOrigin.translation.z +
            jawOpen.floatValue * 0.05
        // 3
        if !isPlayingSound,
            jawOpen.floatValue >= 0.5 {
            isPlayingSound = true
            steelHead.notifications.playBearSound.post()
        }
    }
}
```

Here's the code breakdown:

1. Safely unwrap the jaw open blend shape coefficient. It's possible that ARKit can detect an ARFaceAnchor but not including your jaw. For example, you can cover your mouth, and ARKit can still recognize components of your face beside the mouth.

2. Move the mouth by the coefficient times a
   multiplier. You can play around with the multiplier
   to get the mouth move range you want.

3. In the instance that the sound is playing and
   the jaw stretched at least half-opened, then set
   isPlayingSound to true and notify RealityKit to
   execute playing the bear sound.

Next, you'll do something similar but for the eyebrows. Add the
following code to the end of updateSmileyFace(from:):

```
if !isPlayingEyebrowsAnimation,
    let browOuterLeft = blendShapes[.browOuterUpLeft],
    browOuterLeft.floatValue >= 0.5,
    let browOuterRight = blendShapes[.browOuterUpRight],
    browOuterRight.floatValue >= 0.5 {
    isPlayingEyebrowsAnimation = true
    steelHead.notifications.jiggleHat.post()
}
```

Similar to the logic you've implemented for the jaw, you check blend
shape coefficients of eyebrows and eyebrows animation state. If the
right conditions are met, notify RealityKit to post a Face.SteelHead
notification to execute the jiggle hat animation. Afterward, update the
animation state. That's pretty cool!

To complete the update of your Animoji, replace the code inside of
session(_:didUpdate:) with the following:

```
for case let faceAnchor as ARFaceAnchor in anchors {
    updateSteelHead(from: faceAnchor)
}
```

Here, you're using the `ARFaceAnchor` to update your steel head with the helper method you've implemented earlier.

Build and run.

Open your mouth and roar like a bear!

Raise your eyebrows!

Tap your head to make your hat spin!

You'll learn how to create your own 3D content and interactions using RealityKit from an incoming chapter.

Congratulations on finishing this chapter, hope you've had fun!

# Where to Go from Here?

You've learned how to utilize face tracking in augmented reality using `ARKit`. You've unlocked the capability to create fun Animoji experiences. Can't wait to see the Animoji experiences you've built!

# CHAPTER 17

# Reality Composer: Creating AR Content

Reality Composer can help you generate gorgeous and performant AR experiences easier than most existing 3D content creation tools. Prior to the release of Reality Composer, developers and designers would have to make design or performance trade-offs.

Sometimes, great-looking contents aren't performant or can easily integrate into your project. Other times, content with complex behaviors (some custom animations) created using third-party tools isn't compatible without writing hundreds of more code lines. Reality Composer takes pain points away from content creation for augmented reality.

Hence, if you want to make augmented reality content, you should start with RealityKit for performance and seamless integration with ARKit.

After creating your content in Reality Composer, you can load the content from a framework called RealityKit. You'll learn how to load your content and behavior in the next chapter.

In this chapter, you'll learn the ropes for working with Reality Composer. The topics include

- Designing for face anchors

- Creating content using primitive shapes

- Utilizing Apple's content library

- Creating custom behaviors

© Jayven Nhan 2022
J. Nhan, *Mastering ARKit*, https://doi.org/10.1007/978-1-4842-7836-9_17

- Activating sound

- Adding animations

- Sending notifications

By the end of this chapter, you'd have created an Animoji. And you'd understand how to navigate Reality Composer and begin creating your own 3D content.

# Getting Started

Open the **starter project**.

You'll now begin and create your Animoji.

Click **File ➤ New ➤ File...**. Select **Reality Composer Project**. Click **Next**.

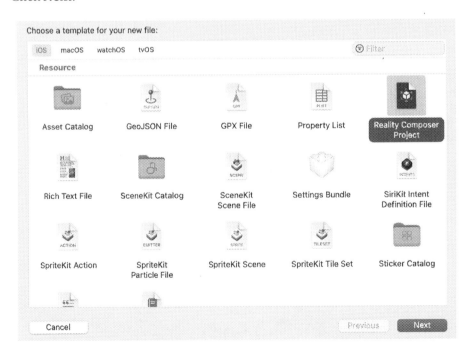

Name the file as **Face.rcproject**. Click **create**.

Next, you should see the following window. At the top-right corner, click **Open in Reality Composer**.

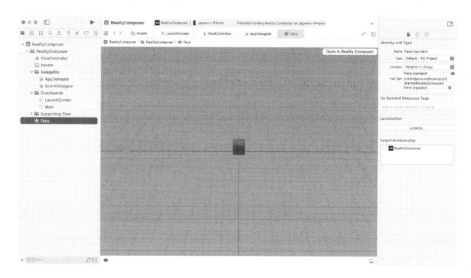

Afterward, you'll be presented with the following screen.

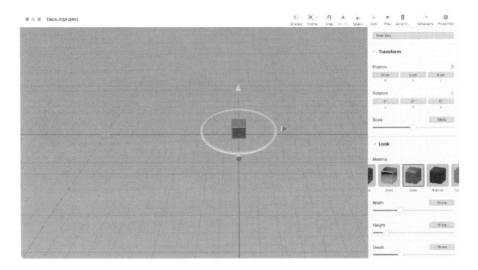

Select the **box**. Once selected, the box will be highlighted. Click **delete**.

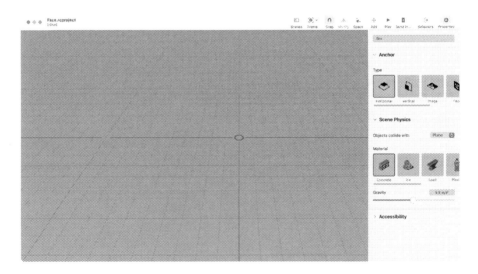

Next, you'll start using primitive shapes to create your Animoji!

# Designing for Face Anchors

In Reality Composer, you can choose from various anchors as your design template. Currently, the anchor type is horizontal. You can also choose vertical, image, face, and object anchors. Because you'll build an Animoji, it makes sense to use the face anchor.

On the right-hand side, you'll see the properties pane. Under the Anchor, there's the type section. Select **Face** from the type section.

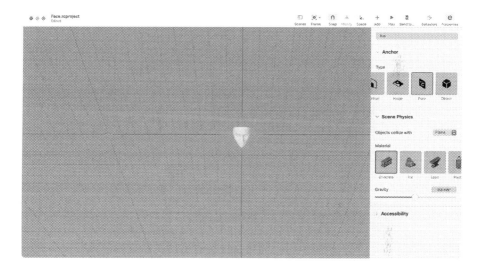

By using the face anchor as your design template, you can adjust the shape/size of your content to fit the face appropriately and with much greater ease. You don't want to use the horizontal design template and complete your design. Then, find out that your design is too big, small, incorrectly positioned, etc. You want to design for and on an actual face model. The face anchor put away a lot of the guesswork for content sizing and positioning.

# Making Your Animoji Using Primitive Shapes

Primitive shapes plus creativity equal cool stuff. Primitive shapes are like Lego blocks. It's up to your imagination to come up with a fire-breathing dragon, Eiffel Tower, virtual world, or whatever you want essentially!

With great content to come from you in the foreseeable future, you'll now lay down the first brick. Click the + button in Reality Composer. Then, select the **sphere** object.

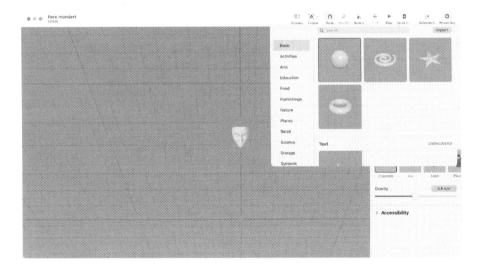

Now, select the **sphere**. Set the x-position to **0** and z-position to **-3** to move the head up from the neck. Set the material to **Steel**. Set the diameter to **25**.

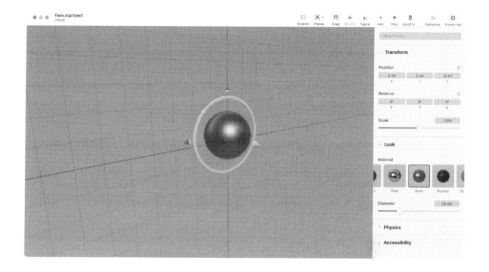

The units are generally in centimeters. Sometimes, when you increase the number large enough as determined by Reality Composer, you'll be working with units of meters. At that time, you'll need to divide by 1000. For your 3D design, you can play around with the numbers until you like what you see.

Look! You already have your Animoji's head. Next, you'll add facial features to the head.

# Implementing Content Library's 3D Models

In addition to primitive shapes, Reality Composer's content library includes an array of 3D models created by Apple. The 3D models are categorized and searchable using the search bar.

Here are some examples of 3D models created by Apple in the places category.

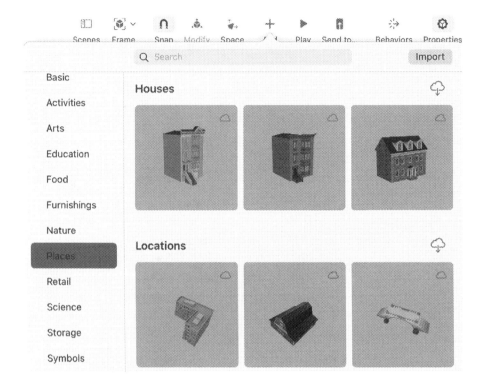

Apple provides a bunch of 3D content for you to use. Each of them is customizable, and it's much more than just the position and size. You seem super excited already! One of the last things a developer wants to do is to design 3D content. Maybe it's just me.

Designing 2D content takes time. Designing 3D content takes significantly more time. Before moving on, you can see that there's an import button at the top-right hand corner. You can import your 3D model into Reality Composer as well.

Now, onto building the facial features. Click the + button to display the content library. In the search bar, enter **hat**.

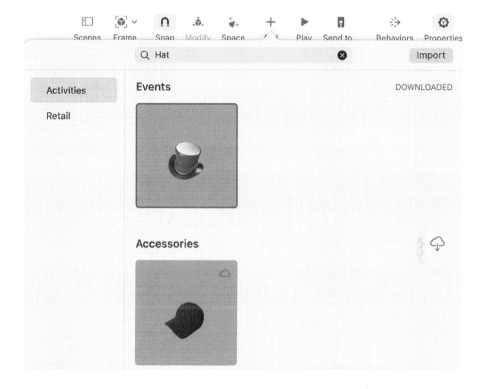

Double-click the **hat** to add it onto your scene.

Next, you'll learn to give your hat personality!

# Setting 3D Content Materials

3D content with personality stands out. When you give your 3D content personality, it stands for something. The virtue that it stands can connect with people. Think about your favorite superhero, action movie star, or cartoon character.

I love Rick from *Rick and Morty* because he's a nonchalant grandpa who goes on wild adventures. He basically creates the universe that he wants to live in. And he's sort of considerate, unless you're a space-invading alien.

Back to the project. Select the **hat**. Set the x-position to **0** and z-position to **-9.12**. Set the x rotation to **-90**. Set the scale to **120**. Set the style to **Realistic**.

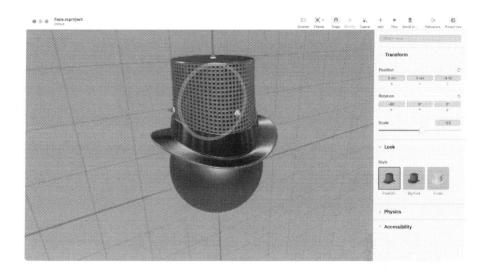

There are many ways you can play around with the materials. You can set the style to **Iconic** and with a **matte paint** finish.

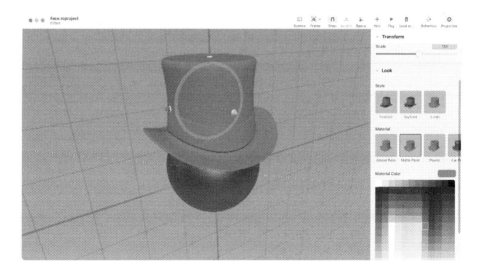

You can also give the hat a **gold** material finish.

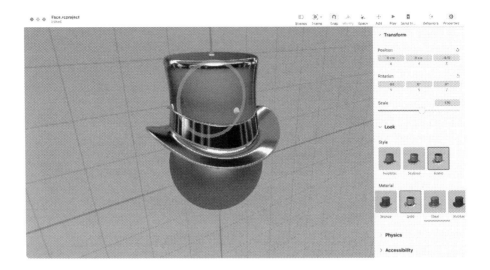

It's your hat, so personalize it to your heart content! It's all yours.

# Making Facial Features with Content Library's 3D Models

Now, you're going to give your Animoji a happy face. There's so much great 3D content to choose from in the content library. It's incredible!

You're going to create the eyes of your Animoji using billiard balls.

Open the **content library**; enter **ball** in the search bar.

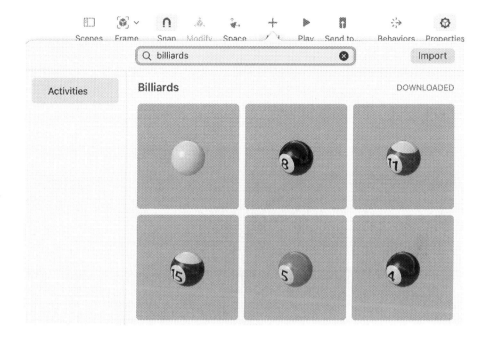

You should see a collection of billiard balls. One at a time, add the **black** and **orange** billiard balls onto the scene.

Select the **black billiard ball**. Name the object **leftEye**. Set the position to **(x: -5, y: 11.93, z: -3.13)**, x rotation to **-90**, and the style to **Realistic**.

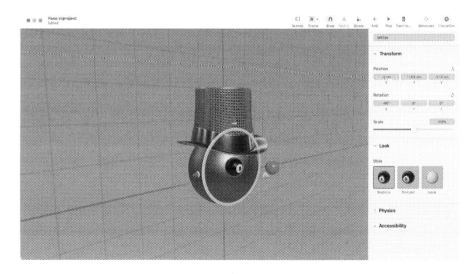

Select the **orange billiard ball**. Name the object **rightEye**. Set the position to (**x: 5, y: 11.93, z: -3.13**), x rotation to **-90**, and the style to **Realistic**.

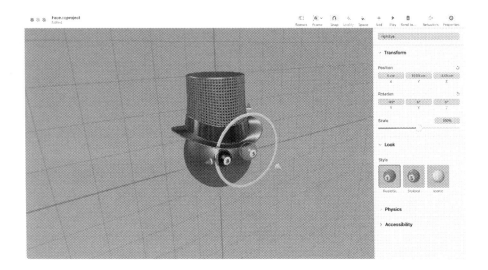

Your Animoji has the eyes. Now, you can give it a smile!

Open the **content library**; enter **banana** in the search bar. Add the **banana** onto the scene.

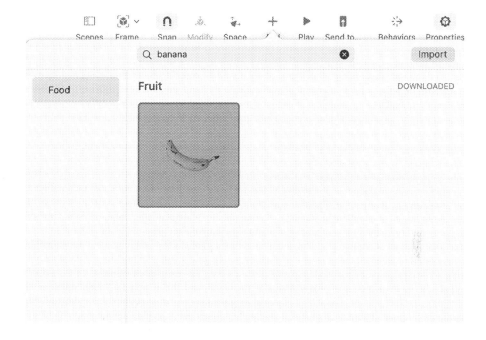

Name the object **mouth**. Set the position to **(x: 0, y: 10.85, z: 5.37)** and z rotation to **-180**.

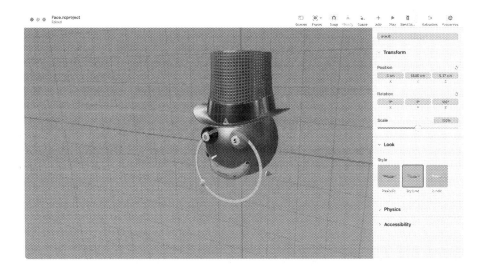

Your Animoji is smiling! Looking good. To give your Animoji even more personality, you're going to learn to provide it with some behaviors next.

# Adding Behaviors to Objects

Once you have your 3D model, you can add behaviors to various parts of the model. You can implement sound sources to come from the object, animation when the object is tapped, add force the object in the physics engine, add notifications, and more.

Reality Composer has built-in behaviors. This means you can work with an existing collection of behavior components. You don't necessarily need to code up your own custom animation, user interaction with an object, object reaction with other object(s), etc. Reality Composer has a collection of common behaviors, and you can just use them. It's wonderful!

You're going to add a tap and spin behavior. In the top-right hand corner, click the **Behaviors** button. Select the **hat**. In the bottom-left corner, you'll see the behaviors panel. Click the + button to open up a collection of behavior options. Select **Tap & Flip**.

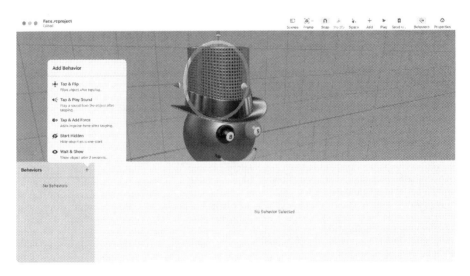

You can see that the trigger for the behavior is a tap. The action sequence that follows is a flip. You can click the play button to preview an individual action. Or if you have multiple actions, you can click the play button to the right of the Action Sequence label.

So you want a different motion. You want the hat to spin. Hence, in the **Action Sequence** section, click the **motion type** drop-down menu. From here, select **spin**.

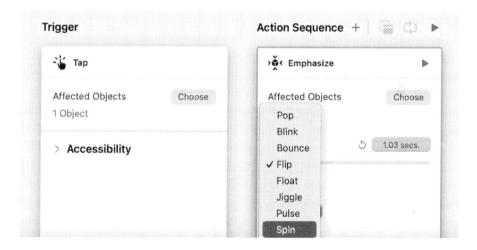

Now, you can preview the spin motion by clicking the play button. Apple didn't stop there with Reality Composer. If you look right below the motion type, you'll see the style. From the style drop-down menu, you can choose variations of your selected motion. You can choose from basic, playful, or wild.

Choose **playful**. Your emphasize action's settings should look like this.

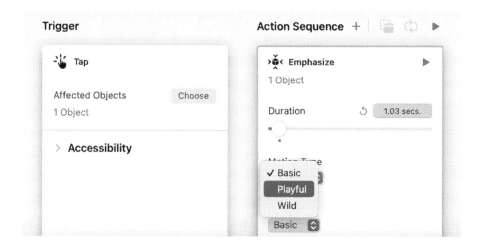

Click the action sequence's play button to preview to see the hat's playful-spin animation!

# Renaming Behaviors

Naming your behaviors organizes your project. Naming various components of your work becomes exponentially important for maintainability as your project grows. Descriptive and succinct naming shouldn't be overlooked, like GitHub commits, for your future self and team's sanity.

You can rename your behavior. Click the **Behavior** label.

Type **Tap & Spin**. Press the **return** key.

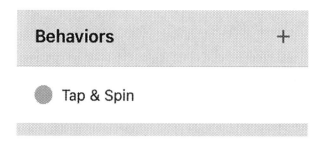

Next, you're going to learn about adding custom behaviors.

# Implementing Your Custom Behaviors

Engineers love to engineer. Sometimes, engineers overengineer, and that's what engineers do. Engineers like to test the limit of technologies. Similarly, at the moment, you're going to open yourself up to a new world of possibilities with custom behaviors. Buckle up. You're about to create your own behaviors.

Click the **add behavior** button. **Scroll all the way down** on the add behavior pop-up menu. Click **Custom**.

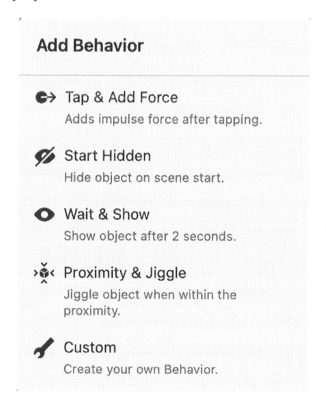

Rename the custom behavior as **Hat Jiggle**. Click the **Add a Trigger to this Behavior** label. In the Add Trigger pop-up menu, scroll all the way to the bottom and click **Notification**.

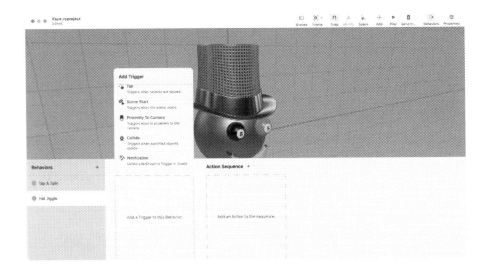

Next, add an **Emphasize** action.

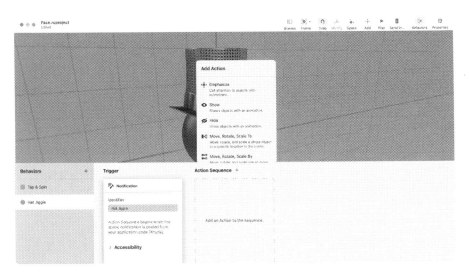

Add the **hat** to the action's affected objects. Then, press **Done**.

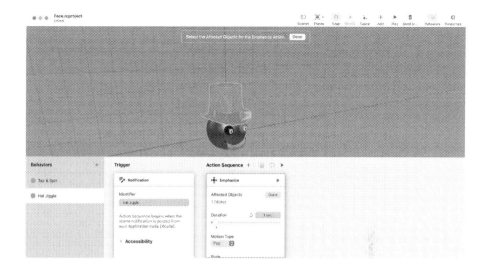

Set the emphasize action's motion type to **Jiggle** and style to **Playful**.

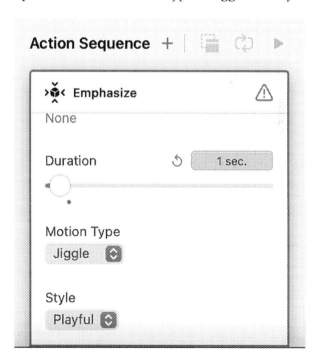

Next, select the **hat**. Then, add a **Play Sound** action to the behavior's action sequence.

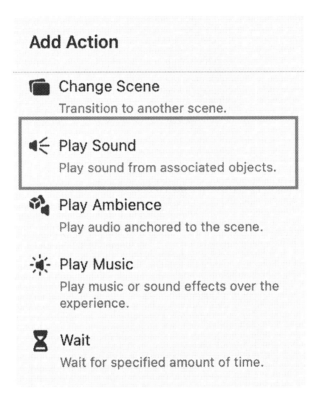

By doing what you've done, you should see that the play sound action's affected objects include the hat.

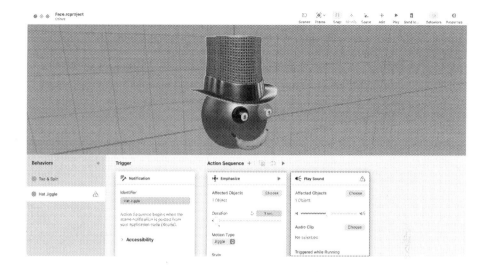

Next to the **Audio Clip** label, click the **Choose** button.

You'll be presented with a library of audio clips. You can download the ones that you want to use for your project. Now, either scroll down to or search for **Filter Sweep FX 10**. Then, **select** the audio clip.

Now, you're going to combine the emphasize and play sound action.

Click-and-drag the **Play Sound** action on top of the **Emphasize** action. You should see a blue highlight indicating that you're about to merge the two.

**Release your touch** on the trackpad/mouse.

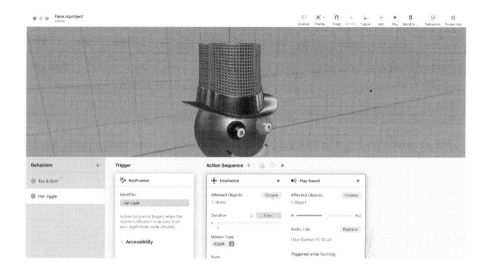

At this point, the action sequence consists of the emphasize and play sound actions running simultaneously.

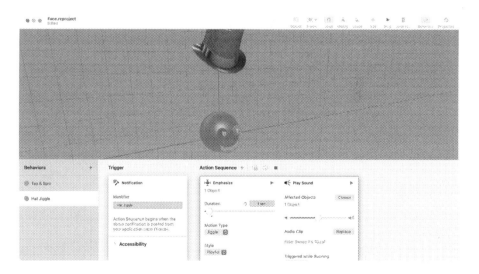

Finally, to finish off, select the **hat**. Add a **Notify** action.

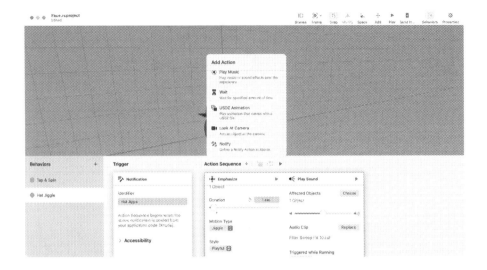

Set the notify action identifier to **Hat Jiggle Has Ended**.

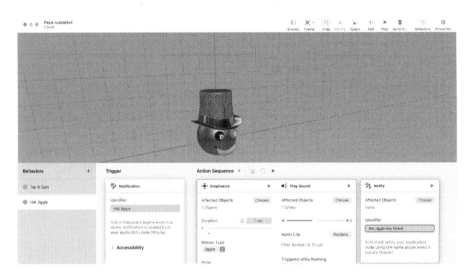

Right before the Hat Jiggle behavior's action sequence ends, it will post a notification to notify your application. You've also selected the hat as one of the objects. Hence, upon the application receiving the notification, it can deduce information from the hat.

That's a handful of information! Play around with Reality Composer. See what you can come up with. If you've had difficulty creating and integrating 3D content into ARKit in the past, Reality Composer might just be the tool to make you fall in love with creating 3D content for ARKit.

# Where to Go from Here?

You've learned how to navigate Reality Composer. You've unlocked the capability to create 3D content, built-in behaviors, and your own behaviors. Hope this chapter has made creating and integrating 3D content easier than ever. It's up to your imagination to build whatever you want. If you have something interesting, tweet me about it on Twitter (@TheJayvenNhan)!

# CHAPTER 18

# Simultaneously Integrate Face Tracking and World Tracking

Creating augmented reality experiences for face tracking and the virtual world are fun things to do. Hence, it only makes sense to double the fun by combining the face tracking and the virtual world into a bigger fun packaged experience!

Devices running on iOS 13 or later can utilize the front-facing and rear cameras in their augmented reality experience.

The requirements for face tracking to function are as follows:

- Devices running iOS 14 and iPadOS 14 and later require Apple Neural Engine.

- Devices running iOS 13 and iPadOS 13 and earlier require a TrueDepth camera.

For simultaneous front and back camera support, a device needs to contain an Apple A12 Bionic chip or later.

© Jayven Nhan 2022
J. Nhan, *Mastering ARKit*, https://doi.org/10.1007/978-1-4842-7836-9_18

CHAPTER 18    SIMULTANEOUSLY INTEGRATE FACE TRACKING AND WORLD TRACKING

In this chapter, you'll learn about the following augmented reality topics:

- Setting up ARSession for both face tracking and world tracking

- Extrapolating a Reality file from a RealityKit project scene

- Expanding beyond the default RealityKit entity's object representations

- Creating a RealityKit entity class

- Encapsulating custom entity properties

- Creating custom interfaces for an entity class

- Integrating the custom entity with the view controller

- Integrating custom entity notification triggers

- Integrating custom entity action notifiers

By the end of this chapter, you'd have created an Animoji. After learning to integrate face tracking and world tracking simultaneously, you'll have a unique tool in your arsenal to delight your audience.

# Getting Started

Open the **starter project**.

Build and run.

There's an implementation for Face.RobotHead to play a roaring bear sound when ARKit detects a wide enough open-jaw. Go ahead and open your mouth in front of your front-facing camera.

You shouldn't hear a bear roar just yet, although the logic for handling an open-jaw and playing sound exists.

To enable face tracking in ARKit, you need to configure the world tracking property to include it. You'll let ARKit know that face tracking from the front-facing camera will be included in your AR session with the world tracking from the rear camera.

Open **ViewController**. Replace the following property:

```
private let worldTrackingConfiguration =
ARWorldTrackingConfiguration()
```

With the following property:

```
private let worldTrackingConfiguration:
ARWorldTrackingConfiguration = {
    // 1
    guard ARWorldTrackingConfiguration.
    supportsUserFaceTracking else {
        fatalError("Application requires support for user face
        tracking.")
    }
    // 2
    let worldTrackingConfiguration = ARWorldTrackingConfiguration()
    worldTrackingConfiguration.userFaceTrackingEnabled = true
    return worldTrackingConfiguration
}()
```

You're doing a couple of things here:

1.  Ensure the property only initializes when the hardware is capable of supporting user face tracking. Besides having a device running on iOS 13, the device needs to have a front TrueDepth camera. ARKit extends face tracking support to devices with a regular front camera running on an A12 Bionic chip or later in iOS 14.

2.  Initialize a world tracking configuration. Then, enable the face tracking property. By doing this, you'll let `ARKit` know to also use the front-facing camera and recognize facial features.

With face tracking enabled in the world tracking configuration, you can expect the essence of a mighty grizzly bear when you open your mouth. It's time to give this a try.

Build and run. Open your mouth. And thankfully, the essence of a mighty grizzly bear is here.

Now, hearing the bear roar is fun and all. However, what if you can bring the face model that you'll typically find on your head onto other places in the world? Yes, it's time to take that head of yours and potentially put it in weird places.

# Exporting a Reality File from a RealityKit Project

To reduce the amount of ongoing logic in the view controller, particularly retaining the steel head entity, you can encapsulate the entity and its logic into its separate model. The encapsulation reduces overall complexity in the view controller and compartmentalizes entities related code into distinct objects as your project grows. Besides, you'll know exceptionally well about what goes into your entity model and customize it to your heart's content.

Open **Face.rcproject**. In Reality Composer, click **Scenes** from the middle-right area. Select the **steel head** scene.

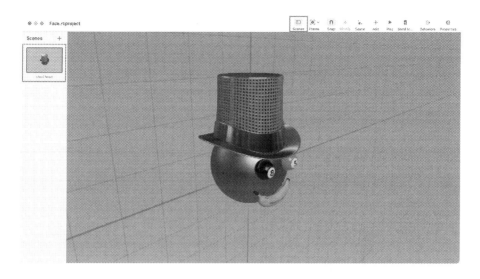

To export the scene into a Reality file, click **File/Export....** Select **Current Scene**. Click **Export**.

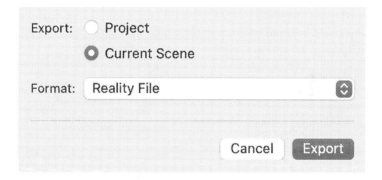

Save set the file as **SteelHead**. Select **Desktop** as the file destination. Click **Export**.

Save As:  SteelHead

Tags:

Where:  📁 Desktop  ◆  ⌄

Cancel    **Export**

The RealityKit project is no longer needed. Hence, remove **Face. rcproject**.

You'll refactor the entity related logic into its separate file. But first, you'll remove extraneous code. Remove the following properties in **ViewController**:

```
private let steelHead: Face.SteelHead
private var isPlayingSound = false
private var mouthEntity: Entity
private var mouthEntityTransformOrigin: Transform
```

Without needing to initialize the removed properties, remove **init(coder:)** from ViewController.

Next, remove the following entity methods in ViewController:

```
private func setupSmileyFaceActionHandlers() {
    steelHead.actions.bearSoundHasEnded.onAction = {
        [weak self] _ in
        self?.isPlayingSound = false
    }
}

private func updateSteelHead(from faceAnchor: ARFaceAnchor) {
    let blendShapes = faceAnchor.blendShapes
```

```
if let jawOpen = blendShapes[.jawOpen] {
   mouthEntity.transform.translation.z =
      mouthEntityTransformOrigin.translation.z +
      jawOpen.floatValue * 0.05
   if !isPlayingSound,
      jawOpen.floatValue >= 0.5 {
      isPlayingSound = true
      steelHead.notifications.playBearSound.post()
   }
}
}
```

You'll encapsulate these properties in the entity instance that you'll construct later.

Then, remove the call to **setupSmileyFaceActionHandlers()** in viewDidLoad() since it's no longer needed.

Finally, remove the following delegate methods in **ViewController**:

```
func session(_ session: ARSession, didAdd anchors: [ARAnchor]) {
   for case let faceAnchor as ARFaceAnchor in anchors {
      let anchorEntity = AnchorEntity(anchor: faceAnchor)
      anchorEntity.addChild(steelHead)
      arView.scene.addAnchor(anchorEntity)
   }
}

func session(_ session: ARSession, didUpdate anchors:
[ARAnchor]) {
   for case let faceAnchor as ARFaceAnchor in anchors {
      updateSteelHead(from: faceAnchor)
   }
}
```

You'll implement these delegate methods similarly later with your own interfaces to keep your code clean.

Now that you've exported your scene as a Reality file, it's time to incorporate the logic relating to the file into your project.

# Encapsulating Custom Entity Properties

Potentially, your RealityKit project can grow massively depending on how much content you've created inside of it. To remedy this contingency, you've exported an individual scene. However, customization comes at a cost. You don't get all the default controls and code that Apple would've generated for you using a RealityKit project. On the other hand, you can control all the systems that interact with your RealityKit file and potentially do more than Apple's RealityKit generated code.

You'll need to add the RealityKit file into your project first. Drag **SteelHead.reality** into the project's directory. Ensure **Copy items if needed** is checked. And ensure the file is accessible to the **FaceAndWorldTracking** target.

Then, click **Finish**.

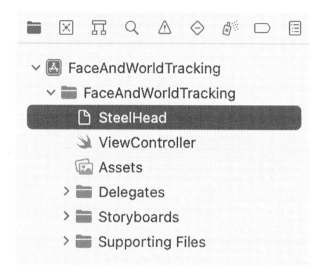

With the RealityKit resource a part of your project, you'll move on to creating the entity model to incorporate the resource and handle the custom interactions.

Create a new Swift file named **SteelHead**. Add the following code to the file:

```
import ARKit
import RealityKit
// 1
final class SteelHead: Entity {
  // MARK: - Properties
    // 2
  private let leftEyeEntity: Entity
  private let rightEyeEntity: Entity
  private let mouthEntity: Entity
```

```
    // 3
  private let mouthEntityTransformOrigin: Transform
    // 4
  private var isPlayingSound = false
}
```

Here's what you've done:

1.  You've created a class of type `Entity`.

2.  You've added private properties that would reference the various parts of the `SteelHead` model.

3.  In addition, you've created a property to store the original transform of the mouth. This way, you update the mouth's movement later on the z-axis using a recognized `ARFaceAnchor`.

4.  You've added a variable to keep track of the bear roar audio player state. This will determine whether an opened jaw from a face anchor triggers or ignores playing a sound.

With the properties created, you've moved many of controller logic to the model itself. This is a massive benefit for your code maintainability and mitigate for mitigating a bloated view controller. Next, you'll initialize these properties in your custom initializer.

Add the following required initializer to `SteelHead`:

```
// MARK: - Initializers
// 1
required init() {
    // 2
    guard let steelHead = try? Entity.load(named: "SteelHead"),
        let leftEyeEntity = steelHead.findEntity(named: "leftEye"),
```

```
    let rightEyeEntity = steelHead.findEntity(named:
    "rightEye"),
    let mouthEntity = steelHead.findEntity(named:
    "mouth") else {
        fatalError()
  }
self.leftEyeEntity = leftEyeEntity
self.rightEyeEntity = rightEyeEntity
self.mouthEntity = mouthEntity
    // 3
mouthEntityTransformOrigin = mouthEntity.transform
super.init()
    // 4
addChild(steelHead)
}
```

Here's the breakdown of the code:

1. You need the required modifier because Entity
   uses a required initializer, indicating that every
   subclass must implement it. Hence, you'll need
   to follow suit to conform to Entity initialization
   protocol.

2. Initialize the entities within the RealityKit file to
   reference later on. For example, trigger a bear roar
   or distancing the face model relative to the front-
   facing camera. These are also properties which you
   would have initially store in the view controller.

3. Set the initial transformation of the mouth entity.

4.  Add the steel head entity from the RealityKit file
    to the list of entities within SteelHead. Upon
    initialization, the model will be a part of SteelHead.
    Consequently, you'll also be able to manipulate and
    visualize the model and its components.

You've added and initialized properties for SteelHead. You'll create its
API for other objects to manipulate the components in the entity.

# Creating the Entity's API

With the entity components in place, you can create some API to
manipulate these properties. You're going to re-create the bear roar sound
and a parallax effect with the face model to distance the model from the
camera. The visualization of the latter effect will be more apparent later on
with the demo.

Now, add the following method:

```swift
// MARK: - Helper
private func getFaceZPositionRelativeToCamera(
    _ faceAnchor: ARFaceAnchor) -> Float? {
    // 1
    guard let parent = parent else { return nil }
    // 2
    let cameraPosition = parent.transform.matrix.columns.3
    // 3
    let faceAnchorPosition = faceAnchor.transform.columns.3
    // 4
    let zPosition = cameraPosition - faceAnchorPosition
    return zPosition.z
}
```

Here's the breakdown of the method. You

1.  Retrieve the parent node. Later, you'll add SteelHead relative to the camera node, and you can move from or away from the front-facing camera to move your face model forward or backward on the z-axis.

2.  Extract the camera's z-position from the transform matrix.

3.  Extract the face anchor's z-position from the transform matrix.

4.  Return the difference in z-position between the camera and face anchor positions.

As the method name suggests, you'll use the method to retrieve the face's z-position relative to the camera. This will help create a parallax effect later on.

Now, add the following method:

```
// MARK: - Update Face Anchor
func updateSteelHead(from faceAnchor: ARFaceAnchor) {
    // 1
  let blendShapes = faceAnchor.blendShapes
  if let jawOpen = blendShapes[.jawOpen] {
    mouthEntity.transform.translation.z =
        mouthEntityTransformOrigin.translation.z +
        jawOpen.floatValue * 0.05
    if !isPlayingSound,
        jawOpen.floatValue >= 0.5 {
        isPlayingSound = true
            // TODO: - Trigger bear roar notification
    }
  }
}
```

```
    // 2
  if let zPosition = getFaceZPositionRelativeToCamera(
  faceAnchor) {
      position.z = zPosition
  }
}
```

The two event occurrences here from the face anchor are:

1. Execute the bear roar notification trigger flow.

2. Position the entity relative to the camera with the given face anchor in the parameter.

Note that there's a TODO comment in the code block you've just added. You'll need to set up a notification object for the entity in the context of RealityKit. This integration will happen later in the chapter.

With these codes in place, you have enough to present your face model in the front-facing camera. You'll accomplish this next.

# Integrating the Custom Entity with the View Controller

Now, you'll integrate SteelHead in ViewController. Open **ViewController**. Add the following property:

```
private var steelHead: SteelHead?
```

You'll use this property to reference your steel head.

Now under // MARK: - Entity, add the following method to initialize SteelHead and add it onto the scene relative to a camera entity:

```
private func addSteelHeadToCamera() {
    // 1
    let cameraEntity = AnchorEntity(.camera)
    // 2
    let steelHead = SteelHead()
    // 3
    cameraEntity.addChild(steelHead)
    // 4
    steelHead.position.z = -1
    // 5
    self.steelHead = steelHead
    // 6
    arView.scene.addAnchor(cameraEntity)
}
```

Here's the code breakdown:

1. Initialize an entity that's anchored to the camera.

2. Initialize a SteelHead.

3. Add the initialized SteelHead as a child of the camera entity.

4. Position the SteelHead 1 meter away from the camera as the initial position.

5. Assign ViewController's steelHead to the recently initialized SteelHead.

6. Add the camera entity you've initialized onto the AR scene.

You've created a method to anchor your face model onto the camera. Next, you'll implement the method and update the model with the latest face anchor during the ongoing ARSession.

351

Inside the ARSessionDelegate extension block, add the following delegate methods:

```
// 1
func session(_ session: ARSession,
             didUpdate anchors: [ARAnchor]) {
   for case let faceAnchor as ARFaceAnchor in anchors {
      steelHead?.updateSteelHead(from: faceAnchor)
   }
}
// 2
func session(_ session: ARSession,
             didUpdate frame: ARFrame) {
   if steelHead == nil,
      case .normal = frame.camera.trackingState {
      addSteelHeadToCamera()
   }
}
```

You've added two methods. Here's what they're for:

1. Whenever an ARAnchor can classify as an ARFaceAnchor in the ARSession, you'll update steelHead with the latest face anchor properties.

2. During every frame update, you'll check if steelHead hasn't initialized, and the camera tracking state is normal. If these two conditions are true, you'll call the method to add steel head relative to the camera.

# Preparing the Custom Entity for Notification Triggers and Actions

Open **SteelHead**. Below import RealityKit, add the following value type and extension:

```
fileprivate enum NotificationKey: String {
    case trigger = "RealityKit.NotificationTrigger"
    case action = "RealityKit.NotifyAction"
}

fileprivate extension Notification.Name {
    static let notificationTrigger =
     Notification.Name(NotificationKey.trigger.rawValue)
    static let notifyAction = Notification.Name(NotificationKey.
    action.rawValue)
}
```

Here, you've created a value type to identify the RealityKit notification trigger and action. NotificationKey identifies reality notification triggers and actions. These are naming conventions you've set to use later on to play the bear sound. The extension creates a convenient and reusable notification name that you'll use to trigger and receive notifications.

By setting up your code this way, you'll have a better time maintaining the project. Next, you'll move onto the implementation of setting up the custom entity notification triggers.

# Setting Up the Custom Entity Notification Triggers

The purpose of the entity notification trigger is to trigger the notifications you've created within a RealityKit scene. For the scene you've exported, this includes the bear roar sound.

Add the following static constant to SteelHead:

```
private static let notificationCenter =
NotificationCenter.default
```

You'll use this property within the object to post and observe notifications.

Above // MARK: - Properties, add the following class instance to SteelHead:

```
// MARK: - Value Type
class NotificationTrigger {
    // 1
    private let identifier: String
    private weak var rootEntity: Entity?
    // 2
    fileprivate init(identifier: String, root: Entity?) {
        self.identifier = identifier
        self.rootEntity = root
    }
    // 3
    func post() {
        guard let scene = rootEntity?.scene else { return }
        let userInfo: [AnyHashable: Any] = [
            "\(NotificationKey.trigger.rawValue).Scene": scene,
            "\(NotificationKey.trigger.rawValue).Identifier":
            identifier
```

```
    ]
    notificationCenter.post(
        name: .notificationTrigger,
        object: self,
        userInfo: userInfo)
  }
}
```

Here's the code breakdown:

1. Every `NotificationTrigger` encompasses two properties—the name to identify the notification trigger and the root entity it's acting upon. In the case of `SteelHead`, this will be the enclosing object itself.

2. Initialize the properties of the object.

3. Post the notification with notification parameters.

Next, you'll handle the entity action notifiers.

# Setting Up the Custom Entity Action Notifiers

When the bear play sound has ended, you want the action to notify the object to handle custom logics. You'll set this up now.

In `SteelHead` and under `// MARK: - Value Type`, add the following value type to `SteelHead`:

```
class NotifyAction {
    // 1
    private let identifier: String
    private weak var root: Entity?
    var onAction: ((Entity) -> Void)?
```

```
    // 2
fileprivate init(identifier: String, root: Entity?) {
    self.identifier = identifier
    self.root = root
    notificationCenter.addObserver(
        self, selector: #selector(actionDidFire(notification:)),
        name: .notifyAction,
        object: nil)
}
    // 3
deinit {
    notificationCenter.removeObserver(self)
}
    // 4
@objc private func actionDidFire(notification:
Notification) {
    guard let onAction = onAction,
        let userInfo = notification.userInfo,
        let scene = userInfo["\(NotificationKey.action.
        rawValue).Scene"] as?
          Scene,
        root?.scene == scene,
        let identifier =
          userInfo["\(NotificationKey.action.rawValue).
          Identifier"] as? String,
        identifier == self.identifier,
        let entity = userInfo["\(NotificationKey.action.
        rawValue).Entity"] as?
          Entity else { return }
    onAction(entity)
    }
}
```

Here's the code breakdown:

1. Declare the properties which you'll use. This includes an identifier for the action, the root entity, and a completion handler of the action.

2. Create an initializer for the object properties and observe the action occurrences within the object.

3. Upon object de-initialization, remove observing notifications from the object.

4. Handle action fired from a notification. You also safely unwrap properties to ensure that an entity object is observing the enclosing object. And you ensure that the user info matches the notification expectations. Afterward, you return the entity to the completion handler.

Now, add the following properties to initialize the notification trigger and action notifier:

```
private(set) lazy var playBearSoundTrigger =
NotificationTrigger(identifier:
   "playBearSound", root: self)
private(set) lazy var bearSoundHasEndedAction =
NotifyAction(identifier: "bearSoundHasEnded", root: self)
```

In order to notify other objects of a notification, you'll create action callbacks within SteelHead for playing the bear roar sound. Add the following method to SteelHead:

```
// MARK: - Overheads
private func setupSmileyFaceActionHandlers() {
   bearSoundHasEndedAction.onAction = { [weak self] _ in
      self?.isPlayingSound = false
   }
}
```

Then, call the following method at the end of init():

```
setupSmileyFaceActionHandlers()
```

Finally, replace updateSteelHead(from:) with the following body:

```
let blendShapes = faceAnchor.blendShapes
if let jawOpen = blendShapes[.jawOpen] {
    mouthEntity.transform.translation.z =
        mouthEntityTransformOrigin.translation.z +
        jawOpen.floatValue * 0.05
    if !isPlayingSound,
        jawOpen.floatValue >= 0.5 {
        isPlayingSound = true
        playBearSoundTrigger.post()
    }
}
if let zPosition = getFaceZPositionRelativeToCamera(faceAnchor) {
    position.z = zPosition
}
```

In addition to handling face position, you also trigger the notification to play the bear sound. Now, it's time to test the notifications work you've done in the project.

# Testing the Notification Triggers and Actions Integration

Build and run.

Now, you have a steel head with a high-top hat in front of the rear camera! You have enough knowledge to do a lot with the user's facial expressions and bring them into the real world. Whether you decide to implement it using the front-facing or both the front-facing and the rear camera, you bring the experience you imagine into reality. Augment reality.

# Where to Go from Here?

You've learned how to integrate face tracking and world tracking simultaneously. Plus, you've learned how to create a RealityKit entity class and expand beyond the default RealityKit entity's object representations. You've unlocked a unique tool in your arsenal to delight your audience. Your audience awaits your performance. Good luck!

# CHAPTER 19

# Scanning 3D Objects

There's image recognition and there's object recognition. Unlike image recognition, object recognition is more complex since it is three-dimensional. Being at a three-dimensional state carries higher variabilities than a two-dimensional image. Variables include

- Light differentiation at various parts of an object

- Angle contrasts with objects close by which could be or not be part of an object

- Greater feature points variabilities captured in different environments

When it comes to object detection, a lot more can go wrong. However, ever since ARKit 2.0, Apple has continuously improved the various facets of image and object detections. The technology is rather young and improving at a rapid pace. Hence, your image/object detection results will only improve over time!

The chapter starts off perhaps a bit more on the part of the dark cloud. But this is to set the expectation of what you need to consider when building out an augmented reality application given the technical capacity. For example, perhaps you would build an augmented reality application for a more consistent environment than one where the environment changes dramatically.

© Jayven Nhan 2022
J. Nhan, *Mastering ARKit*, https://doi.org/10.1007/978-1-4842-7836-9_19

This isn't to say that you can't account for various environments; it may take a large sum of work or a creative solution to scale the application to account for great environment variabilities. And you can use `ARSession` feedbacks to guide the users for object detection as well.

Object detection is more exciting than image detection. After all, most of the objects that I interact with are three-dimensional—hence the seamless integration of the virtual and physical worlds.

This chapter focuses primarily on scanning objects. And you'll learn about the following augmented reality topics:

- What's a reference object
- Environment optimization for object scanning
- Object scanning at home
- API for making a referenced object
- API for applying a transform to a referenced object
- API for merging referenced objects into a single entity
- Exporting a referenced object a .arobject file with Apple's sample code

By the end of this chapter, you'd know the inner workings of creating a referenced object and can turn it into a reusable AR object file.

# What's a Reference Object

In this section, you'll walk through the step-by-step process before running in a reference object. This will give you a better context of a reference object once you know where it derives from.

As you've seen from previous chapters, there are a mass array of anchors depending on the tracking configuration you set your `ARSession` to run on. When it comes to object scanning, you run `ARObjectScanningConfiguration` and likely with a `horizontal` plane detection setting.

By running the object scanning configuration, the ARSession aggregates high-fidelity spatial mapping data on physical objects. At this point, you can collect feature points on an object. You collect feature pointing the camera at the object at different angles. Before making a reference object, you need to specify a bounding box.

A bounding box is a rectangular prism with a position and volume. Because you can scan and come across so many objects during your ARSession, you need to tell ARKit where to focus its attention to when creating a referenced object that you want. With the bounding box, you can say that you want to create a reference object with these feature points within the bounding box's premises.

Say, you have an iPhone and an iPad laying 0.3 m apart. You want to only scan the iPad, but the ARSession picks up feature points of the iPhone as well. You could specify the reference object creation process to account for all feature points, max-width, height, and depth. Or you can be specific on the bounding box that you only want the iPad's occupied space to be used as reference object creation.

After scanning the object, you'll call an ARKit API to create a reference object. This reference object consists of a structured map of feature points from a specified space of an ARSession. With this reference object, you can reuse it for object recognition or merge this object with another object. By combining spatial information from two objects, you can create a more detailed reference object or even a larger object. Typically, the former is more common.

Because ARKit works like human eyes, it needs light. Not as incredible as the human minds to discern color and space, ARKit works better in a certain environment with object scanning than humans. You'll look into optimizing your environment for object scanning next.

# Environment Optimization for Object Scanning

You want to scan objects to encode three-dimensional spatial features to let ARKit know when and where a recognized real-world object is detected. The recognized real-world object is known as a referenced object. As you can imagine, an object appearing in one place can look different in another place, especially to the camera. For example, if you illuminate an object with 200 lux in an environment vs. a 2,000 lux environment, each of the scenarios will result in a different visual outcome. Hence, it'll make recognizing the referenced object challenging.

For optimal object recognition results, you can follow some of Apple's guidelines for the object scanning phase. Here are the conditions that are instrumental for ARKit object scanning:

- **Light illuminance**: Light your object on from all sides with an illuminance of 250–400 lux. Lux, an SI photometry unit, measures luminous flux per unit area or one lumen per square meter. Luminous flux measures the power of light to the perceiving entity. The unit weights the perceived power of the light source to the human eyes. Imagine a light bulb. A higher lumen capacity light bulb can exert more energy. Thus, you'll see a brighter environment.

- **Light temperature**: Scan your object in cooler colors similar to daylight at around 6500 Kelvin. Expressed in units of kelvins, light temperature describes how warm or white visible light is. Yellowish or lower color temperatures (2700–3000 Kelvin) are known as warm colors. While bluish or high color temperatures (5000+ Kelvin) are known as cool colors.

- **Background**: Place your object in front of a matte, middle gray background. Matte is a surface that is dull, flat, and without a shine. Middle gray is a tone halfway between black and white on a lightness scale. Typically defined in photography, it is visible light with an 18% reflectance.

These recommendations aren't exactly helpful unless there are instructions on how to provide this environment for people who are perhaps at home. You'll look into this next.

# Preparing Your Environment for Object Scanning

Depending on the device you run the scan on, the performance can vary in creating a high-quality scan. You can scan an object on any ARKit-supported device. But for a smoother and more rapid high-quality scan, a more recent high-performance device is recommended.

For my home workstation environment, I've done the following to optimize the scan performance:

1. Open the window blinds to allow natural light in. This helps with light illuminance and creating a daylight temperature.

2. Find light gray objects like a laptop case, iPad Pro keyboard cover, or Bose speaker packaging, anything you can find that's as much mid-gray color as possible. Then, position them in a way to form a backdrop.

3.   Download Lux Light Meter Pro from the App Store to measure the light luminosity. My environment's average luminosity sits at around 300 lux. [Image of the Lux Meter Pro app]

4.   Find an object that isn't gray and has more excellent contrast with the color gray. Also, find an object that's nontranslucent and a small enough form factor to position within the walls of your background. I originally wanted to use Nando's hot sauce bottle as a nice little object. However, I've finished the entire bottle recently and needed to find a replacement. Hence, I've opted for an egg. Then, I cracked the egg. Made scrambled eggs. And I also realized that a reasonably sized item has is 500 cubic cm in Apple's sample code. So an average egg won't suffice. Therefore, I've opted for a cocoa powder container in the end.

Beyond utilizing these recommendations when setting up your environment, I've found that having enough space to move your device around an object is also important. Although finding a matte middle gray background is recommended for scanning, don't fret if you can't seem to find one around the house. For reference, here's the color of middle gray.

I've found that having a contrasting and textured background like a wooden floor can do wonders for your scan.

# Making a Reference Object

At the time of this writing, Apple has yet to release a standardized way of creating a referenced object in ARKit. Apple provides a sample app that showcases how you can generate a referenced object using a bounding box and feature points. In the end, you'll want to use the following API to generate your scanned reference object:

```
ARSession.createReferenceObject(transform:center:extent:
completionHandler:)
```

In the preceding method, you pass in the following parameters:

- **Transform**: Relative to the local coordinate system, this is a matrix consisting of origin and orientation definitions in the form of `simd_float4x4`. This will be where your object is situated in an `ARSession`.

- **Center**: Relative to the transform's origin from the previous parameter, this is a value that defines the bounding box's center. Typically, you'd pass in zeroes in the form of `simd_float3` unless you'd like to offset the center.

- **Extent**: Relative to the center and orientation from the previous two parameters, this value defines the width, height, and depth of an `ARSession` for extraction. For example, after capturing a bounding box's position and orientation, you specify that you want to capture an area of 10 cubic centimeters. Then, ARKit will go to work and try to create that `ARReferencedObject` for you.

- **Completion handler**: You can use this closure to pass back two parameters to the caller, `ARReferenceObject` and `ARError`. The former is a referenced object you created as a result of your `ARSession` and the specified location and size of the captured volume within the session. The latter object returns when you encounter a failure to create a referenced object. Examples of such errors include insufficient feature points, unusable reference objects, or failure to merge two or more reference objects.

You've learned about the API that makes a reference object. Next, you'll learn about another API that you may want to use.

# Merging Two Reference Objects

Merging two reference objects is a great way to make your final reference object more robust. Your object can show up in various environments, such as lighter or darker lights and everything in between. Your object can also show up in areas where there are green or blue lights shining toward it. For these reasons, merging reference objects gives ARKit an easier time recognizing the same object in more conditions.

To merge two reference objects into one, you call the following ARKit API:

```
ARReferenceObject.merging(_:)
```

This method is called on a reference object, and you pass in another reference object. ARKit then attempts to combine the spatial mapping data of the two reference object into a single reference. The method will either return an `ARReferenceObject` or throw an `ARError` describing why the merge has failed.

Next, you'll look at in which scenarios you may want to apply transform on a reference object.

# Applying Transform to a Reference Object

When the referenced object's bounding box isn't positioned as intended, you can use the following API:

```
ARReferenceObject.applyingTransform(_:)
```

With a new transform you pass into the parameter, applying a transform to a reference object returns a new reference object. Because your reference object is taken from a specific `ARSession` with its environment coordinates, you may want to reposition your reference object. For example, if a reference object is scanned sitting on top of the box, you probably want the reference object to position flushed to a surface (e.g., horizontal plane).

You want to use this API, especially when you have other virtual content that is of the child reference object. This may disorientate the virtual content where they are presented higher than you would like them to be. Or if for some reason an object is scanned tilted, you can also apply a transform to reorientate to the position that you find the reference object in another ARSession.

The reference object transform API is more niche. However, it's there for you when you need it. Next, you'll look at exporting a reference object into a format that you can conveniently save and reuse.

# Exporting a Referenced Object

You can save a reference object for future use by exporting it. An exported reference object takes the file format of **.arobject**. With this file, you can drag it into your Xcode project's AR Resource Group in the asset catalog.

To export a reference object, you can use the following ARKit API:

```
ARReferenceObject.export(to:previewImage:)
```

This method takes in two parameters, URL and UIImage?. Then, it will either be successful in exporting a reference object or throw an error describing the export failure. You specify URL as the location for writing the reference object (e.g., File app at a specific document directory).

You can pass in an UIImage that becomes your file's preview image. When you deal with the file in places such as Files, Xcode, or Finder, having a preview image can help you easily identify a reference object from the others. Passing in a preview image is optional but benefits the users handling the .arobject files.

You can generate a preview image from making a snapshot on an `ARView`:

```
private func makePreviewImage() {
    arView.snapshot(saveToHDR: false) { [weak self] (image) in
        guard let self = self, let cgImage = image?.cgImage else
        { return }
        let previewImage = UIImage(cgImage: cgImage)
    }
}
```

Next, you'll look at using Apple's sample project to export a reference object.

# Using Apple's Sample Project to Export a Referenced Object

To get started, download Apple's object scanning project using the following URL:

```
https://developer.apple.com/documentation/arkit/scanning_and_
detecting_3d_objects
```

Open the project in Xcode. Open the project's settings. Under **TARGETS**, click **Scanning App**. Then, click **Signing & Capabilities**. Finally, select your signing **Team**.

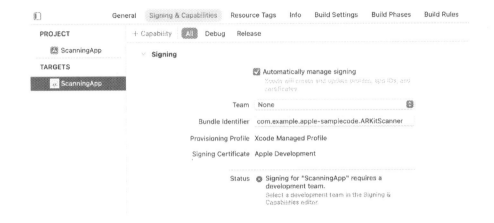

Before running the app on your device, you can test your environment's luminosity using the Lux Meter Pro app.

Build and run the project on a physical device.

In your so optimal scanning environment, pick an object that you'd like to scan.

Nando's hot sauce? Translucent, not the best.

An egg? Might be a bit small for scanning and the lack of texture makes it more difficult for ARKit to capture feature points. Maybe...

Well, it's cracked. That's becoming a scrambled egg, not a
reference object.

A cocoa powder container? It seems like a good choice. It has distinct definitions, such as the cap's rigidness, texts, images on the label, and various colors. In a way, I am picking objects that are different enough to make the ARKit object scanning process easier.

Before walking through the app's scanning process, you'll first look over what a successful scan looks like and how you can export a reference object.

After a successful scan, you'll see something like this.

Then, you can move the device around to move away from the
previous object's captured feature points angles for an object scan reset.

Then, move around your object to see the detection of your object.

You can then tap the **Share** button. And tap the **Save to Files** button.

Save to **On My iPad** or your preferred document directory.

Now, you can scan an object more than once and merge objects together.

Run **ScanningApp** on your device.

Move the device around to capture some feature points of your object.

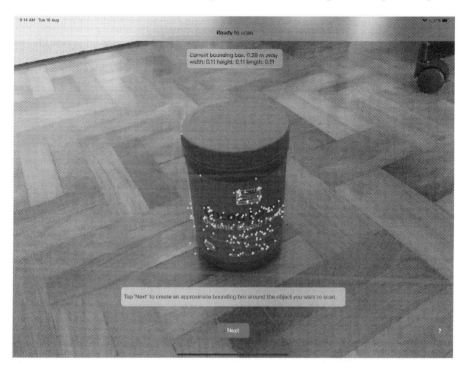

Tap **Next**. Adjust the bounding box of the object.

You can position and size the bounding box with pan and pinch gestures, respectively.

Next, tap **Scan**. Move the device around the object. You'll see rectangles get highlighted around the object helping you keep track of surface area scanned from various angles.

Go ahead and highlight all the rectangles from your scans.

After all rectangles are filled, you'll see something like this.

At this stage, you can apply a transform on the object's origin by moving the 3D-axis object around. If you scan the object on a flat surface, you shouldn't need to apply any transform. If you do apply a transform, the app will look something like this.

Now, move your device around to test that ARKit can detect the object you've scanned.

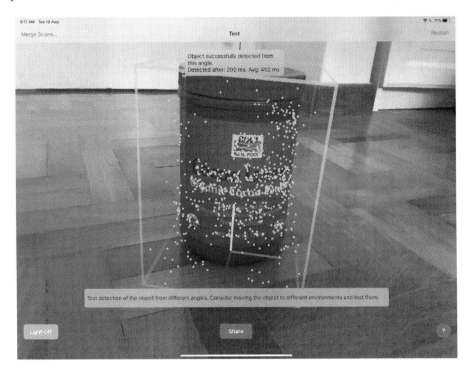

If this is your second scan of the object, you can merge the previous scan with the current scan. Tap the **Merge Scans...** button.

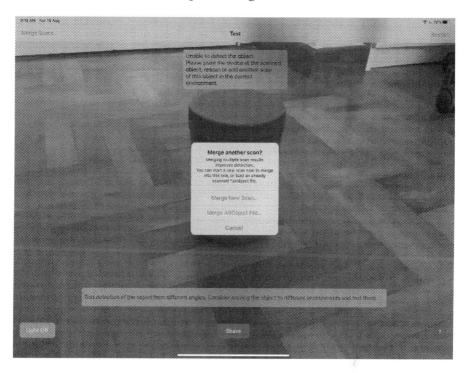

Tap **Merge ARObject File...** if you have an existing ARObject file. Alternatively, you can tap **Merge New Scan...** for a second scan. The next step assumes you have an existing ARObject file.

Select the **ARObject file** from your device.

The app will then begin merging the current reference object with the reference object from the selected **ARObject file**.

On a successful merge, you'll be prompted with a success message.

Now, when you detect your object, it should be more robust and capable of accounting for more environmental conditions. And you'll likely see more feature points on the merged reference object.

You can export this reference object again for future use.

# Where to Go from Here?

In this chapter, you've learned how object scanning works and a way of creating and saving a reference object with an app. Next, you'll learn how to implement object detection and add virtual content onto a detected object. See you soon!

# CHAPTER 20

# Detecting 3D Objects

When it comes to the real world, you'll encounter 3D objects more time than not. It's a power move when your app can detect a 3D object and have a spatial mapping of it as well. The latter is especially crucial if you want to add virtual content to the physical world.

Since ARKit 2.0, devices running on iOS 12 and above can detect 3D objects embedded from reference objects. Upon object detection, you can initiate augmented reality content. In a technology shop, you may pop up a trailer of a gadget, while in a culinary store, various kitchenware show images of what each appliance is suitable for when you point at it with your finger.

Perhaps, you can even recognize luggage and then see if your items fit in your luggage. That would be super handy, wouldn't it? If your items are standardized or weighted, you could even know how much your luggage would weigh in total. No more finding a scale, weighing yourself, and weighing yourself and the luggage, hoping that your luggage is within the weight limit. Although Emirates and Singapore Airlines have been very kind to me in the past.

© Jayven Nhan 2022
J. Nhan, *Mastering ARKit*, https://doi.org/10.1007/978-1-4842-7836-9_20

In this chapter, you'll work on a project that'll allow you to do things after scanning a 3D object. You'll learn about the following ARKit topics:

- Setting up reference objects to the project

- Configuring ARKit for detecting reference objects

- Presenting virtual content on reference objects

- Utilizing reference objects to create model entities

- Implementing simple and unlit materials

- Leveraging mesh resource in RealityKit for generating custom text

By the end of this chapter, you'd have created a project that can detect reference objects. In addition, the project becomes capable of presenting virtual content anchored to the 3D object.

---

**Note**   Ensure the project targets a device. Otherwise, the exposure of `AnchorEntity` APIs will be limited and the compiler will show a compilation error.

---

# Getting Started

Before moving further, please use the previous chapter as a guide to export a 3D object of your choice. Afterward, feel free to return here.

For the project, I've decided to use a cocoa powder container. You can use a 3D object of your choice.

For my 3D objects, I've scanned a cocoa powder container.

And an instant noodle cup.

Once you have your reference object in the form of `.arobject`, you're ready to begin.

# Adding Reference Objects to the Project

Open the **starter project**. Open **Assets.xcassets**.

In the asset folder, click the + button. Click **AR and Textures/New AR Resource Group**.

Drag and drop the objects into the **AR Resources** group.

Great! The objects for detection are in place. Next, you'll handle the fun stuff. Code!

# Configuring ARKit for Object Detection

Similar to image detection, object detection requires you to let it know the objects that ARKit should be interested in. In this case, they are the objects which you've just added to the **AR Resource Group** in the main bundle.

At the moment, worldTrackingConfiguration is only running a horizontal plane detection configuration. You'll change that to also detect objects. Replace worldTrackingConfiguration with the following code:

```
private let worldTrackingConfiguration:
ARWorldTrackingConfiguration = {
   let worldTrackingConfiguration =
ARWorldTrackingConfiguration()
   worldTrackingConfiguration.planeDetection = .horizontal
   // 1
   guard let detectionObjects = ARReferenceObject.
   referenceObjects(inGroupNamed: "AR Resources", bundle:
   .main) else {
      fatalError("Missing reference objects from main bundle.")
   }
   // 2
   for detectionObject in detectionObjects {
      print(detectionObject.name ?? "")
   }
   // 3
   worldTrackingConfiguration.detectionObjects =
   detectionObjects return worldTrackingConfiguration
}()
```

With the code you've added, here's a breakdown:

1. Request the app to search in its directory for a list of `ARReferenceObject` in the main bundle with a group named `AR Resources`. Otherwise, you'll throw a fatal error with a message explaining that reference objects are missing. The app will also come to a halt there and then.

2. With the list of detection objects retrieved from the app's reference object directory, print out the detected object's name. This is more for debugging purposes and showing what each object name is. If you have more than one object, the loops will print multiple names. Otherwise, you'll see a single object name printed. The name should be the same as you see in the AR resource group.

3. Set the tracking configuration detection objects to those that you've retrieved recently.

Next, you'll handle what happens when object anchors are detected.

# Handling Objects Detection

In the `ARSessionDelegate` extension block, add the following delegate method:

```
// 1
func session(_ session: ARSession, didAdd anchors:
[ARAnchor]) {
    // 2
    for case let anchor as ARObjectAnchor in anchors {
        // Add Buy Item Anchor Entity
    }
}
```

Two things to take note here:

1. When an anchor is detected, the protocol method triggers.

2. Looping over the anchors, enter the loop only when the anchor can be cast as `ARObjectAnchor`.

There's a comment in the code you've added. You'll add a buy item anchor entity. Upon detection of an object, you'll generate a combination of visual elements that basically provide information for the user to buy the item.

# Making the Buy Item Anchor Entity

You'll create the main anchor entity that acts like it's the center of the universe because it is. Oh yeah, it's important!

Basically, other visual elements will sit around this anchor entity.

In `ViewController`, add the following code under `// MARK: - Object Entity Factory`:

```
private func makeBuyItemAnchorEntity(
    from objectAnchor: ARObjectAnchor) -> AnchorEntity {
    let referenceObject = objectAnchor.referenceObject
    // Make Sphere Model Entity
    // Make Price Tag Text Model Entity
    // Make Buy Text Model Entity
    // Make Final Buy Item Model Entity
    let anchorEntity = AnchorEntity(anchor: objectAnchor)
    return anchorEntity
}
```

One interesting occurrence here is you extract the reference object from an ARObjectAnchor. With this extracted property, you'll be able to do things like reading the size, position, feature points making up the object, name of the object, AR Resource group name the anchor belongs to, etc. There's a lot that you can do with this information and more. I've only presented a couple, which I think will be helpful more often than not when developing object detection applications. The main anchor entity is created from the ARObjectAnchor passed in and makes a copy of its properties.

To let the main anchor entity feel like it's the center of the universe, you'll begin adding objects around it. First, you'll make a sphere model entity!

# Making the Sphere Model Entity

You'll add an orange sphere object to the detected object. The challenge is to have the orange sphere sit nicely on top of the detected object.

In makeBuyItemAnchorEntity(from:), add the following code under // Make Sphere Model Entity:

```
// 1
let sphereMesh = MeshResource.generateSphere(radius: 0.05)
// 2
var sphereMaterial = SimpleMaterial(color: .customOrange,
                                    isMetallic: true)
// 3
sphereMaterial.roughness = 1
// 4
let sphereEntity = ModelEntity(
   mesh: sphereMesh,
   materials: [sphereMaterial])
sphereEntity.position = SIMD3(
```

```
0,
referenceObject.extent.y
    + sphereMesh.bounds.extents.y/2
    + 0.04,
0)
```

Here's a breakdown of the code you've added:

1.  Initialize a sphere `MeshResource` with a
    0.05 m radius.

2.  Initialize a material for the sphere with a custom
    color and a metallic surface.

3.  Set the roughness of the material to 1. This gives the
    material rougher and a better light conductor. In
    other words, lights are better reflected off of these
    surfaces. It will closely resemble materials like
    aluminum, copper, gold, silver, and titanium.

4.  Initialize a `Model Entity`. Set the mesh and
    materials to the values you've recently initialized.
    For the entity's x-position, you set it to zero because
    you want it to be centered relative to the detected
    object. For the y-position, you sum the reference's
    size, half the sphere mesh height, and an addition
    of 0.04 m. This makes the sphere sit nicely on top
    of the detected object with a bit of root between
    the detected object's max height and the bottom of
    your virtual content. The z-position is zero since you
    don't need to move the virtual content forward or
    backward relative to the referenced object.

There you have it. An orange sphere ready to float on top of the
detected object! You'll let the orange sphere do what it's made to do next.

Beneath `let anchorEntity = AnchorEntity(anchor: objectAnchor)`, add the following code:

```
anchorEntity.addChild(sphereEntity)
```

Okay `anchorEntity`. It looks like you're more like the center of the universe already.

Now in `session(_:didAdd:)`, add the following code right below `// Add Buy Item Anchor Entity`:

```
let buyItemAnchorEntity = makeBuyItemAnchorEntity(
    from: anchor)
arView.scene.addAnchor(buyItemAnchorEntity)
```

Upon detecting an object anchor, you add the buy item anchor entity made from the anchor entity factory method you've created. With the created anchor entity, add it onto the scene.

Build and run. Detect your 3D object.

ARKit should be able to detect your 3D object without needing to scan the entire 3D object. It will require just enough feature points to recognize the object.

Upon detection, you should see an orange sphere sitting on top of the detected object. Awesome!

Next, you'll create a price tag text model entity.

# Making the Price Tag Text Model Entity

Here, you want to create a price tag that floats directly on top of the orange ball.

In makeBuyItemAnchorEntity(from:), add the following code under // Make Price Tag Text Model Entity:

```
// 1
let randomNumber = Int.random(in: 1..<10)
// 2
```

```
let priceText = "$\(randomNumber)9.99"
// 3
let priceTextMesh = MeshResource.generateText(
   priceText,
   extrusionDepth: 0.01,
   font: .systemFont(ofSize: 0.1),
   containerFrame: .zero,
   alignment: .center,
   lineBreakMode: .byTruncatingTail)
// 4
let textEntity = ModelEntity(mesh: priceTextMesh)
// 5
textEntity.position = SIMD3(-priceTextMesh.bounds.extents.x/2,
                            sphereMesh.bounds.extents.y/2, 0)
```

Here's the code breakdown:

1. Generate a random integer.

2. Initialize the price text string. The price text is a
   dollar sign followed by a random integer and 9.99
   using string interpolation.

3. Create a price text mesh using the text you've
   initialized. The extrusion depth of the text is 0.01 m.
   You can make your text extrude further in space
   with a higher value or stick closer to a 2D text with
   a lower value. You also set mesh resource with a
   system font of size 0.1. The default container size
   is (0,0), and you'll keep it that way. The container
   frame creates a local coordinate system to contain
   the text. By setting this value to zero, the text will
   generate a frame large enough to contain the text.

Set the text alignment to center within the container frame and truncate the tail in the scenario where the container frame doesn't have enough space to contain the text.

4. Create a `ModelEntity` with the recently initialized text mesh.

5. Position the text entity to the center of the sphere mesh. For the x-position, move to the left by half of the price text mesh bounds' x-extent, half of its width. For the y-position, move it upward by the sphere mesh bounds' y-extent, half of its height. The z-position is kept the same to mitigate moving the text entity forward or backward relative to the detected object.

Now, it's back to adding objects around the main anchor entity.

Beneath `let anchorEntity = AnchorEntity(anchor: objectAnchor)`, add the following code:

```
sphereEntity.addChild(textEntity)
```

Build and run. Detect your 3D object.

This time, you should see a randomized price tag too!

Next, you'll let the user know that the detected object is for purchase.

# Making the Buy Text Model Entity

You'll position a buy text model entity in front of the orange sphere entity.

In makeBuyItemAnchorEntity(from:), add the following code under
// Make Buy Text Model Entity:

```
// 1
let buyTextMesh = MeshResource.generateText(
    "Buy",
    extrusionDepth: 0.01,
    font: .systemFont(ofSize: 0.05),
    alignment: .center)
```

```
// 2
let buyTextMaterial = SimpleMaterial(color: .white,
                                     isMetallic: true)
// 3
let buyTextEntity = ModelEntity(mesh: buyTextMesh,
                                materials: [buyTextMaterial])
// 4
buyTextEntity.position = SIMD3(
    -buyTextMesh.bounds.extents.x / 2,
    0,
    sphereMesh.bounds.extents.z / 2 + 0.01)
```

Here's what you've done:

1. Initialize a text mesh resource with a buy text. It will have the same extrusion depth and alignment settings as the price text mesh but a smaller font size.

2. Initialize a `SimpleMaterial` that's white and metallic.

3. Initialize a `ModelEntity` using `buyTextMesh` and `buyTextMaterial`.

4. Position the buy text entity to half of its width to the left and move it forward by the sphere mesh's radius plus 0.01 m.

Beneath `let anchorEntity = AnchorEntity(anchor: objectAnchor)`, add the following code:

```
sphereEntity.addChild(buyTextEntity)
```

Build and run. Detect your 3D object.

# Where to Go from Here?

You did a wonderful job mastering some ARKit's intricacies! With so many objects in the world, having the ability to detect and amplify physical object is no joke. The power is in your hand. Choose wisely Obi-Wan Kenobi.

# CHAPTER 21

# Body Motion Capture

One of the most overpowered moves in fiction is the Sharingan from the Uchiha clan in *Naruto*. The Sharingan allows an individual to outright copy every action a person does. In this chapter, you'll give your device the Sharingan ability. You'll have a rigged model that does exactly as you move.

Capturing body motion is first introduced in ARKit 3 and iOS 13. The device capability prerequisite is an A12 chip or later for neural engine processing and making use of machine learning. ARKit's body motion capture allows the device to track a person's body movement, as the name implies. With the tracked human's information, you can replicate this into a rigged model—this is kind of like the people who wear black suits to play characters with CGI effects.

ARKit 3 uses machine learning to decipher the person in the camera image to build out a skeleton. This skeleton can then be combined with a rigged model to copy everything a person does in real time.

In this chapter, you'll learn about the following body motion capture topics:

- Understanding the skeleton

- Capturing a person's body motion in real time using RealityKit

- Integrating the body motion capture feature with a rigged model

- Deciphering a skeleton to spot various joints

J. Nhan, *Mastering ARKit*, https://doi.org/10.1007/978-1-4842-7836-9_21

- Placing objects relative to various joints captured on a body

- Calculating distances between joints

By the end of this chapter, you'll learn how to use a rigged model to simulate a person's body motion. You'll also know how to work with various joints found on a person's skeleton through ARKit's image processing. And you'd have created an exercise app that counts the number of shoulder raises a person does! No cheating the repetition!

# Understanding the Skeleton

The outcome of body motion capture in ARKit is the skeleton. And a skeleton is made up of joints. In the skeleton model generated from ARKit 3, you get an astounding 91 joints. Here are some of the 3D skeleton joints:

- Hips

- Leg

- Foot

- Toes

- Spine

- Hand

- Shoulder

- Neck

- Eye

- Nose

- Jaw

- Chin

The list consists of some of the joints described in the high-level joints. Whereas looking into a 3D skeleton specific joints, you'll find joint names like `left_foot_joint`, `right_upLog_joint`, `spine_7_joint`, `left_handIndex_3_joint`, `left_handThumb_2_joint`, `left_eyeUpperLid_joint`, etc. In ARKit, a thumb is divided into two joints, and a spine is divided into seven joints.

`ARBodyAnchor` has a captured body's `Skeleton`. A `Skeleton` holds the joint transforms. You can get a list of the full list of available joints from ARKit from the following value type: `ARSkeleton3D.JointName`.

With the number of recognizable joints, ARKit can represent a person well enough where a rigged model moves as a person would. Body motion capture is a compelling feature in ARKit.

# Capturing a Person's Body Motion in Real Time Using RealityKit

Open the **starter project**.

Since body motion capture integrates with RealityKit, you'll use the framework to construct your project. To set up and run the body tracking configuration, add the following property to `ViewController` first:

```
private let bodyTrackingConfiguration =
ARBodyTrackingConfiguration()
```

This is the augmented reality tracking configuration for body tracking. With this configuration, you have `ARFrameSemanticBodyDetection` enabled. Having this option enabled asks ARKit to detect a body in 2D from the camera image. With the information obtained, estimate a person's joints relative to the screen space from the camera feed.

Then, add the following property to `ViewController`:

```
private var bodyTrackedEntity: BodyTrackedEntity?
```

415

This property will hold the skeleton attributes in memory and for updates. Next, add the following code to `resetTrackingConfiguration()`:

```
guard ARBodyTrackingConfiguration.isSupported else {
    fatalError("Device doesn't support ARBodyTracking
    Configuration.")
}
arView.session.run(bodyTrackingConfiguration)
```

The code block checks that the device supports body tracking or runs on an A12 chip or later. Since this is necessary for body tracking in ARKit, the guard statement will prevent further code execution for unsupported devices and return a fatal error message. If the body tracking configuration is supported, the method continues and gets the view controller's ARView to run the body tracking configuration. The method is called on viewDidAppear(_:).

# Integrating the Body Motion Capture Feature with a Rigged Model

Before integrating the rigged model in RealityKit, it's helpful to learn about BodyTrackedEntity. This is because a BodyTrackedEntity is what you'll load into ARKit to copy a person's body motion.

As the name implies, BodyTrackedEntity is an entity. This entity type's specific use case is for animating a rigged model in AR from tracking a person's body movement. The entity's model component makes up the physical appearance, and the body tracking component dictates the positioning and movements.

Overall, BodyTrackedEntity is an entity with a rigged model visualization, and the body motion dictates the relative positioning of the model's components such as a leg or a hand.

416

Now that you've understood the specific entity's role, add the following code to `loadRiggedModelAsync()`:

```
do {
    // 1
    let robotBodyTrackedEntity = try Entity.loadBodyTracked(
    named: "robot")
    // 2
    robotBodyTrackedEntity.scale = [1, 1, 1]
    // 3
    bodyTrackedEntity = robotBodyTrackedEntity
    // 4
    let bodyAnchorEntity = AnchorEntity(.body)
    bodyAnchorEntity.addChild(robotBodyTrackedEntity)
    // 5
    arView.scene.addAnchor(bodyAnchorEntity)
} catch {
    // 6
    print("Error:", error.localizedDescription)
}
```

Here's the breakdown of the code:

1. Using a `do-catch` statement, you ask the app to load a `BodyTrackedEntity` named robot using the `Entity` API. This will either result in a loaded rigged model or not.

2. Set the scale of the rigged model. You can make the rigged model smaller/bigger/the same here relative to the person's body that the rigged model mimics. Setting the scale to [1, 1, 1] across the x, y, and z coordinates produces a one-to-one scale on all axes.

3. Upon successfully loading a `BodyTrackedEntity` onto the `ARView` scene, add a body anchor entity that tells the ARKit to locate the tracked body.

4. On top of the body anchor entity, place the body tracked entity (rigged model) on top of it. Now that the rigged model is a child of the `bodyAnchorEntity`, the rigged model will follow it according to the user's body motion.

5. Add `bodyAnchorEntity` onto the `ARView`. This makes the body anchor entity part of the augmented reality scene.

6. If the rigged model isn't successfully loaded as a `BodyTrackedEntity`, print the error's localized description.

Build and run.

Should Raise Stage: Raised                Repetition: 5

Walk around in front of the camera. I use QuickTime Player to see the screen of the iPad. And don't forget to almost fall flat on your face to limit test ARKit's capability to capture quick motions.

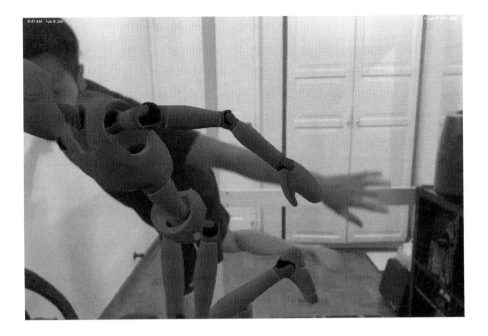

Just like that, you have a rigged model on top of a tracked body.

# Generating Your Rigged Model

Since most of us reading this book are engineers, designs don't always come as intuitively. However, that should not stop us from creating unique-looking content—not even a rigged model. Essentially, you'll want your rigged model to be a USDZ file for seamless integration with RealityKit.

There are three main methods that I've found most applicable for generating your rigged model. Here are the three methods:

1. With your imagination and RealityKit Composer, mesh basic shapes into a rigged model.

2. On a Mac, use Apple's USDZ converter tool from the developer portal's download page to convert an existing rigged model.

3. On an iOS/iPadOS device, use Adobe Aero to export a USDZ file on an iPad.

You can learn more about rigging a model here:

> https://developer.apple.com/documentation/arkit/rigging_a_model_for_motion_capture

And then validating the rigged model to ensure compatibility here:

> https://developer.apple.com/documentation/arkit/validating_a_model_for_motion_capture

Feel free to take a pause here to explore creating your rigged model. Or keep going to learn about deciphering different joints from a skeleton.

# Deciphering a Skeleton Using Lower-Level APIs to Spot Various Joints

When body motion tracking is active with a visible person on screen, ARKit generates an ARSkeleton composed of many joints. By deciphering the various joints, you can achieve things like placing virtual objects at various joints, calculating distances between joints, etc. You'll get to find your ARSkeleton of interest in one of ARKit's protocol methods and from extracting ARBodyAnchor.

ARBodyAnchor is the object that contains an ARSkeleton. ARKit gets a new ARBodyAnchor when a person's body is first detected and second after.

Similar to other anchors you've seen in the past, you set session(_:didUpdate:) to receive updates about your anchor of interest.

In session(\_:didUpdate:), add the following code:

```
for anchor in anchors {
    guard let bodyAnchor = anchor as? ARBodyAnchor else {
    continue }
    // TODO
}
```

Here, you iterate through the available ARAnchors and continue code execution only if the ARAnchor can cast as an ARBodyAnchor. In cases where you are detecting more than just a human body, you'll add more conditional checking to account for other specific anchor types.

Now, add the following properties to ViewController:

```
private let rootAnchorEntity = AnchorEntity()
private let leftShoulderAnchorEntity = AnchorEntity()
private let rightShoulderAnchorEntity = AnchorEntity()
private let leftHandAnchorEntity = AnchorEntity()
private let rightHandAnchorEntity = AnchorEntity()
private let rootModelEntity = makeBoxModelEntity()
private let leftShoulderModelEntity =
makeBallModelEntity(color: .systemBlue)
private let rightShoulderModelEntity =
makeBallModelEntity(color: .systemBlue)
private let leftHandModelEntity = makeBallModelEntity()
private let rightHandModelEntity = makeBallModelEntity()
```

Here, you initialize anchor entities and model entities for five different joints. You'll add a ball or box model to the tracked body depending on the joint. Also, various joints consist of various colors.

To map the various joint names to the respective anchor entity and model entity, add the following value type and computed property to ViewController:

```
// 1
typealias JointAnchorTuple = (anchorEntity: AnchorEntity,
                              modelEntity: ModelEntity)
// 2
private var jointAnchorSphereMap: [
  ARSkeleton.JointName: JointAnchorTuple
  ] {
  [
    .root: (rootAnchorEntity, rootModelEntity),
    .leftShoulder: (leftShoulderAnchorEntity, leftShoulder
    ModelEntity),
    .leftHand: (leftHandAnchorEntity, leftHandModelEntity),
    .rightShoulder: (rightShoulderAnchorEntity, rightShoulder
    ModelEntity),
    .rightHand: (rightHandAnchorEntity, rightHandModelEntity)
  ]
}
```

Here, you

1.  Create a typealias to define a custom type using existing types. This is for convenience, clarity, and reusability. Otherwise, it'll become cumbersome to type out AnchorEntity and ModelEntity continually. And you'll miss out on the context for the role each value plays. For example, when you type out the custom tuple type, there's the context that the tuple is related to a joint. Afterward, accessing an anchor or model entity, this shows the context that these properties are related to a particular joint.

2.  Map out the various joints to their respective anchor and model entities. All the joint names are self-explanatory except for root. The root joint is the hip joint.

Now, you'll add a method to update the joint positioning as new information arrives from ARKit. Add the following method to ViewController:

```
private func updateJointPosition(
    bodyAnchor: ARBodyAnchor,
    jointName: ARSkeleton.JointName,
    jointAnchorTuple: JointAnchorTuple) {
    // 1
    guard let transform = bodyAnchor.skeleton.modelTransform(
                for: jointName) else { return }
    // 2
    let position = simd_make_float3(transform.columns.3)
    let jointAnchorEntity = jointAnchorTuple.anchorEntity
    jointAnchorEntity.position = position
    // 3
    guard jointAnchorEntity.parent == nil else { return }
    let modelEntity = jointAnchorTuple.modelEntity
    jointAnchorEntity.addChild(modelEntity)
    bodyTrackedEntity?.addChild(jointAnchorEntity)
}
```

Here's a breakdown of the code:

1.  First, to retrieve the joint position, you safely unwrap and retrieve the transform matrix of jointName from bodyAnchor.

2.  Second, using the four-dimensional transform matrix, extract the position from there and update the joint with the latest position.

3.  Third, if the joint anchor entity doesn't have a parent, it has yet to be added to the user's tracked body. When this is the case, add the joint's model entity to joint's anchor entity. Then, add the joint's anchor entity onto the body tracked entity of the user.

Now that you have all the joint anchor and model entities in place, you visualize how ARKit captures and processes the various joints of a human body.

# Placing Objects Relative to Various Joints Captured on a Body

Sometimes, you'll wonder why a model looks a certain way, and other times it looks like other ways. At the end of the day, it comes down to how well ARKit can capture your body motion and decipher the joints through image processing with the neural engine. In order to visualize what ARKit understands, you'll add landmark objects to various joints of the user.

In session(_:didUpdate:), replace // TODO with the following code:

```
jointAnchorSphereMap.forEach { jointName, jointAnchorTuple in
    updateJointPosition(bodyAnchor: bodyAnchor,
                        jointName: jointName,
                        jointAnchorTuple: jointAnchorTuple)
}
// TODO
```

Using a `forEach` loop, you iterate through `jointAnchorSphereMap` to update the various joints of interest. In total, there are five; the joints are essentially the hip, hands, and shoulders.

Build and run.

[Image]

You can locate various joints on a human body in augmented reality. That's an achievement itself. On top of that, you're able to map virtual objects onto different joints too. Amazing, Sharingan, and visual effects!

Next, you'll learn to calculate distances between joints to create an app that simulates a personal coach to count your exercise repetition!

# Calculating Distances Between Joints

One of the tedious activities an athlete does at the gym by himself/herself is to count the exercise's repetition. If only it's possible to delegate this task off to a person or a machine, that'll free up the mind to focus on the repetition quality. In this section, you'll learn to implement a repetition counter for shoulder raises.

To keep track of the current stage of a shoulder raise, add the following value type to `ViewController`:

```
enum ShoulderRaiseStage: String {
   case raised, finished
}
```

For the shoulder raise, there will be two states. For exercises that evolve more than point A to B, like point A to B to C, you can add more states accordingly and handle them accordingly.

Now, you'll add a repetition counter and exercise stage tracker. In addition, you'll add a property that dictates the maximum y-distance margin between the left/right hand and the left/right shoulder.

Add the following properties to `ViewController`:

```
// 1
private var repetition = 0 {
   didSet {
      repetitionLabel.text = "Repetition: \(repetition)"
   }
}
// 2
private var shoulderRaiseStage: ShoulderRaiseStage =
.finished {
   didSet {
      shoulderRaiseStageLabel.text = "Should Raise Stage:
      \(shoulderRaiseStage.rawValue.capitalized)"
   }
}
// 3
private let maximumYDistanceMargin: Float = 0.05
```

Here's what you've done with the code:

1.  Start the repetition at 0. Upon updating the repetition, you'll update the repetition label's text to the latest value.

2.  The initial shoulder raise stage is finished. Similar to the previous property, you'll use `didSet` to observe changes on the property and update the shoulder raise stage label's text.

3.  The biggest difference in distance between the shoulder and the hand is 0.05 m for repetition to count. This means that a person will have to raise their hand almost at shoulder height for repetition to count—nothing but full repetition on the exercise!

Now, you'll implement the logic to make all these things work together. In session(_:didUpdate:), replace // TODO with the following code:

```
// 1
guard
    let lhsUpperDifference = yDifferenceBetweenJoints(
        .leftShoulder, .leftHand, relativeToBodyAnchor:
        bodyAnchor),
    let rhsUpperDifference = yDifferenceBetweenJoints(
        .rightShoulder, .rightHand, relativeToBodyAnchor:
        bodyAnchor),
    let lhsLowerDifference = yDifferenceBetweenJoints(
        .root, .leftHand, relativeToBodyAnchor: bodyAnchor),
    let rhsLowerDifference = yDifferenceBetweenJoints(
        .root, .rightHand, relativeToBodyAnchor: bodyAnchor)
else { continue }
// 2
if shoulderRaiseStage == .finished,
    lhsUpperDifference <= maximumYDistanceMargin,
    rhsUpperDifference <= maximumYDistanceMargin {
    shoulderRaiseStage = .raised
    // 3
} else if shoulderRaiseStage == .raised,
        lhsLowerDifference <= maximumYDistanceMargin,
        rhsLowerDifference <= maximumYDistanceMargin {
    shoulderRaiseStage = .finished
    repetition += 1
}
```

Here's a breakdown of the code:

1. The shoulder raise exercise will have to be done simultaneously using both arms. And the distance between the shoulder and the hand of each side must respect the maximum distance margin allowed.

2. The shoulder raise exercise will have to be done simultaneously using both arms on the way up. And the distance between the shoulder and the hand of each side must respect the maximum distance margin allowed. If these two requirements are met when the shoulder raise stage is finished, update the shoulder raise stage to `raised`. Congratulation, you've reached the top of the repetition.

3. The shoulder raise exercise will have to be done simultaneously using both arms on the way down. And the distance between the shoulder and the hand of each side must respect the maximum distance margin allowed. If these two requirements are met when the shoulder raise stage is at `raised`, update the shoulder raise stage to `finished` and increment the repetition count. Congratulation, you've completed the full range of motion of a repetition!

Build and run.

Making a shoulder raise count looks something like this.

Should Raise Stage: Raised                                    Repetition: 11

At rest, it looks something like this.

A repetition that doesn't count and looks something like this.

And one handed rep doesn't count and looks something like this.

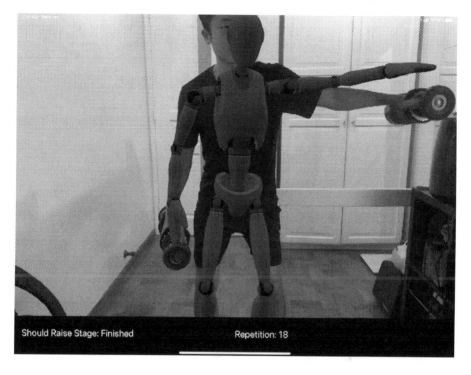

Yes, you can use water bottles as weights.

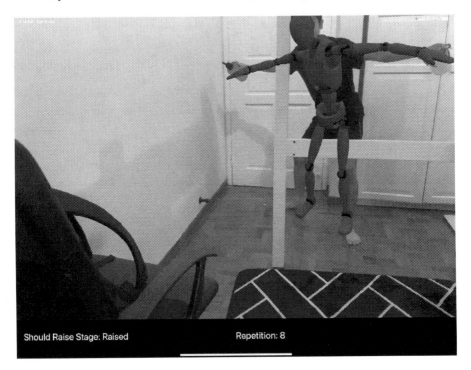

Should Raise Stage: Raised                          Repetition: 8

Awesome! You've created an augmented reality app that automates the counting of shoulder raises. This is my second favorite shoulder exercise behind the shoulder press. You can solidify your understanding by creating a counter for that exercise as well.

# Where to Go from Here?

You've learned how to capture a person's body motion in real time. Also, you've integrated the body motion capture feature with a rigged model. And you've learned how to decipher a skeleton in code using lower-level APIs to spot various joints and place objects relative to them.

Using what you've learned, you can definitely create some exciting apps that can recognize and analyze activities. Plus, you can even create apps that interact with virtual objects from body motion.

# CHAPTER 22

# People Occlusion

People occlusion is the effect of hiding virtual content when accounting for the relative distance between physical human and virtual content. When a person stands in front of virtual content, he/she should hide the parts of the content which he/she covers. When the same person stands behind the virtual content, the virtual content should conceal the human's parts that the virtual content covers. That's the gist of people occlusion.

People occlusion adds realism to an augmented reality experience. Thus, it also greatly enhances user engagement. When people in a frame play an essential role in your app, which inevitably will with the Apple AR Glass when you take it with you everywhere, people occlusion is vital for the realism and natural integration of virtual content onto the physical world.

First introduced in ARKit 3 along with iOS 13, people occlusion is made possible for devices running on Apple A12 and later devices. The illusion effect is achieved, thanks to advances in machine learning and understanding of depth in real time. In this chapter, you'll learn about the following people occlusion topics:

- Understanding the inner workings of people occlusion

- Understanding pixel buffers

- People occlusion features

- The places where people occlusion shines in ARKit

- Configuring RealityKit for people occlusion

© Jayven Nhan 2022
J. Nhan, *Mastering ARKit*, https://doi.org/10.1007/978-1-4842-7836-9_22

- Implementing people occlusion with RealityKit

- Setting frame semantics for person segmentation with depth

- Toggling people occlusion for performance

By the end of this chapter, you'll have an app that adds realism when people are involved with people occlusion effect.

# Under the Hood of People Occlusion

If you take a step back and think about how occlusion works in real life, it's simply about what's in the way of your view. That's occlusion. In the context of people occlusion, you have a device with a camera that recognizes depth from images or camera frames.

Using camera frames, ARKit deciphers each frame into individual depth frames with visual-inertial odometry and machine learning applications.

You have ARKit that's capable of understanding depth from images. In a practical example, imagine you have an augmented reality app. You detect a horizontal plane with ARKit. On the detected horizontal plane, you place a virtual model of Apple Park. This virtual Apple Park model is a rendered frame. Not real.

Within an image frame recorded by ARKit (ARFrame), there are pixels. Within each pixel, there are pixel buffers. The pixel buffers consist of depth, segmentation, and people buffers. You use depth to detect planes. In people occlusion, it gives you the depth of the person. However, people occlusion is made possible with the latter two pixel buffers' inclusion— segmentation and people buffers.

Segmentation buffer helps ARKit decide where a pixel part of a person is within an image frame. Keep in mind that the segmentation and depth buffers are generated from only the image frame; this is an impressive feat!

The people buffers are what you see on an image frame from the first two introduced buffers. From detecting the edges of a person entity, the neural network isn't able to catch all the pixels on magnification. In other words, the edges look pixelated when zoomed in. So Apple introduced an additional process, applying matting.

A matted person entity has smooth edges as a result of the matting solution. The key players here are the segmentation buffer that detects the edges of a person. Using a person's edge, ARKit outlines the person first. Then from the image of the person, finish off the edges using the actual image frame. The matting process begins with an outline of a person with the help of the neuro-engine. Then, using the outline of a person, compare with the original image, and fill in the details. As a result, you have a matted person entity.

With a matted person entity, you have successfully extract different people from an image frame. In combination with the depth data, you have a natural-looking blend of the virtual content with people. At this point, virtual and people layer on top of each other as if everything is physical.

# Knowing People Occlusion Features

When using any technology, it's vital to know how far you can stretch the technology to understand the boundaries of what can and cannot be done. From this, you can deduce the places where technology shines. Now, you'll look at the three key people occlusion considerations.

First, people occlusion is more optimally built for indoor environments. Second, ARKit recognizes and can occlude your hands and feet without the entire person on the image frame.

Third, people occlusion works with multiple people on an image frame.

Fourth, start off on the happy path with RealityKit. You get great performance benefits and more built-in features than the alternative solutions right out of the box. SceneKit integrates with people occlusion, but the technology not built from the ground up for AR isn't optimized specifically for AR. You can create and tailor your renderer with Metal for graphics-intensive applications, but a lot can go wrong, and maintenance is a must. So pick your weapon for your battle.

With these considerations in mind, you can better work backward from a problem and find a solution that's fitting. If you want an AR app to adopt people occlusion with transparent objects in an outdoor environment using SceneKit, you may want to reconsider your options. But if you are building for an indoor environment with other requirements holding true, then you may want to proceed with rebuilding the app using RealityKit for the optimal user experience.

Now, you know what's possible with people occlusion and the places where the technology shines. Next, you're going to build!

# Configuring RealityKit for People Occlusion

Since RealityKit is built for AR apps from the ground up, it's recommended to default your app production in RealityKit. Using RealityKit instead of perhaps SceneKit, you'll also get the augmented reality optimal performance, thanks to the framework optimization. For example, Apple mentioned that rendering transparent objects with people may not work well in SceneKit due to postprocessing of the image composition. In contrast, RealityKit has a deep integration of composition processing built-in. That's the reason for choosing RealityKit with people occlusion.

Open the **starter project**. Open **ViewController**. Add the following property to ViewController:

```
private let worldTrackingConfiguration:
ARWorldTrackingConfiguration = {
   let worldTrackingConfiguration = ARWorldTracking
   Configuration()
```

```
worldTrackingConfiguration.planeDetection = [.horizontal]
    return worldTrackingConfiguration
}()
```

The configuration you run is a world tracking configuration. However, you will need to toggle the frame semantics configuration to retrieve the information with people segmentation.

Now, call the following method in resetTrackingConfiguration():

```
arView.session.run(
    worldTrackingConfiguration,
    options: [.removeExistingAnchors])
```

Every time the view appears, the ARView will run the world tracking configuration and reset any existing anchors. As you can see here, the world tracking configuration doesn't include anything related to people occlusion because this isn't the place to configure it. Your world tracking configuration will standardize to the tracking settings of your desire. Your people occlusion settings come when dealing with frame semantics.

# Setting Frame Semantics for Person Segmentation with Depth

Each frame provides you with semantics. Semantics are information about the frame. On a default world tracking configuration, you set frame semantics to require ARKit to provide additional frame information. With additional processing, it will require more power from your device. Hence, choose what you need and when you need it. Afterward, turn off what you don't need—more on this later.

In **ViewController**, add the following method to ViewController:

```
private func setupWorldTrackingConfiguration() {
  // 1
  let frameSemantics: ARConfiguration.FrameSemantics =
  [.personSegmentationWithDepth]
  // 2
  guard  ARWorldTrackingConfiguration.supportsFrameSemantics
  (frameSemantics)
   else {
     fatalError("Device isn't able to support \
     (frameSemantics)")
  }
  // 3
  worldTrackingConfiguration.frameSemantics = frameSemantics
}
```

Here's the code breakdown:

1. Person segmentation and depth semantics occlude virtual content when a person is standing in front of it. This is what you want for people occlusion in general.

2. Ensures that the device supports the frame semantics that you want to run. Otherwise, throw a fatalError.

3. Set the frame semantics of the world tracking configuration to the semantics you defined earlier.

In viewDidLoad(), call the following method:

```
setupWorldTrackingConfiguration()
```

Now, you have a world tracking configuration with person segmentation and depth semantics every time the view loads.

Before you can see occlusion in action, you'll need to add virtual content. To achieve that, add the following method to ViewController:

```
@objc func didTapARView(_ sender: UITapGestureRecognizer) {
    let tapLocation = sender.location(in: arView)
    let raycastResults = arView.raycast(
        from: tapLocation,
        allowing: .estimatedPlane,
        alignment: .horizontal)
    guard let firstRaycastResult = raycastResults.first else {
    return }
    let anchor = ARAnchor(name: anchorName,
                          transform: firstRaycastResult.
                          worldTransform)
    arView.session.add(anchor: anchor)
}
```

This method will take care of adding an anchor named anchorName with transform derived from the first raycast result's world transform from the user's tap gesture recognition.

Now, add the following method to ViewController:

```
private func registerTapGestureRecognizer() {
    let tapGesture = UITapGestureRecognizer(
        target: self, action: #selector(didTapARView(_:)))
    arView.addGestureRecognizer(tapGesture)
}
```

This method register a tap gesture recognizer which calls didTapARView(_:) when triggered.

To register the ARView with the tap gesture recognizer, call the following method in viewDidLoad():

```
registerTapGestureRecognizer()
```

441

Next, you'll handle loading a RealityKit scene onto the ARView after your tap gesture recognition triggers the anchor addition. Add the following code to the ARSessionDelegate extension block:

```
func session(_ session: ARSession, didAdd anchors:
[ARAnchor]) {
    for anchor in anchors {
        guard anchor.name == anchorName else { return }
        Avatar.loadAluminumAsync() { [weak self] result in
            switch result {
            case .success(let aluminum):
                self?.arView.scene.anchors.append(aluminum)
            case .failure(let error):
                print("Error:", error.localizedDescription)
            }
        }
    }
}
```

Here, you load a scene from the Avatar RealityKit project named **aluminum** asynchronously. You do this whenever an anchor name matches from the one that gets added by your tap gesture.

Build and run.

Place your hand behind the virtual content.

Place your hand in front of the virtual content.

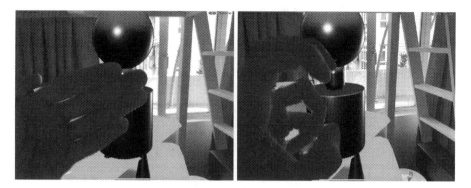

If you use a LiDAR camera, the occlusion will work more magically! Welcome to snappy world and instantaneity.

# Turning Off People Occlusion for Performance

If you think about the amount of processing a device does for people occlusion, it's remarkable. With a big Neural Engine brain and high-fidelity camera frames, Apple can create advance augmented reality features like people occlusion. This happens 60–120 frames per second on Apple mobile devices in 2020. The features are remarkable, but the energy consumption from frame processing is a crucial consideration for a performant app.

Frame semantics don't come for free. Hence, it would be best if you considered what's deliberately needed and when it's needed. You've learned how to set frame semantics. Now, you'll learn how you can pick and choose which frame semantic to insert and remove.

In addition to setting multiple frame semantics at once, you can also insert and remove specific frame semantic into the world tracking configuration.

Open **Main.storyboard**. In the document outline, select **Switch**. Set the switch's **hidden** property to **unchecked**.

Open **ViewController**. Add the following code to switchValueDidChange(_:):

```
if sender.isOn {
  worldTrackingConfiguration.frameSemantics.remove(
      .personSegmentationWithDepth)
} else {
  worldTrackingConfiguration.frameSemantics.insert(
      .personSegmentationWithDepth)
}
arView.session.run(worldTrackingConfiguration)
```

Here, the switch's isOn property dictates the insert/remove person segmentation with depth frame semantic from the world tracking configuration running on the ARView. After updating the world tracking configuration, you rerun the ARSession with the world tracking configuration to see the latest frame semantics changes in effect.

You add what you need. Afterward, turn off what you don't need to mitigate unnecessary memory allocation, optimize frame rate performance, decrease thermal heating, reduce battery drain, etc. Overall, happy users with a user-centric implementation.

Build and run. Now, you should be able to control the on/off state of the occlusion effect using the switch. More power to performance!

# Where to Go from Here?

Augmented reality is a technology that bridges the virtual and physical worlds. When people occlusion is combined with apps like an exercise app tracks the human body, the illusion of hiding part of the virtual/physical content is vital for realism. All these little things add to the whole package of a well-designed app that feels real and engaging.

If you are interested in learning more about people occlusion, I encourage you to play around with the various frame semantics and discover the various achievable feats. For example, you can explore person segmentation without depth where a person always occludes virtual content despite relative positioning. The world is your oyster.

Hope you've enjoyed learning about people occlusion in this chapter. In the next chapter, you'll learn about AR Quick Look to make your AR universally content accessible on Apple's platforms.

# CHAPTER 23

# Create System-Wide Accessible AR Content: Quick Look with USDZ

What if you can allow your users to preview your AR content without downloading your app? And what if your users can preview AR content directly from the Web? With the Quick Look framework, these features are available.

Quick Look is first introduced in iOS 4 and isn't a new technology. However, Quick Look has advanced year after year and adding new capabilities with each iteration of the framework. Quick Look allows users to preview various common file types inside your app and other apps such as Mail, Notes, File, Safari, and more. Some file types that Quick Look can preview right out of the box include:

- Images
- Live Photos
- Audio files
- Video files

© Jayven Nhan 2022
J. Nhan, *Mastering ARKit*, https://doi.org/10.1007/978-1-4842-7836-9_23

- Text files

- .docx

- PDFs

- USDZ

Each operating system release may support a different set of file types. Some file types may be deprecated, and other file types get added. When a file type isn't supported, you can create an extension to present your custom file format with system-wide support on iOS.

Now, you'll look at some of the places where you can explore and find Quick Look in action.

Here's a video sent to the Mail app.

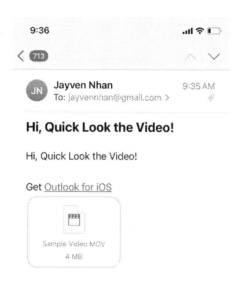

You can see that Quick Look generates a thumbnail for the supported file type. As mentioned earlier, if you were to send a custom file type, you can create an extension to support it too. Then, a tap on the thumbnail presents the following.

In this preview, you can play the video, scroll through the video, and even share the video.

Or perhaps you find yourself often taking screenshots. Here's a screen of the Notes app opened.

Then, taking a screenshot or multiple screenshots presents a floating thumbnail preview on the device. Upon tapping on the thumbnail, you are presented with an editor to create markups, crop images, share images, etc.

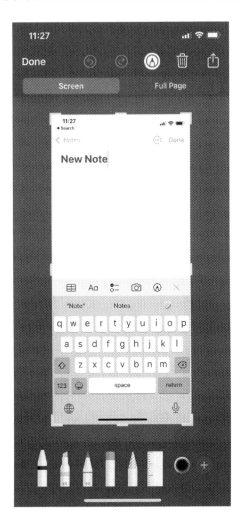

Do note that Quick Look previews are very simple in nature. As the framework name suggests, it's supposed to be quick in getting to the content.

Similarly, you can preview AR content quickly. You know you can do this when you see an AR badge on the top-right corner of a thumbnail. Like on the following Quick Look gallery, where Apple showcases some of their AR content, you can see the badge on the top-right corner of the thumbnail:

```
https://developer.apple.com/augmented-reality/quick-look/
```

Open the site on your iOS device. Tap on the thumbnail with the AR badge. Then, you'll be brought straight into the AR object viewer.

From a system-wide location like a website/app, you can launch straight into an AR viewer.

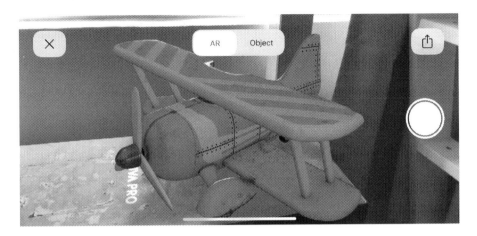

Within this Quick Look browser and by selecting the object option, you can inspect the 3D content in a virtual space without the real world as the backdrop.

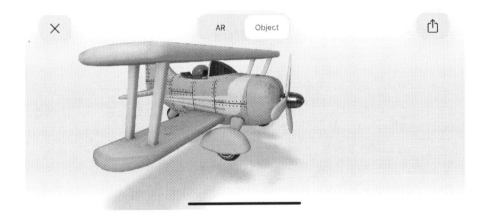

Evidently, users will have a lesser immersion experience, lose sight of the real-world content scale, etc.

In this chapter, you'll build out an app that utilizes Quick Look and USDZ. By building this app, you'll gain a more robust understanding of the mechanics behind Quick Look and USDZ. The chapter covers the following topics:

- Building Quick Look into an iOS app

- Conforming to QLPreviewControllerDataSource

- Creating ARQuickLookPreviewItem to obtain AR specific features

- Universal Zoom Animation with QLPreviewControllerDelegate

- Setting the QLPreviewController Delegates

- Determining AR Quick Look canonical web page

- Forcing Content Size to Origin in Preview

Quick Look and USDZ are a massive step-up to creating accessible AR content, especially for retails that have reported four times to increase in sales due to funneling immersive Quick Look content into their customers' devices. Particularly for retails and during a pandemic, you can literally bring the products from your store to your customers' home.

I know you're just as excited as I am! Without further ado, it's time to dive in.

# Getting Started

Open the **starter project**.

In this section, you'll add the controller that's the presenter of your Quick Look item, `QLPreviewController`. Built on top of a

`UIViewController`, `QLPreviewController` contains built-in features to present Quick Look item with a consistent experience system-wide. To have Quick Look in your app, you'll need to

1.  Initialize `QLPreviewController`

2.  Set the number of Quick Look items to present

3.  Tell `QLPreviewController` which item to present

These are the fundamental building blocks that will get Quick Look up and going. There will be more advanced topics that you'll touch on, and even those more specific to AR Quick Look as the chapter progresses.

To begin, add the following property to `ViewController`:

```
private let quickLookPreviewController = QLPreviewController()
```

You've initialized a `QLPreviewController` inside of `ViewController`. Next, add the following code to `previewARContentButtonDidTap(_:)`:

```
present(quickLookPreviewController, animated: true,
completion: nil)
```

Here, tapping on the **Preview AR Content** button will present **QLPreviewController**.

Great. Now that you have a Quick Look preview controller, it's time to feed it data.

# Conforming to QLPreviewControllerDataSource

You use `QLPreviewControllerDataSource` to feed `QLPreviewController` information.

Conform `ViewController` to `QLPreviewControllerDataSource` with the following block of code:

```
// MARK: - QLPreviewControllerDataSource
extension ViewController: QLPreviewControllerDataSource {
    // 1
  func numberOfPreviewItems(in controller:
  QLPreviewController) -> Int {
    return 1
  }
    // 2
  func previewController(_ controller: QLPreviewController,
  previewItemAt
   index: Int) -> QLPreviewItem {
    let resourceName = "gramophone"
    let resourceExtension = "usdz"
        // 3
    guard let previewItemURL = Bundle.main.url(
          forResource: resourceName,
          withExtension: resourceExtension) else {
      fatalError("Unable to locate \(resourceName).
      \(resourceExtension)")
    }
        // 4
     return previewItemURL as QLPreviewItem
  }
}
```

Here's the code breakdown:

1.  Set the number of items to preview in the Quick
    Look preview controller. You would set this number
    to one for your AR content because you're going to
    present a single AR content file.

2.  Decide which content to show. You can use `index`
    to iterate through a list of content. However, since
    there's a singular virtual content to display, it makes
    sense to directly and always show the same content
    which is the gramophone.

3.  Safely unwrap the preview item URL within the
    project's directory, given the resource name and
    extension.

4.  Cast and return the expected generic object type,
    `QLPreviewItem`.

Inside `setupQuickLookPreviewController()`, add the following code:

```
quickLookPreviewController.dataSource = self
```

Here, you set `ViewController` to provide the data source for
`QLPreviewController`.

Build and run.

9:23

Preview AR Content

Tap the **Preview AR Content** button.

There you go! You can explore and see all the built-in features into AR
Quick Look mentioned earlier in the chapter.

Selecting using object mode, your users can also preview the item in a contained virtual 3D space as well.

In the next section, you'll look into implementing an animation feature that makes the feel of AR Quick Look consistent across the board.

# Universal Zoom Animation with QLPreviewControllerDelegate

If you notice the current transition, it doesn't represent those that you'll find in apps such as File. It's not exactly the native Quick Look preview controller transition experience that users expect. Instead of the standard modal transition, you'll find that Quick Look items transition with a specific zoom animation, especially when opened from a list of items. This is the feature to implement next.

Open **ViewController**. Conform ViewController to QLPreviewControllerDelegate with the following block of code:

```
// MARK: - QLPreviewControllerDelegate
extension ViewController: QLPreviewControllerDelegate {
    func previewController(_ controller: QLPreviewController,
    transitionViewFor
      item: QLPreviewItem) -> UIView? {
        return stackView
    }
}
```

Before QLPreviewController invokes, previewController(_:transitionViewFor:) gets called. Here, you declare the stackView as the view to provide the zoom transition from and to as you open and close Quick Look preview controller, respectively. If you are using a collection view, you can choose the specific collection view cell.

Inside setupQuickLookPreviewController(), add the following code:

```
quickLookPreviewController.delegate = self
```

Here, you set ViewController to be the delegate for QLPreviewController. Build and run.

Tap the **Preview AR Content** button.

Notice that the transition is not the modal transition. Instead, it's the familiar and system-wide Quick Look zoom transition coming into effect!

As recommended by Apple, it's best to create a universal experience where possible and appropriate for a fantastic user experience.

Next, you're going to look at two helpful configurations that you may find helpful to customize your AR Quick Look preview item.

# Determining AR Quick Look Canonical Web Page

For devices running on iOS 13 and later, developers and users have the ability to utilize ARQuickLookPreviewItem. ARQuickLookPreviewItem is built on top of QLPreviewItem. On top of the existing features from QLPreviewItem, you get some features only specific to AR. The first ARQuickLookPreviewItem exclusive feature is setting a canonical web page. A canonical web page allows you to set the content sharing link. Typically, as the name suggests, a canonical web page allows the users to track the origin URL of the virtual content.

Open **ViewController**. In previewController(_:previewItemAt:), replace the following:

```
return previewItemURL as QLPreviewItem
```

With the following:

```
// 1
let previewItem = ARQuickLookPreviewItem(fileAt: previewItemURL)
// 2
guard #available(iOS 13.0, *) else {
    return previewItem as QLPreviewItem
}
```

```
// 3
guard let canonicalWebPageURL = URL(string: "https://www.
appcoda.com") else {
    fatalError("Unable to construct canonical web page URL.")
}
// 4
previewItem.canonicalWebPageURL = canonicalWebPageURL
return previewItem
```

Here's the code breakdown:

1.  Initialize an ARQuickLookPreviewItem using the
    preview item URL declared earlier.

2.  Using version conditional guard statement, only
    proceed further if the user runs on iOS 13 or
    above. Otherwise, return the preview item as a
    QLPreviewItem for devices below iOS 13.

3.  Safely unwrap the canonical web page URL.

4.  Set the canonical web page URL on the AR Quick
    Look preview item. You can do this only on devices
    running iOS 13 and above. An earlier guard
    statement ensures that to be true.

Build and run.

In the Quick Look preview controller, tapping the **share** button will let you see the canonical web page URL as the sharing link instead of the USDZ file.

At this point, users can copy the link, share directly onto Notes, messaging platforms, AirDrop, etc.

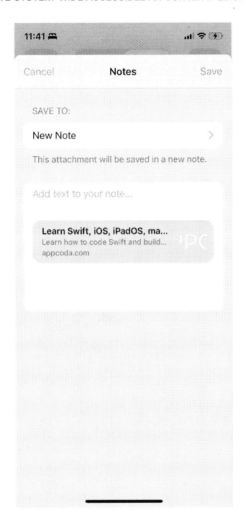

Next, you'll take a look at another AR Quick Look preview item exclusive feature.

# Forcing Content Size to Origin in Preview

There will be times where you don't want the users to scale the virtual content. In those scenarios, you'll want to disable content scaling. For example, when showing furniture like a refrigerator in the customer's home, you'll want the users to see the item in the real environment as true to scale. In addition, for branding purposes, you may want to present a product a certain way consistently from the retail world all the way to the virtual world. Fortunately, this feature is possible and can be easily implemented with ARQuickLookPreviewItem.

Below the following code:

```
previewItem.canonicalWebPageURL = canonicalWebPageURL
```

Add the following code:

```
previewItem.allowsContentScaling = false
```

Simply setting the allowsContentScaling to false will disable content scaling. Again, this feature is possible for devices running iOS 13 and above using ARQuickLookPreviewItem. You've placed a guard statement to check that earlier.

Build and run.

Now, whenever the user pinches to scale the virtual content up or down, the virtual content will resist the size change and always bounce back to 100%. This is possible because you're using ARQuickLookPreviewItem.

# Where to Go from Here?

Quick Look allows users to have a consistent AR experience system-wide on Apple platforms. Depending on the specification and depth of custom AR integration you want, it may actually be an amazing idea to implement AR Quick Look instead of almost building everything from the ground up by yourself using the ARKit framework. By using AR Quick Look, you can leverage a system-wide experience and many built-in AR features. AR Quick Look is a fast and effective way to present content in AR.

# CHAPTER 24

# Advancing AR Quick Look for Commerce on the Web

Oh iOS developers, today you're going to advance AR Quick Look on the Web. AR Quick Look is a system-wide AR content preview framework, and it's definitely not limited to just your app. Particularly with websites that want to leverage AR content in commerce, your iOS device can leverage some magic.

Here's a quote from Bang & Olufsen's Customer Experience Senior Manager, Jakob Kristoffersen:

> Users who engage with the AR experience in our iOS
> app or on the website are 4X more likely to seek out
> our Store Finder to visit B&O store and has aided
> our sales effort to great extents.

Early adopters of AR in commerce have an advantage in that the company offering the products oozes out innovation juice. In addition, the company allows customers to see products at their place (like home). It's like letting the customers visualize products at their home. Because customers can see it at their home, they are more likely to purchase something that fits.

© Jayven Nhan 2022
J. Nhan, *Mastering ARKit*, https://doi.org/10.1007/978-1-4842-7836-9_24

For AR Quick Look to work with Apple Pay, you'll need a device running iOS 13.3 or later. Apple Pay allows users to make purchases conveniently from their devices. As Amazon touted in the past, fewer steps equal easier purchasing, which equals more sales.

In this chapter, you'll learn about the following AR Quick Look in web topics:

- Creating a website for AR Quick Look

- Integrating Apply Pay to receive payments

- Creating custom action to create a more personal experience

- Using custom banner for branding

This chapter won't go into the details of web-specific technologies like HTML. Rather, it'll focus on AR Quick Look. Without further ado, it's time to dive in.

# Getting Started

Open a **text editor** like Atom, Sublime Text, or TextMate. Add the following code:

```html
html
<!DOCTYPE html>
<html>
<head>
    <title>AR Quick Look</title>
</head>
<body>
    <h1>Preview a Model in AR Quick Look</h1>
</body>
</html
```

Here, you have a simple HTML file with a web header name and a header body. Save the **file** as **ARQuickLook.html**.

Open **ARWeb.html**. Opened in Safari, here's what you'll see.

### Preview a Model in AR Quick Look

Great! Next, you'll add the quick look buttons in the website.

# ARQuickLook Buttons

ARQuickLook buttons are standardized buttons with the ARKit logo. You can find this in recent places, such as previewing the Pro Display XDR.

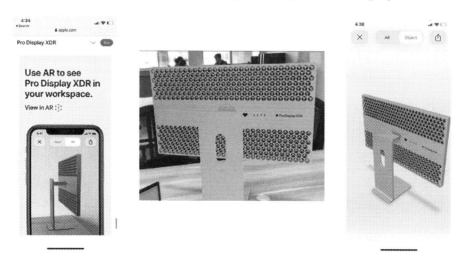

Add the following code below the `<h1>` tag:

```
<a href="gramophone.usdz" rel="ar">
    <img src="gramophone.png" width=160 height=160>
</a>
```

Inside the hyperlink tag, the most important thing to note here is `rel="ar"`. The relationship tag specifies `gramophone.usdz` as `ar`. After the hyperlink tag, you've added an image which sources from `gramophone.png` with a width and height of 160.

Your HTML file should now look like this:

```
<!DOCTYPE html>
<html>
<head>
    <title>AR Quick Look</title>
</head>
<body>
    <h1>Preview a Model in AR Quick Look</h1>
    <a href="gramophone.usdz" rel="ar">
        <img src="gramophone.png" width=160 height=160>
    </a>
</body>
</html>
```

You can find more of Apple's USDZ models at

`https://developer.apple.com/augmented-reality/quick-look/`.

Open the **HTML** file in a web browser. And you should be able to see the following.

**Preview a Model in AR Quick Look**

Next, you'll learn how to deploy your website with GitHub Pages.

# Deploying Website with GitHub Pages

GitHub Pages are websites for showcasing your projects. Typically, GitHub Pages consist of an accumulation of your GitHub work. As a matter of fact, you can leverage GitHub Pages to display your augmented reality artistry.

Wow, I'm excited. To begin, open **www.github.com**. Create a GitHub profile if you've yet to create one. In the top-right corner, click the + button. Then, click the **New repository** button.

Now, name your GitHub repository with the following convention:

username.github.io

It will look like this.

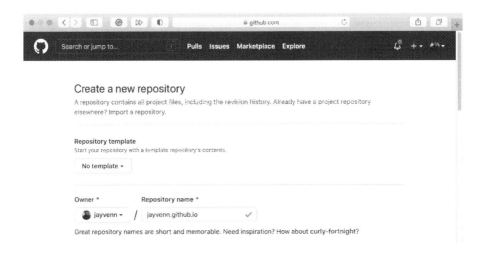

Scroll down to the bottom of the page; create **Create repository**.

Afterward, look to the top-right corner. Click your **profile**. Then, select **Settings** from the drop-down menu.

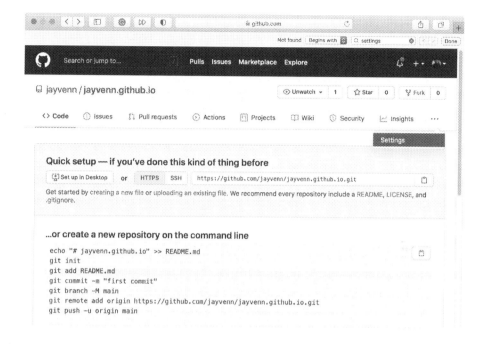

Here's the Settings page.

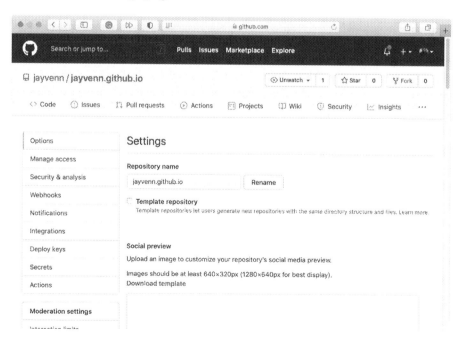

Scroll down to the GitHub Pages section.

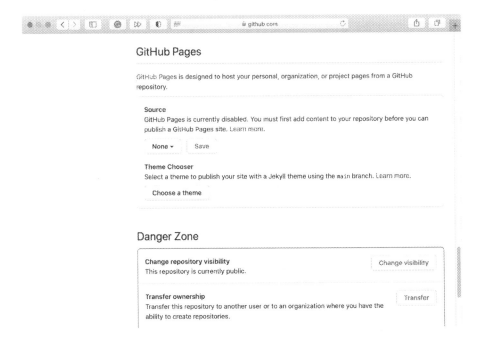

Click **Select theme** to choose your theme.

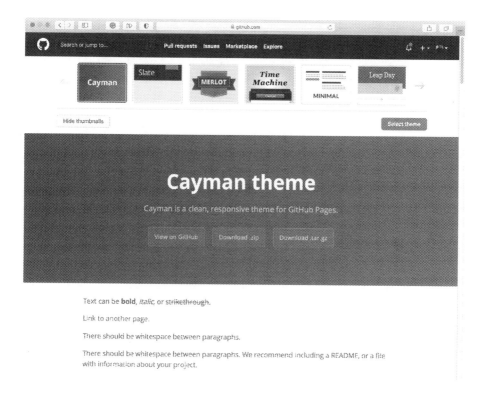

Replace the markdown file with the following:

```
## AR Showcase
```

```
[QuickLook](ARQuickLook.html)
```

So it'll look like this.

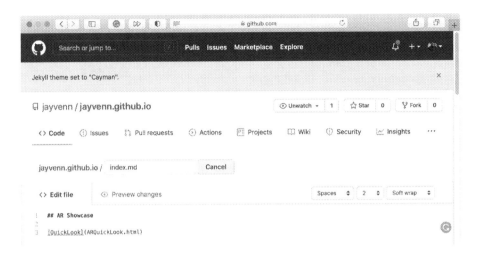

Now, scroll down and **commit** the changes.

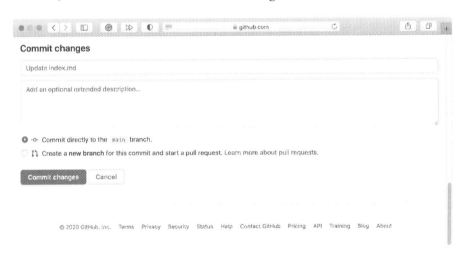

Next, you'll upload the website and its resources you created locally onto your website.

# Uploading Resources to GitHub Pages

Click **Code** to open the repository's main page.

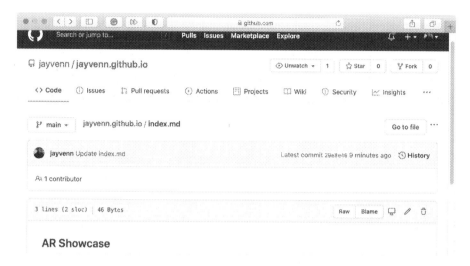

Next, click **Add file** drop-down menu. Click **Upload files**.

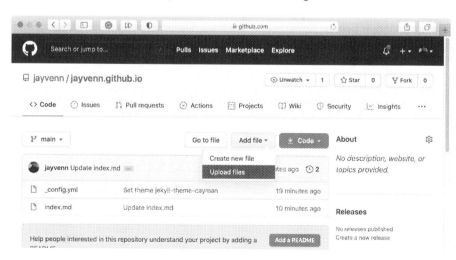

Select the USDZ, thumbnail, and HTML **files**.

Once the files have completed uploaded, click **Commit changes**.

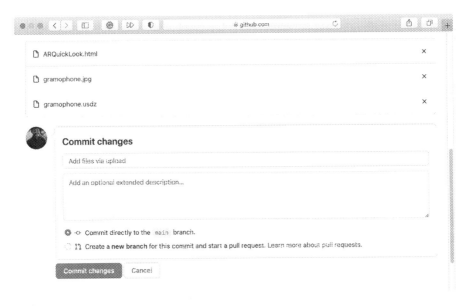

GitHub will process your newly added files. Now, on your iOS or iPadOS device with an A12 chip or later, open your deployed website. Click **QuickLook** to see the framework in action from the next page.

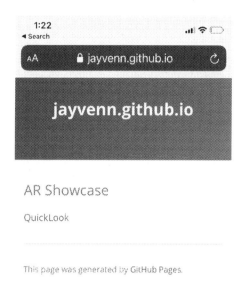

On the QuickLook page, you'll see a gramophone image with an ARKit badge, thanks to the AR relationship tag you've set earlier.

Tap on the gramophone. And you can preview the gramophone model in AR.

You can see a lot of built-in features in ARQuickLook such as plane detection, lighting, shadow, and environment texturing, to name a few. ARQuickLook creates a universal platform experience for iOS and iPadOS users.

But there's more, especially with commerce integration.

# Making a Merchant ID for Apple Pay with Web

Apple Pay integration on the Web requires a number of prerequisites. It's not straightforward, like add a button with an Apple Pay tag and call it a day. To begin, you'll handle the noncoding logistics side of Apple Pay. In this section, you'll walk through the process of creating a merchant identifier. The merchant identifier specifies who the merchant is. You can use the merchant identifier interchangeably between native and web apps, and it never expires.

First, log in to your developer account.

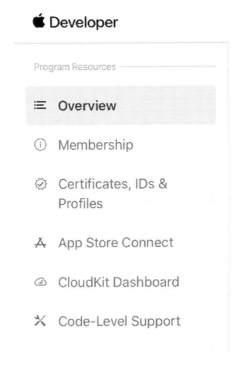

Second, under the program resources section, select **Certificates, IDs & Profiles**.

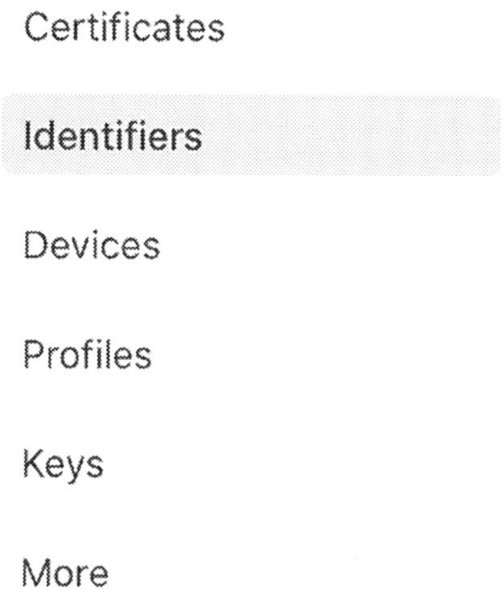

Certificates

Identifiers

Devices

Profiles

Keys

More

Third, click **Identifiers** and click the + button.

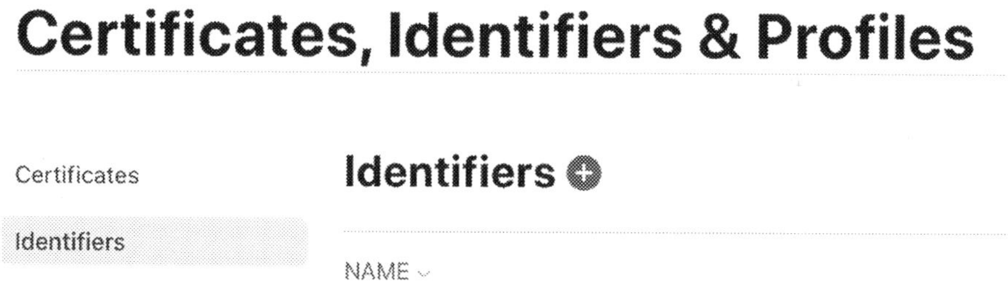

# Certificates, Identifiers & Profiles

Certificates

Identifiers

## Identifiers ⊕

NAME ⌄

Fourth, select **Merchant IDs** and click **Continue**.

### Certificates, Identifiers & Profiles

‹ All Identifiers

#### Register a new identifier

Continue

○ **App IDs**
Register an App ID to enable your app, app extensions, or App Clip to access available services and identify your app in a provisioning profile. You can enable app services when you create an App ID or modify these settings later.

○ **Services IDs**
For each website that uses Sign in with Apple, register a services identifier (Services ID), configure your domain and return URL, and create an associated private key.

○ **Pass Type IDs**
Register a pass type identifier (Pass Type ID) for each kind of pass you create (i.e. gift cards). Registering your Pass Type IDs lets you generate Apple-issued certificates which are used to digitally sign and send updates to your passes, and allow your passes to be recognized by Wallet.

○ **Website Push IDs**
Register a Website Push Identifier (Website Push ID). Registering your Website Push IDs lets you generate Apple-issued certificates which are used to digitally sign and send push notifications from your website to macOS.

○ **iCloud Containers**
Registering your iCloud Container lets you use the iCloud Storage APIs to enable your apps to store data and documents in iCloud, keeping your apps up to date automatically.

○ **App Groups**
Registering your App Group allows access to group containers that are shared among multiple related apps, and allows certain additional interprocess communication between the apps.

⦿ **Merchant IDs**
Register your Merchant Identifiers (Merchant IDs) to enable your apps to process transactions for physical goods and services to be used outside of your apps. Generate a Apple Pay Payment Processing certificate for each registered Merchant ID to validate transactions initiated within your app.

Fifth, enter the merchant ID's details. Give it a description and an identifier in the format of `merchant.com.domainname.appname`. Click **Continue**.

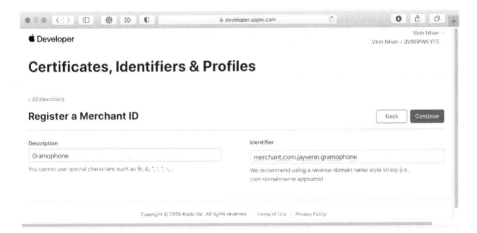

488

Sixth, click **Register** to finalize your merchant ID details.

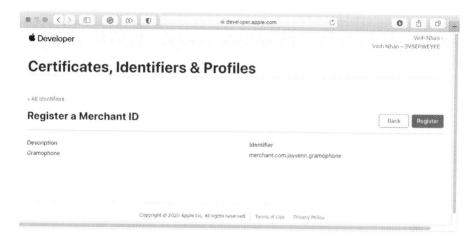

Now, you'll see something like this in your list of merchant IDs.

Great, now that you have your first piece of logistics out of the way. There are two more to go!

# Creating Your Certificate Signing Request (CSR) File

Now, you'll need to create a payment processing certificate and associate it with your merchant identifier for payment information encryption.

To create the certificate, you'll need to get a Certificate Signing Request (CSR) file from your Mac. Open **Keychain Access**.

In the upper-left corner, click Keychain Access ➤ Certificate Assistant ➤ **Request a Certificate From a Certificate Authority...**.

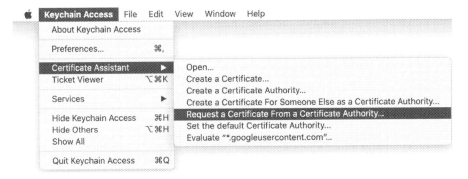

First, fill in the **User Email Address** and **CA Email Address** with your email. Second, select the **Saved to disk** option. Third, enable the **Let me specify key pair information**. Fourth, click **Continue**.

Save the **.csr** file to your computer. Click **Save**.

In the Key Pair Information page, set the algorithm to **RSA** and key size to **2048 bits**. Click **Continue**.

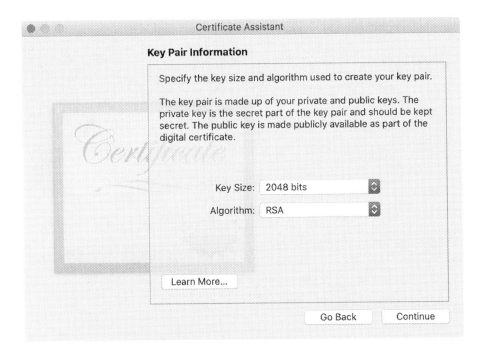

At the Conclusion page, click **Done**.

You have a CSR file generated using the RSA algorithm and with 2048 bits key size. You'll use this CSR file to create a **payment processing certificate**.

# Generating the Apple Pay Payment Processing Certificate

Open your developer account. Under the program resources section, select **Certificates, IDs & Profiles** again.

Click **Identifiers**. Click the **Merchant ID** you've created earlier.

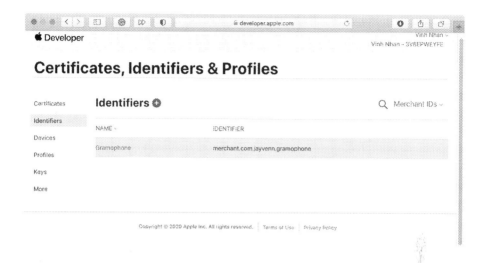

To integrate Apple Pay Payment Processing into your website, you'll need to agree to the Apple Pay Platform Web Merchant Terms and Conditions. Click **Review Agreement**.

## Certificates, Identifiers & Profiles

⚠ You must agree to these Apple Pay Platform Web Merchant Terms and Conditions in order to incorporate Apple Pay Payment Processing into your website.

Review Agreement ›

‹ All Identifiers

### Edit or Configure Merchant ID

Remove    Save

Name

Gramophone

You cannot use special characters such as @, &, *, ', ", -, .

Identifier

merchant.com.jayvenn.gramophone

### Apple Pay Payment Processing Certificate

To configure Apple Pay Payment Processing for this merchant ID, create a Payment Processing Certificate. Apple Pay Payment Processing requires this certificate to encrypt transaction data. Use the same certificate for Apple Pay Payment Processing in apps or on the web.

Create an Apple Pay Payment Processing Certificate for this Merchant ID.

Create Certificate

Agree to the **Terms and Conditions**.

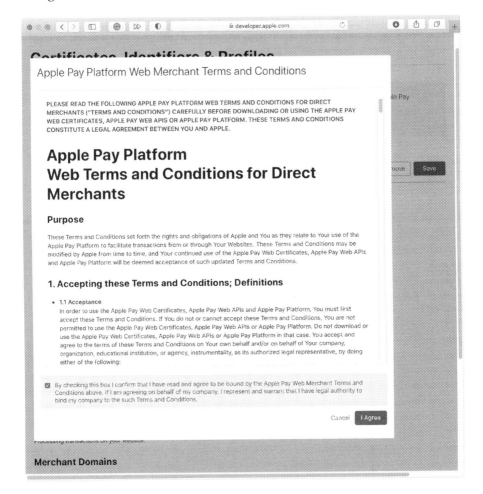

Under the Apple Pay Payment Processing Certificate section, click **Create Certificate**.

## Apple Pay Payment Processing Certificate

To configure Apple Pay Payment Processing for this merchant ID, create a Payment Processing Certificate. Apple Pay Payment Processing requires this certificate to encrypt transaction data. Use the same certificate for Apple Pay Payment Processing in apps or on the web.

Create an Apple Pay Payment Processing Certificate for this Merchant ID.

Create Certificate

Choose the **CSR** file. Click **Continue**.

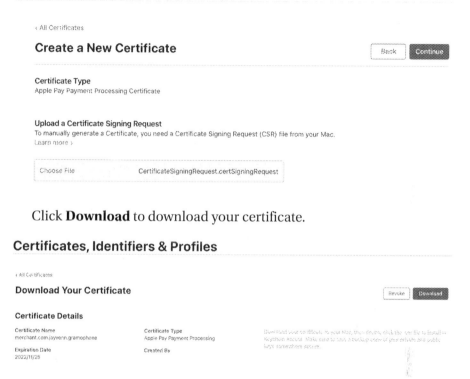

Click **Download** to download your certificate.

The downloaded certificate should be named **apply_pay.cer**.

# Registering a Merchant Domain

In Certificates, Identifiers & Profiles, select **Identifiers**. Filter the identifiers
by **Merchant IDs**. Click your **Merchant ID**.

## Certificates, Identifiers & Profiles

| Certificates | Identifiers ⊕ | | Q Merchant IDs ˅ |
|---|---|---|---|
| Identifiers | | | |
| Devices | NAME | IDENTIFIER | |
| Profiles | Gramophone | merchant.com.jayvenn.gramophone | |

Under the Merchant Domains section, click **Add Domain**.

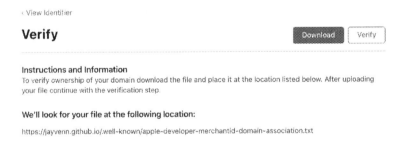

Enter your **domain**. Click **Save**.

Click **Download** to download your **Apple Developer Merchant ID Domain Association** text file.

In a new tab, open your website repository and upload the **verification text** file to your website. Then, **commit** the new changes to deploy the website.

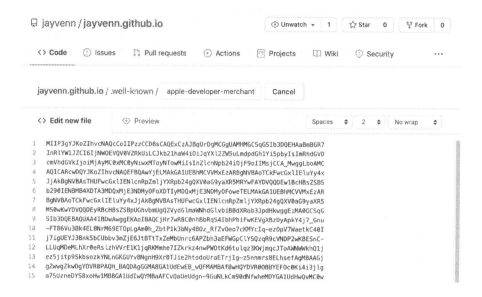

In addition to the text file, you'll need to edit **_config.yml for Apple to discover your .well-known directory. Replace the content inside the file with the following**:

```
theme: jekyll-theme-cayman
```

```
include: [".well-known"]
```

The first line of code sets the theme of your website. The second line ensures the website includes and makes the **.well-known** directory to the client system.

Now, your repository should look like this.

Open back to the **Verify** page; click **Verify**.

### Merchant Domains

Domain: jayvenn.github.io
Status: Verified
Verification Expires:  Apr 14, 2022

Add a domain for use with this Merchant ID.

Add Domain

Now, you've verified your domain.

# Creating an Apple Pay Merchant Identity Certificate

Specific to registering yourself as a merchant using Apple Pay, you'll create an Apple Pay Merchant Identity Certificate.

### Apple Pay Merchant Identity Certificate

Create an Apple Pay Merchant Identity Certificate for this Merchant ID.

Create Certificate

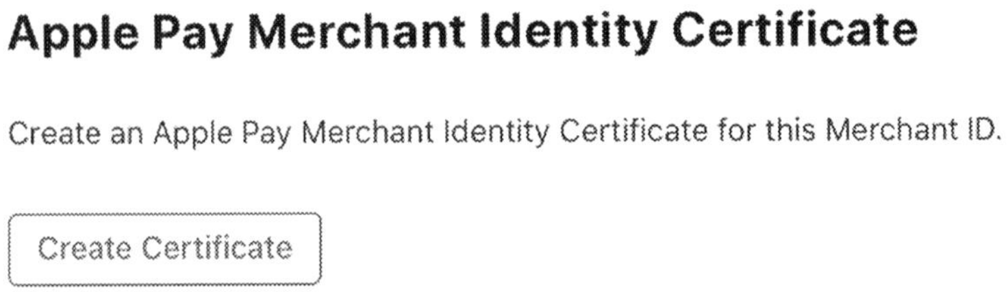

This time, you'll need an **RSA(2048)** CSR file created from **Keychain Access** as you did earlier. The only difference here is the Key Pair Information.

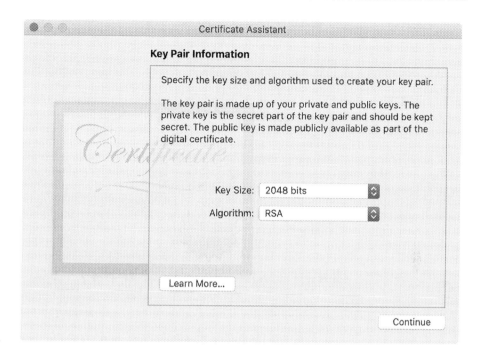

Then, upload the RSA file.

# Certificates, Identifiers & Profiles

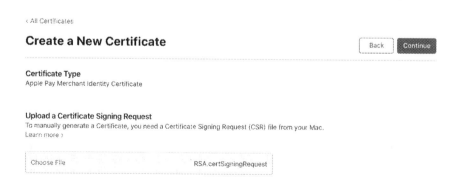

Now, download and install Apple Pay Merchant Identity file on your computer.

You probably don't need to make use of this file at the moment. But it may come in handy when you need to integrate Apple Pay on an iOS/iPadOS/macOS app.

# Commerce Integration with Apple Pay

As stated earlier in the chapter, one of the clearest industry disruptors that AR is going to have is on commerce. With AR, you can bring any product into the customer's home.

At this point, you've learned how to deploy your website into the public Internet. To make changes, you can either create clone your repository, make changes, and push it. Or you can also make changes directly to the HTML file from GitHub.com.

Open **ARQuickLook.html**. Before the closing body tag, add the following code:

```
<a rel="ar" id="ApplePay"
 href="gramophone

 .usdz#applePayButtonType=plain&checkoutTitle=Gramophone&check
 outSubtitle=Gold&
 price=$900.00">
  <img src="gramophone.jpg">
</a>
```

Hence, your HTML file should look like this:

```
<!DOCTYPE html>
<html>
<head>
   <title>AR Quick Look</title>
</head>
<body>
   <h1>Preview a Model in AR Quick Look</h1>
   <a href="gramophone.usdz" rel="ar">
     <img src="gramophone.jpg" width=320 height=320>
   </a>
   <h2>Preview a Model with Apple Pay</h2>
   <a rel="ar" id="ApplePay"
    href="gramophone

    .usdz#applePayButtonType=plain&checkoutTitle=Gramophone&
    checkoutSubtitle=Gol
    d&price=$900.00">
      <img src="gramophone.jpg">
   </a>
</body>
</html>
```

Similar to the AR button, you have the AR relationship tag. In addition, you've added an Apple Pay ID tag to indicate its role. In addition to referencing the gramophone model, you specify the Apple Pay button type, checkout title, subtitle, and price.

Commit the **changes**. Open your website in **Safari**. Tap on the **saxophone with Apple Pay** button.

You should be able to see that Apple Pay is integrated into your AR Quick Look!

There's your 900 dollars saxophone ready for sale. Woo-hoo!

# Where to Go from Here?

Now, you can sell products and get rich off of AR Quick Look. It's time for you to make money. Go ahead and make money. Cheers.

# CHAPTER 25

# Working with SwiftUI and ARKit

With the introduction of SwiftUI, iOS developers have the ability to create apps using declarative syntax. SwiftUI doesn't support ARKit in the declarative format. Nonetheless, this shouldn't stop developers from working with the latest technologies even when ARKit is built primarily for UIKit.

In this tutorial, you'll learn about the following working with SwiftUI and ARKit topics:

- Understanding the mechanism for integrating ARKit with SwiftUI

- Displaying ARView in SwiftUI

- Integrating the Coordinator architecture

- Handling delegate methods

- Integrating SwiftUI views with ARView

Without further ado, it's time to dive into the future with SwiftUI!

© Jayven Nhan 2022
J. Nhan, *Mastering ARKit*, https://doi.org/10.1007/978-1-4842-7836-9_25

# Getting Started

In this chapter, you'll build an augmented reality app in SwiftUI from the ground up.

Open **Xcode**. In the toolbar, click **File ➤ New ➤ Project...**.

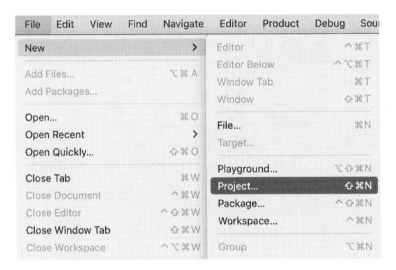

Select the **App** template. Click **Next**.

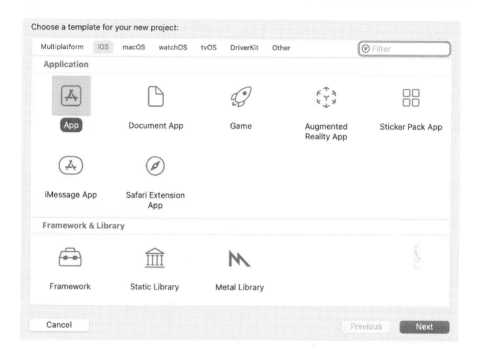

In the new project options, set the product name to **ARKit-SwiftUI**. Set the interface to **SwiftUI**. Set the life cycle to **SwiftUI App**.

Your project options should look like this.

Choose options for your new project:

| | |
|---|---|
| Product Name: | ARKit-SwiftUI |
| Team: | None |
| Organization Identifier: | com.jayvennhan.app |
| Bundle Identifier: | com.jayvennhan.app.ARKit-SwiftUI |
| Interface: | SwiftUI |
| Language: | Swift |

Use Core Data

Host in CloudKit

Include Tests

Cancel                                    Previous      Next

Choose a directory to save your project. Then, click **Create**.

Now, set the scheme to **Any iOS Device (arm64)** or an **actual arm64
iOS/iPadOS device**. You'll need this build scheme to compile and access a
certain RealityKit code. In addition, set the project's **development team** in
the project's settings to sign the build.

Open the project's **ARKit-SwiftUI** target settings. Select the
**Info** tab. Under the **Custom iOS Target Properties** section, add
**NSCameraUsageDescription** and **For Augmented Reality.** key-value pair.

Great, you're reading to build a SwiftUI app with ARKit integration!

# Understanding the Mechanism for Integrating ARKit with SwiftUI

## Setting Up a Custom ARView

Create a new **Swift** file named **CustomARView**. Add the following code to the file:

```swift
import SwiftUI
import ARKit
import RealityKit

final class CustomARView: ARView {
    // 1
    let label: UILabel = {
        let label = UILabel()
        label.translatesAutoresizingMaskIntoConstraints = false
        return label
    }()
```

```
// 2
var didTapView: ((_ sender: UITapGestureRecognizer)
-> Void)?
// 3
@objc required dynamic init(frame frameRect: CGRect) {
    super.init(frame: frameRect)
    commonInit()
}
required init?(coder: NSCoder) {
    super.init(coder: coder)
    commonInit()
}
convenience init() {
    self.init(frame: .zero)
    commonInit()
}
private func commonInit() {
}
}
```

Here's the code breakdown:

1.  You initialize a UILabel to be placed on top of
    ARView. You can customize your ARView with all
    manner of user interfaces and to your heart's
    content.

2.  One way to send data between views is to use a
    closure. This is a great way to pass data back and
    forth when the data complexity is low. When the
    complexity increases, such as requiring multiple
    method calls or data types, you may want to opt for
    the delegate pattern instead of the closure pattern.

3.  ARView initializes several ways as created by
    Apple, one for programmatically and the other
    for interface builder. In addition to those two,
    you create a convenient initializer whereby you
    can call CustomARView. All the initializers will use
    commonInit() as part of the initialization code
    execution.

Now, you'll add methods that you want to execute inside of the class.
Add the following methods to CustomARView:

```
// 1
private func registerTapGesture() {
    let tapGesture = UITapGestureRecognizer(
        target: self,
        action: #selector(didRegisterTap(_:)))
    addGestureRecognizer(tapGesture)
}
// 2
@objc private func didRegisterTap(_ sender:
UITapGestureRecognizer) {
    guard let didTapView = didTapView else { return }
    didTapView(sender)
}
```

Here are the methods' functionalities:

1.  Add a tap gesture recognizer to ARView to call
    didRegisterTap(_:) when the tap gesture
    recognizes.

2. First, the tap gesture action ensures that the didTapView closure binds to an object. Otherwise, the code execution stops. Second, when an object binds to the didTapView closure, call the closure and pass the UITapGestureRecognizer to the object bound to the closure.

Next, you'll handle the events that you want to take place in all initializers. Inside commonInit(), add the following code:

```
// 1
addSubview(label)
NSLayoutConstraint.activate(
    [
        label.topAnchor.constraint(equalTo: topAnchor),
        label.leadingAnchor.constraint(equalTo: leadingAnchor),
        label.trailingAnchor.constraint(equalTo: trailingAnchor),
        label.bottomAnchor.constraint(equalTo: bottomAnchor)
    ]
)
// 2
registerTapGesture()
```

Within the common initializer, you

1. Add label as a subview of ARView. Then, pin the edges of the label to the edges of self or the enclosing ARView.

2. Register the tap gesture recognizer on ARView.

Next, you'll create a view model to encapsulate the data logic of ARView into an observable object.

# Making a View Model Observable Object for ARView

In SwiftUI, you use an observable object to publish event changes within the object. You also use it to encapsulate logic in the form of a view model with SwiftUI. In the current case, you'll create a view model to store the log.

Create a new **Swift** file named **ARContainerViewManager**. Add the following code to the file:

```
import SwiftUI
import ARKit
import RealityKit
// 1
final class ARContainerViewManager: ObservableObject {
    // 2
    var arView = CustomARView()
    // 3
    private let worldTrackingConfiguration:
    ARWorldTrackingConfiguration = {
        let worldTrackingConfiguration =
        ARWorldTrackingConfiguration()
        worldTrackingConfiguration.planeDetection = .horizontal
        worldTrackingConfiguration.isLightEstimationEnabled = false
        return worldTrackingConfiguration
    }()
    // 4
    func resetTrackingConfiguration(options: ARSession.
    RunOptions = []) {
        arView.session.run(
            worldTrackingConfiguration,
            options: options)
    }
}
```

Here's the code breakdown:

1. Declare a view model object that's observable in SwiftUI.

2. Initialize a `CustomARView` within the containing object.

3. Initialize a world tracking configuration property to detect horizontal planes.

4. Declare a method with the option for the caller to choose the session run options.

You've contained the tracking logic within a view model named `ARContainerViewManager`.

Next, add the following methods to the `ARContainerViewManager`:

```
// 1
func appendTextToScene(anchor: ARAnchor) {
    // 2
    let textMeshResource = MeshResource.generateText(
        "AppCoda.com\nx\nMastering ARKit",
        extrusionDepth: 0.02,
        font: UIFont.systemFont(ofSize: 0.05),
        alignment: .center)
    // 3
    let modelEntity = ModelEntity(
        mesh: textMeshResource,
        materials: [
            SimpleMaterial(color: .systemOrange, isMetallic: false)
        ]
    )
```

```
// 4
let anchorEntity = AnchorEntity(anchor: anchor)
anchorEntity.transform.translation.x = -textMeshResource.
bounds.extents.x / 2
anchorEntity.addChild(modelEntity)
// 5
arView.scene.anchors.append(anchorEntity)
}
```

Here's the code breakdown:

1. Take in an ARAnchor to inherit its world position.

2. Initialize a text mesh resource.

3. Initialize a model entity consisting of the text mesh resource and simple orange material.

4. Initialize an AnchorEntity from the ARAnchor in the parameter. Then, translate the anchor entity's transform by half of the text mesh resource's x bound.

5. Append the initialized AnchorEntity onto the ARView scene.

With a method like this, you can easily add RealityKit virtual content onto ARView. You'll see this in action later in the chapter.

# Creating a UIViewRepresentable to Contain ARView

With the introduction of SwiftUI, it's not a surprise that people will miss many of the beautiful creations from UIKit. Plus, many of the wonderful UIKit creations have yet to have an equal match in SwiftUI. For that reason,

Apple engineers have come up with a solution to use UIKit elements interchangeable in SwiftUI. To achieve this, developers will encapsulate UIKit elements in a `UIViewRepresentable`. Wrapping a UIKit view in this object allows you to integrate the view into your SwiftUI view hierarchy.

Create a new **Swift** file named **ARContainerView**. Add the following code to the file:

```
import SwiftUI
import ARKit
import RealityKit
// 1
struct ARContainerView: UIViewRepresentable {
   // 2
   @ObservedObject var containerViewManager =
   ARContainerViewManager()
   var sessionRunOptions: ARSession.RunOptions
   // 3
   func makeUIView(context: Context) -> CustomARView {
      containerViewManager.arView.didTapView = didTapView(_:)
      containerViewManager.resetTrackingConfiguration(options:
      sessionRunOptions)
      return containerViewManager.arView
   }
   // 4
   func updateUIView(_ uiView: CustomARView, context: Context) {
   }
   // 5
   func didTapView(_ sender: UITapGestureRecognizer) {
      let arView = containerViewManager.arView
      let tapLocation = sender.location(in: arView)
      let raycastResults = arView.raycast(
```

```
        from: tapLocation,
        allowing: .estimatedPlane,
        alignment: .horizontal)
     guard let firstRaycastResult = raycastResults.first else
     { return }
     let anchor = ARAnchor(name: "anchorName",
                           transform: firstRaycastResult.
                           worldTransform)
    arView.session.add(anchor: anchor)
  }
}
```

Here's the code breakdown:

1. Declare a custom UIViewRepresentable subclass.

2. Add two properties to the struct, a view model, and another to decide the ARSession run options.

3. One of the UIViewRepresentable protocol methods is makeUIView(context:); here, you configure the UIKit view. In this case, you set up the CustomARView. For the custom AR view, you set the closure and the tracking configuration run options.

4. Another UIViewRepresentable protocol method is updateUIView(_:context:); you use this when you want to pass data from SwiftUI back to your UIKit view for processing. In this case, there isn't anything to pass back to CustomARView. Hence, it's safe to leave the body empty for now.

5.  Decide what to do when the tap view method
    triggers. In this case, simply extract the tap location
    for the first raycast result. Using the raycast result,
    initialize an ARAnchor with an anchor name and
    transform before adding the anchor onto the ARView
    session.

Great. Now, what about integrating protocols from UIKit with SwiftUI?
You'll look into this in the next section.

# Integrating the Coordinator Pattern

There are many ways to pass data between SwiftUI objects. A similar
but currently more important story goes for UIKit and SwiftUI due to
SwiftUI's novelty. An integral part of communication between SwiftUI
and UIKit views is the coordinator instance. Making this instance allows
communication between the two user interface frameworks.

In **ARContainerView**, add the following class to ARContainerView:

```
// 1
class Coordinator: NSObject, ARSessionDelegate {
  // 2
  var parent: ARContainerView
  // 3
  init(_ parent: ARContainerView) {
    self.parent = parent
  }
  // 4
  func session(_ session: ARSession, didAdd anchors: [ARAnchor]) {
    for anchor in anchors {
      guard anchor.name == "anchorName" else { continue }
```

```
        parent.containerViewManager.
        appendTextToScene(anchor: anchor)
      }
    }
  }
```

Here's the code breakdown:

1. Declare the `Coordinator` class as an `NSObject` that also conforms to `ARSessionDelegate`. The first conformance is part of the practice of implementing a coordinator.

2. Set the parent type as `ARContainerView` because that's the type that this object will work with.

3. In the initializer, take in the appropriate parameters to initialize the properties within the object.

4. Implement one of the `ARSessionDelegate` protocol methods. Whenever new anchors are added onto the scene, the coordinator you're implementing will handle what to do with it. Hence, you conform to and implement the protocol method here. Within the method, you traverse through all the anchors in search of a specific anchor name. When it's found, you use the convenient method you created earlier to append the text mesh resource onto the scene.

To connect the coordinator, add the following method to `ARContainerView`:

```
func makeCoordinator() -> Coordinator {
   Coordinator(self)
}
```

This method creates an instance to pass data between UIKit view and SwiftUI. This method is called before calling `makeUIView(context:)`.

Now in `ARContainerView`, replace the body in `makeUIView(context:)` with the following code:

```
containerViewManager.arView.didTapView = didTapView(_:)
containerViewManager.resetTrackingConfiguration()
containerViewManager.arView.session.delegate = context.coordinator
return containerViewManager.arView
```

The only difference here is that you set the `ARView` session delegate to the coordinate. Now, the coordinator inside of `ARContainerView` will handle the `ARSessionDelegate` protocol methods such as `renderer(_:didAdd:for:)`.

That's quite a number of concepts you've learned about just now! Wouldn't it be wonderful to see your work in action? Time to do just that.

# Displaying ARView in SwiftUI

With the setup of turning a UIKit view into a compatible SwiftUI view completed, displaying your custom SwiftUI UIKit view is rather straightforward.

Open **ContentView**. Replace the content file content with the following code:

```
import SwiftUI

struct ContentView: View {
   var body: some View {
      ARContainerView(sessionRunOptions:  [.removeExistingAnchors,
         .resetTracking])
   }
}
```

```
struct ContentView_Previews: PreviewProvider {
  static var previews: some View {
    ContentView()
  }
}
```

You've encapsulated all the ARKit details inside of ARContainerView.
Anytime you want to instantiate an ARView with the configurations you've
set, you can use ARContainerView. Here, you only expose the session run
options in the property's argument constructor. You can initialize various
properties of concern, create modifiers, bind values, and implement more
SwiftUI features that you see fit.

Build and run.

Scan a horizontal plan and tap on it.

There's a setting that you may want to make to take advantage of the entire screen, including the safe area. To achieve this, open **ContentView**. Add the following modifier to ARContainerView:

```
.edgesIgnoringSafeArea(.all)
```

Now, the body should look like this:

```
ARContainerView(sessionRunOptions: [.removeExistingAnchors,
.resetTracking])
    .edgesIgnoringSafeArea(.all)
```

By default, SwiftUI accounts for the safe area automatically. By instructing ARContainerView to ignore all safe area edges, you'll allow the ARView to cover the entire screen inclusive of the safe area.

Build and run.

Now, you can do everything you've previously could. And the `ARView` takes up the entire screen inclusive of the safe area.

# Where to Go from Here?

When it comes to developing apps declaratively, SwiftUI is Apple's answer. With the knowledge you've learned from this chapter, you can integrate ARKit components into a SwiftUI app. Anything you've learned to do with ARKit using a UIKit app becomes applicable to the bridging mechanism between SwiftUI and UIKit. Even SwiftUI can propel you to build amazing ARKit apps now!

**CHAPTER 26**

# Record Augmented Reality Experiences with ReplayKit

Great experiences are worth living and, perhaps even more important, sharing! Developers and designers sometimes forget that making an app conveniently shareable gives users the ability to spread words of mouth on your app. They can recommend your app and help your business grow. In augmented reality, you can record wonderful experiences using ReplayKit.

In this chapter, you'll learn about the following augmented reality experiences with ReplayKit topics:

- Understanding the purpose of ReplayKit

- Integrating ReplayKit into the project

- Recording augmented reality experiences

- Recording the app display

- Recording the screen and audio

- Sharing video clips of AR experiences

By the end of this chapter, you'll have a grasp on ReplayKit and understand the intricacies of building an ARKit app for sharing.

© Jayven Nhan 2022
J. Nhan, *Mastering ARKit*, https://doi.org/10.1007/978-1-4842-7836-9_26

# Understanding the Purpose of ReplayKit

ReplayKit is a framework first made available to iOS 9 users. It's built to help users record or stream video on your screen. In addition, it also has the capability to record or stream audio from the app and microphone. ReplayKit also makes previewing and sharing video clips a breeze.

In addition to making the framework available to iOS users, the Apple team is also expanding this framework to tvOS, Mac Catalyst, and macOS. Introduced in WWDC20, the macOS and ReplayKit framework integration is still in beta for macOS 11.0 at the time of this writing. Hence, learning to use this framework can help you expand onto other Apple platforms if you choose to take that route.

Plus, you can create livestreaming apps with ReplayKit. Essentially, if you've used the recording features in QuickTime Player, you can audio record, screen record, and app record using ReplayKit. Because you're developing the app, you can give users the customizability to configure microphone settings, pixels manipulation, broadcast settings tailored to your requirements, and more.

Sharing is becoming a must-have feature, especially on gaming platforms. Think about PS4 and PS5, Sony places a dedicated sharing button on the PlayStation controllers. Extraordinary experiences are worth sharing. Life is worth sharing. What's the point of doing what we do if we don't share it with someone in the world, after all.

Without further ado, you'll dive into ReplayKit framework integration in your project!

# Integrating ReplayKit into the Project

In this section, you'll integrate ReplayKit into your project. Also, initialize a screen recorder object.

First, open the **starter project**. Build and run to familiarize the current state of the app.

At the moment, you have an app with an ARView and a record button. This is the base of the project that you'll build on.

Second, add the following import statement at the top of the **ViewController**:

```
import ReplayKit
```

Here, you import ReplayKit into ViewController. You do this to make use of the framework's screen recorder object and protocol methods.

Now, add the following property to ViewController:

```
private let screenRecorder = RPScreenRecorder.shared()
```

RPScreenRecorder is a singleton class for controlling app recordings. This means that there will and should only be one instance of this object at any code execution time. To access the single screen recorder instance, you initialize the object with the shared() property.

At this time, you've imported the ReplayKit framework and have the shared screen recorder instance. You're ready to handle the augmented reality recording experience next.

# Recording Augmented Reality Experiences

With the integration of ReplayKit, you can record augmented reality experiences and essentially anything that happens in your app! To begin, add the following method to ViewController:

```
private func startScreenRecording() {
    // 1
    guard screenRecorder.isAvailable else { return }
    // 2
    recordButton.setTitle("Stop", for: .normal)
    // 3
    screenRecorder.startRecording {
        (error) in if let error = error {
            print("Error:", error.localizedDescription)
            return
        }
    }
}
```

Here's the code breakdown:

1.  Since the ReplayKit isn't always readily available for usage on your device, you need to check the screen recorder's availability. For example, you can hook your device's display onto unsupported hardware such as AirPlay or TVOut session. As stated earlier, with the screen recorder's singleton intent, an ongoing recording session is active in the current or another app. Hence, checking the screen recording availability lets you handle the business logic and user interface logic accordingly.

2.  Update the record button's title to stop.

3.  Start the screen recording with the screen recording object. If there's an error, safely unwrap it and print the error's localized description.

With the app screen ready for recording, you'll need to set up the action the app should take once the user is presented with the video clip preview and is done with previewing the video clip.

# Handling Preview Controller Did Finish Protocol

Before handling the saving augmented reality experience, you'll conform ViewController to RPPreviewViewControllerDelegate. This is to handle the action to take when the user is done using the preview view controller.

In **ViewController**, add the following extension at the end of the file:

```
extension ViewController: RPPreviewViewControllerDelegate {
  func previewControllerDidFinish(_ previewController:
    RPPreviewViewController) {
      previewController.dismiss(animated: true)
  }
}
```

Simply, when the user is done interacting with the preview view controller, you dismiss the preview view controller with animation. Next, you'll craft the business logic to save the recording of the augmented reality experience.

# Saving Augmented Reality Experiences

Now that you've allowed the user to record the augmented reality experience, it's time to save it! Add the following method to ViewController:

```
private func stopScreenRecording() {
  // 1
  recordButton.setTitle("Record", for: .normal)
  // 2
  screenRecorder.stopRecording { [unowned self]
  (previewController, error) in
    // 3
    guard let previewController = previewController else {
    return }
    // 4
    previewController.modalPresentationStyle = .fullScreen
```

```
  // 5
  previewController.previewControllerDelegate = self
  // 6
  self.present(previewController, animated: true)
  }
}
```

Here's the code breakdown:

1. Update the record button's title to record.

2. Stop the recording. And use the unowned reference
   to mitigate a strong reference to ViewController.
   Inside the closure, ViewController will only ever be
   safely unwrapped when it's used.

3. Safely unwrap the preview view controller to ensure
   that the object exists with a guard statement.
   Otherwise, return.

4. Set the preview view controller's presentation
   style to full screen instead of the default modal
   presentation.

5. Set the preview view controller's preview
   controller delegate to ViewController. You're
   telling the compiler that ViewController will
   handle the delegate methods coming from the
   preview view controller. Previously, you instructed
   ViewController to dismiss the preview view
   controller upon user activity completion in the
   extension block.

6. Get ViewController to present the preview view
   controller with animation.

Great. The recording logics are in place. Now, it's time to activate the start or stop recording methods using the recording button.

# Wrapping the Recording Logic Inside IBAction

Now that you've set up the methods to handle the recording and saving of the app, it's time to integrate this logic on the record button tap action. In ViewController, add the following code to recordButtonDidTap(_:):

```
if screenRecorder.isRecording {
    stopScreenRecording()
    return
}
startScreenRecording()
```

With the added code, you decide whether to start or stop the screen recording based on the screen recorder's recording status. When the screen recorder is recording, stop the screen recording and return. Otherwise, start the screen recording.

With everything in place to see ReplayKit in action, build and run. Tap the **record** button.

Tap the **stop** button.

Here, the app presents you with the RPPreviewViewController to preview your recording. You're presented with a video clip preview. You can make edits and changes to the video clip recording.

At the top-left hand corner, you can press the cancel button to dismiss the preview view controller. At the top-right hand corner, you can press the save button to save the video clip to your device.

You also can use the share button at the bottom-left corner to share.

This feature makes sharing video clips of AR experiences convenient and a breeze!

# Where to Go from Here?

From this chapter, you've learned about the benefits and practicality of ReplayKit. You've created an iOS app capable of recording augmented reality experiences. Furthermore, you've learned how to make sharing video clips of AR experiences simple for the users.

Sharing is the best action people can take to give ideas and experiences a longer lifespan. Sometimes, sharing allows your creation to have a permanent footprint in history. With all the amazing AR experiences you have in your head, please turn them into a reality with your AR application building skills. Then, integrate sharing options to share the amazing experiences people will have using your app with the world. And more people will have the opportunity to experience your masterpiece.

# Index

## A

Abstraction layer, 13
Accessibility, 12
Adding light node, 136, 137
Anchor entity, 402, 403
Animoji, 18, 303, 304, 307
Apple A12 Bionic chip, 337
Apple Pay integration, 486
Apple Pay Merchant Identity
    Certificate, 498
Apple Pay Payment Processing
    Certificate, 493, 494
Apple's augmented reality
    platform, 15
Apple's core values, 10, 11
Apple's development
    platform, 13, 14
Apple's documentation, 14
Apple's platform, 12
Apple technologies, 4
ARAnchor, 97
ARBodyAnchor, 421, 422
ARCoachingOverlayView, 265
ARContainerView, 516, 518–522
ARContainerViewManager,
    513, 514
AR experience

ARKit, 171
ARWorldMap object, 173,
    176, 177
Data object, 175
getCurrentWorldMap
    closure, 176
loadBarButtonItem
    DidTouch(_:) method, 178
mapping data, 172
resetTracking
    Configuration(with:), 179
retrieveWorldMapData(_:)
    method, 178
saveBarButton
    ItemDidTouch(_:)
    method, 175
3D space
    ARPointCloud, 180
    ARWorldMap, 182
    viewDidAppear():, 186
    viewDidLoad():, 185
    VisualizationView
        Controller, 181, 183,
        185, 186
    VisualizationView
        Controller, 182
ViewController class, 174,
    175, 177

Printed in the United States
by Baker & Taylor Publisher Services